Proactive and Powerful

Proactive and Powerful

Law Clerks and the Institutionalization of the Norwegian Supreme Court

Gunnar Grendstad, William R. Shaffer,
Jørn Øyrehagen Sunde and Eric N. Waltenburg

eleven
international publishing

Published, sold and distributed by Eleven International Publishing
P.O. Box 85576
2508 CG The Hague
The Netherlands
Tel.: +31 70 33 070 33
Fax: +31 70 33 070 30
email: sales@elevenpub.nl
www.elevenpub.com

Sold and distributed in USA and Canada
Independent Publishers Group
814 N. Franklin Street
Chicago, IL 60610, USA
Order Placement: +1 800 888 4741
Fax: +1 312 337 5985
orders@ipgbook.com
www.ipgbook.com

Eleven International Publishing is an imprint of Boom uitgevers Den Haag.

ISBN 978-94-6236-978-8
ISBN 978-94-6094-352-2 (e-book)

To Carsten Smith

FOREWORD

The word 'clerk' evokes employees who perform routine, administrative, and mostly non-discretionary tasks: the filing clerk who organizes documents, the salesclerk who sells goods to customers, the bank clerk who cashes checks. Indeed, the Oxford English Dictionary defines a clerk as 'one employed in a subordinate position ... to make written entries, keep accounts, make fair copies of documents, do the mechanical work of correspondence and similar 'clerkly' work.'[1] Common synonyms include 'paper-pusher,' 'secretary,' 'bookkeeper,' and the like.

These are not the clerks of the Norwegian nor, for that matter, the U.S. Supreme Court. Nearly three decades ago, the political scientist H.W. Perry shattered (whatever was left of) the myth that U.S. law clerks were unassuming clerical staff who spent their days typing the justices' opinions, filing their documents, and taking dictation.[2]

And so it goes in Norway. Despite important differences in their terms of employment[3] and relations with their bosses,[4] generations of law clerks in the United States and Norway have fundamentally altered their courts. That's easy to see in the justices' workaday world. Perry demonstrated that clerks play a crucial role in aiding the justices to determine which cases to hear and resolve;[5] and Grendstad and his co-authors show much the same for Norway. The clerks review appeals and write memos to the Court's 'gatekeepers' – justices serving on the Appeal Selection Committee – who almost always accept the clerks' recommendations. Assistance, of course, doesn't stop with case selection. Clerks in both countries now help the justices prepare their opinions, though the extent of 'ghostwriting' is far less

1 *Oxford English Dictionary*, current use definition (6b), at: https://www.oed.com.

2 H.W. Perry, Jr., *Deciding to Decide: Agenda Setting in the United States Supreme Court* (Cambridge, MA: Harvard University Press, 1994). Several anecdotal accounts preceding Perry also drew attention to the importance of clerks on the U.S. Supreme Court. *E.g.*, Bob Woodward & Scott Armstrong, *The Brethren: Inside the Supreme Court* (New York: Simon and Schuster, 1979).

3 *E.g.*, Norwegian clerks are offered seven-year fixed contracts, with most serving for about six years (Grendstad, et al, at p. 20-21); U.S. clerks typically work for one term.

4 E.g., Norwegian clerks work for the Court in what Grendstad et al. call a "clerk unit"; U.S. clerks are hired by and work for a justice (in other words, they are "personal" clerks).

5 Perry, note 2; see also Todd C. Peppers, *Courtiers of the Marble Palace: The Rise and Influence of the Supreme Court Law Clerk* (Stanford University Press, 2006); Artemus Ward & David L. Wieden, *Sorcerers' Apprentices: 100 Years of Law Clerks in the United States Supreme Court* (New York: New York University Press, 2006).

in Norway.[6] Then again, Norwegian – but not U.S. – clerks participate in the justices' formal deliberations over the merits of cases.[7]

These day-to-day clerk activities eventually cumulate, empowering and professionalizing courts. McGuire demonstrated that the makeover of the U.S. Supreme Court from an "unassuming tribunal of little consequence" to "an integral part of the national government" traced in no small part to the institutionalization of the law-clerk position[8] – though that was hardly by design. When Justice Horace Gray hired the first U.S. Supreme Court law clerk in 1882, it was at his own expense. Not until 1919 did Congress provide funds for legally trained assistants.[9]

The story Grendstad and his colleagues tell about Norway's clerks is also one of empowerment and professionalization, but haphazard the process was not. Actually the opposite. In 1974, then-Norwegian law professor and future Chief Justice, Carsten Smith, set out a vision for transforming the Court from a "passive receiver of appeals to a proactive policy maker."[10] Crucial to Smith's plan was a dramatic increase in the number of clerks to help ensure a docket "less cluttered with appeals of individual and legally petty cases"[11] so that the justices could devote their time to cases most consequential for law and policy. Smith also envisioned the clerks playing a major role in the drafting of opinions on the theory that their input would generate decisions that were more accurate, more informed, and ultimately more respected.

When Smith's plans eventually came to pass, he was proven right. As Grendstad et al. show, increases in the number of clerks (and in their responsibilities) generated a more efficient appeals process, a merits docket befitting a court of precedent, and higher-caliber decisions. All in all, it's hard to imagine the transformation Smith envisioned occurring without the robust clerk unit that now exists in Norway. As one of Smith's successors,

6 Grendstad, et al. note that clerks draft the fact sections of opinions; Rosenthal & Yoon show that U.S. clerks write up much more than that. Jeffrey S. Rosenthal & Albert H. Yoon, "Judicial Ghostwriting: Authorship on the Supreme Court," 96 *Cornell Law Review* 1307 (2011). See also Ward & Wieden, note 5, at 9 ("the process of [opinion writing] has changed over time, with the justices ceding greater responsibility to clerks in recent years.").

7 Grendstad, et al., at p. 34, 89-90.

8 Kevin T. McGuire, "The Institutionalization of the U.S. Supreme Court," 12 *Political Analysis* 128, 140 (2004).

9 In 1886, Congress providing funding for each justice to hire a "stenographic clerk" to "to assist in such clerical work as might be assigned to him." This work included taking dictation, proofreading documents, and even cutting their hair. See Ward and Wieden, note 5, at 31; and the Federal Judicial Center, "Court Officers and Staff: Law Clerk," at: https://www.fjc.gov/history/administration/court-officers-and-staff-law-clerks.

10 Grendstad et al., at p. 1.

11 Grendstad et al., at p. 9.

Chief Justice Schei, expressed it: "Only by the quality of its decisions, *assured by integrated support of clerks*" can the Court "maintain its institutional legitimacy and ensure the public's confidence in the rule of law."[12]

Bolstered by historical documents, interviews, and quantified data, this is a great story. But more than that *Proactive and Powerful* is a great book – covering all the bases from the history of clerks, to their demographics and responsibilities, to their impact on the justices' decisions and on the Court's legitimacy. No doubt too *Proactive and Powerful* is path-marking, likely to spur research throughout Europe and elsewhere too if only because explanations of judicial behavior and the development of high courts will be incomplete without accounting for law clerks. This is certainly true in the United States and Norway; and based on the penultimate chapter of *Proactive and Powerful*, a systematic survey of clerks in the other Nordic high courts, it also likely holds in Denmark, Finland, Iceland, and Sweden.

Almost needless to write, *Proactive and Powerful* is a must read for anyone interested in judicial staff. But there's much more to the book than law clerks, however important they may be. The breadth of subjects covered is great: the (in)efficacy of Chief Justices; the structuring role of an array of institutions, from those governing panel size to procedures for detecting conflicts-of-interest; and the importance of high-quality lawyers. Grendstad et al.'s discussions of these and other topics will provide grist for many future studies, whether country- or comparatively-focused.

I could go on: *Proactive and Powerful* is that chocked-full of original insights into law and legal institutions. But I won't because Grendstad, Shaffer, Sunde, and Waltenburg's book should be read, not summarized. It's innovative, erudite, lucid and, frankly, downright riveting.

Lee Epstein
Ethan A.H. Shepley Distinguished University Professor
Washington University in St. Louis

12 This is Grendstad's summary of Schei's argument, at p. 100. Emphasis added.

Table of Contents

List of Figures

List of Tables

Preface

This book is about law clerks and the institutionalization of the Norwegian Supreme Court. We analyse how the Court took advantage of the slow and steady growth of clerks to transform itself from a passive court of appeal to a proactive court of precedent in order to position itself as an influential policymaker in a democratic society. Our book tells the story of the introduction of the first clerk in 1957 and the gradual hiring of more clerks over the next decades, and how they first assisted the Court in reducing its almost perennial backlog, how they assisted the Appeals Selection Committee (the Court's gatekeeper) and how they later contributed more directly to the justices' decision-making.

During the last 25 years, the Norwegian Supreme Court has been transformed from a reactive court of appeal to a proactive court of precedent. Fundamental to this transformation were the 1995 and 2008 reforms of the appeals process that gave the Court complete control of its own docket, including managing its backlog of cases, and the significant increase in the number of clerks who were to assist the justices in selecting the most important and principled cases for merits review. These innovations were designed to achieve the Court's goal of 'developing the law', aka policymaking. As of 2019, the Norwegian Supreme Court's clerk unit comprises 23 clerks, and they assist the justices not only in the Court's gatekeeping process, reviewing all types of appeals and making recommendations whether to grant or deny, but also throughout the whole process of decision-making in merits panels.

It took an outsider, law professor Carsten Smith, in 1974 to vocally challenge the established legal order and call for a transformation of the Supreme Court from a passive receiver of appeals to a proactive policymaker through seeking out cases that would contribute to the creation of precedents. Although the legal establishment in 1974 was cool to Smith's policymaking ambitions, he never abandoned his agenda of making 'judicial legislation' the goal of the Supreme Court. His patience was rewarded when the government appointed him as Chief Justice to the Supreme Court in 1991. Again, while many of the associate justices on the Court remained unconvinced by Smith's programme when he stepped down as chief in 2002, they realized that the institutional change that Smith had promoted would not be reversed. The subsequent chief justices and new associate justices had no interest in turning the clock back to overtime, weekend burnouts, crammed offices and little to no assistance from law clerks.

The book is a case study of the role of clerks and the transformation of an apex court. We believe the story of the clerks we tell and the institutionalization of the High Court that we analyse is a harbinger and an example of the general process of building court support functions and strengthening the policymaking role of high courts in Europe. While important books and articles have been published on clerks in the United States (Baum 2014; Baum and Ditslear 2010; Best 2002; Cushman and Peppers 2015; Ditslear and Baum 2001; Kromphardt 2014; Peppers 2006; Perry 2009; Rhinehart 1994; Szmer, Kaheny, and Christensen 2014; Ward 2017; Ward and Weiden 2006), no monograph has been published on the clerks or the clerk system for any apex court in Europe.

Some legal and social science publications on various aspects of clerks (or 'legal assistants') and clerk functions in Europe exist. For example, Holvast (2017) studied clerks ('judicial assistants') in Dutch district courts. Paterson (2013) and Nesterchuck (2013) discuss the 'relatively new phenomenon' of 'judicial assistants' on the UK Supreme Court. Coonan (2006) discusses the tasks of the 'research assistants' in the Irish judiciary. Massing (2016) and Wieland (2002) study legal assistants at the German Federal Constitutional Court. Kenney (2000) compares the 'référendaires' in the European Court of Justice with the clerks in the U.S. Supreme Court. Bieri (2016) studies law clerks in the Swiss judicial system, while Jimeno-Bulnes and Hans (2016) have studied clerks ('secretario judicial') in Spanish provincial courts. This body of research indicates an interest in the clerk institution across nations and legal systems.

In 2017, the Norwegian Supreme Court celebrated its clerk unit's diamond jubilee. All 121 current and former clerks were invited; 80 attended. They were welcomed by two former chief justices, Carsten Smith and Tore Schei, as well as the current chief justice, Toril Marie Øie. Øistein Aamodt, the then head of the clerk unit and a former clerk himself, warmly welcomed the attendees. He underscored the important work that the clerks did and had done over the six decades. His praise was echoed by Justice Arnfinn Bårdsen who pointed out the clerks' crucial role in the Court's transformation to a court of precedent and its emphasis on the development of the law, how the clerks were instrumental in reining in the Court's crushing backlog of appeals and the growing need to recruit clerks as legal specialists. Justice Bårdsen's remarks left little doubt: the clerk unit is now integral to the functioning of Norway's highest court. And the clerks' pivotal role is rippling through the broader Norwegian judicial system. Within the last couple of years, two of Norway's largest courts of appeal – Gulating and Borgarting – have already copied and implemented the clerk unit function of the Supreme Court at their courts. We would be very surprised if the other four courts of appeal do not follow suit in the near future.

Acknowledgements

This research project would not have been possible without the generous help and assistance of several people. We are extremely grateful to Gunnar Bergby, the Director General of the Norwegian Supreme Court, and to Øistein Aamodt, the Head of the Court's clerk unit. They and their staff provided us with detailed and historical information on all the clerks who had worked at the unit since 1957. In addition, Aamodt provided detailed information of applicants for a number of openings at the unit. The information on clerks and applicants was especially useful for our analyses in Chapter 6. We also benefitted greatly from our meeting with Birthe Aspehaug Buset and Chirsti Erichsen Hurlen in August 2017 when both were deputy leaders at the clerk unit. Aamodt sat down with some of us several times, and he and his staff promptly answered the many questions we sent by email during our research.

We are also very grateful to the justices who took time to answer our questions and explain issues. We thank former Chief Justice Tore Schei, current Chief Justice Toril Marie Øie, former Justices Liv Gjølstad and Steinar Tjomsland, current Justices Ragnhild Noer and Knut Kallerud, and former interim Justice Rune Sæbø.

Very valuable to us were the interviews we had with Norwegian law clerks. A total of 16 former and current law clerks sat down with us and patiently explained why they had studied law, why they wanted to be a law clerk at the Court, how the recruitment process worked, how the workplace was organized, how they interacted with the justices and other clerks, what kind of work they did and how they scrutinized the appeals and prepared memos for the justices on the important gatekeeping Appeals Selection Committee.

Both justices and clerks participated in the interviews and provided information on the explicit understanding that interviews were primarily for background information only and that there would be no information that could identify them. If any information or quotes were to be used, the agreement was that we would get back to them and ask for permission to do so. We have not found it necessary to use any quotes in this manner. When we deemed that information was so important that it required a source, we cite the source of this information by referring to our internal document of all interviews. We cite the source by the date of the interview, starting page of the interview and the location where the relevant information is found.

Specifically for the comparative analysis in Chapter 8 we conducted a second round of interviews with Supreme Court clerks in the other Nordic countries. Jørn Øyrehagen Sunde carried out four interviews between September 2018 and February 2019. Each clerk was identified to be interviewed by their respective Supreme Courts. The interviews took place at each Supreme Court and lasted about two hours. The interviewees were Guðlaug

Jónasdóttir from the Icelandic Supreme Court (*Hæstiréttur Íslands*), Christina Berg from the Swedish Supreme Court (*Högsta domstolen*), Casper Sølbeck from the Danish Supreme Court (*Højesteret*) and Teemu Vanhanen from the Finnish Supreme Court (*Korkein Oikeus/Högsta domstolen*).

Several weeks prior to any given interview, the clerks received the interview questions. These were the same set of questions to which Norwegian clerks had responded in our first round of interviews, but the clerks were informed that specific questions might have to be adjusted to the specific circumstances. Vanhanen provided three pages of typed answers to the questions at the start of the interview and referred to the document during the interview. Sølbeck provided a 2014 publication by Supreme Court Chief Justice Børge Dahl (2014) before the interview. Notes were taken throughout the four interviews. The interviews were not recorded. Before each interview began, the interviewees were told that they would have the opportunity to read and correct any part of the text based on the information they had given. All four clerks were given the opportunity to read the first version of Chapter 8 and to make necessary corrections. In this process, Berg also supplied the 2018 annual report from the Swedish Supreme Court (Høgsta Domstolen 2019).

All clerk interviews and the way we conducted them provided unique insight into the role of the clerks in the Nordic Supreme Courts. All courts were happy to arrange for the interviews. The clerk units are not at all a secret part of the Court's inner life. In fact, the Courts have decided to be very open and transparent. For instance, the Norwegian Supreme Court published the name, age, educational background and work experience for each clerk in the Court's 2014 *Annual Report.* Such data were available only for the justices in prior publications of the *Annual Report* (Norges Høyesterett 2015:34-37). The openness and commitment to transparency can be considered a common policy across all five Nordic Supreme Courts.

During our research we also had the opportunity to hire three very helpful research assistants. We thank Olav Laug Bjørnebekk, Mari Skåra Helliesen and Marius Mikkel Kjølstad for excellent work and efficient delivery of small and large tasks alike. We also thank Anne Noddeland who assisted with the index of the book.

An earlier version of Chapter 1 was presented at the Annual Norwegian Political Science Conference, Stavanger, Norway, 4-6 January 2017. Earlier versions of Chapters 3 and 5 were presented at the 75th Annual Conference of the Midwest Political Science Association, Chicago, IL, 6-9 April 2017 and at the CORE-research group at the Department of Comparative Politics on 24 May 2017. An earlier version of Chapter 7 was presented at the 76th Annual Conference of the Midwest Political Science Association, Chicago, IL, 5-8 April 2018 and at the CORE-research group at the Department of Comparative Politics on 12 September 2018. Next to last versions of Chapters 8 and 9 were presented at a workshop titled 'The Role and Legitimacy of Judicial Assistants in European Legal Systems' at the Center for Interdisciplinary Research, Bielefeld University, Germany, 27-28 August 2019.

We thank the participants at these venues, especially Joseph L. Staats and Yvette Peters, for their constructive comments.

The analysis of the growth of the clerk unit and the development of the Norwegian Supreme Court that we present in this book also rests on two independent strands of work. Jørn Øyrehagen Sunde is a legal historian and has studied comparative law over a number of years. On the occasion of the Court's 200-year anniversary in 2015, he was engaged by the Norwegian Court Administration in January 2011 to write the Court's history for the 1965-2015 period. The book *Høgsteretts historie 1965-2015* was published in time for the bicentennial celebration. In 2006, William R. Shaffer and Eric N. Waltenburg became interested in the Norwegian Supreme Court, where no one seemed to have applied political science models of judicial behaviour to the justices' decisional outputs. They brought Gunnar Grendstad on board, and in 2015 Grendstad, Shaffer and Waltenburg published their book, *Policy Making in an Independent Judiciary: The Norwegian Supreme Court.* The Court's 200-year anniversary not only celebrated a revered national institution; as it turned out, it also attracted and aligned scholars from different disciplines. These scholars discovered that with a common interest in the Norwegian Supreme Court they had more in common than what their academic disciplines would predict. This book is the result of a fruitful collaboration that no one of us would have anticipated a decade ago.

In spring 2018 Gunnar Grendstad was a visiting scholar at the Department of Political Science and the Department of Scandinavian Studies, University of Washington, Seattle. He thanks the two departments as well as Meltzer Foundation at the University of Bergen, which supported his stay financially, for the opportunity to work on the book during his visit.

William R. Shaffer is Professor Emeritus of Political Science at Purdue University. He divides his academic time between Santa Cruz and Bergen.

Jørn Øyrehagen Sunde received funding from the Meltzer Foundation for travel to the other four Nordic Supreme Courts to interview clerks.

Eric N. Waltenburg is grateful to the Department of Political Science and the College of Liberal Arts at Purdue University for their support during his work on this book.

Compiling and analysing data on clerks was approved by the *Data Protection Services* of the Norwegian Centre for Research Data (NSD), http://pvo.nsd.no/prosjekt/50633.

All translations from Norwegian to English have been done by the authors unless otherwise indicated. When a Norwegian source already had been translated to English, we used the translated source.

We dedicate this book to Carsten Smith, former law professor and dean of the Faculty of Law at the University of Oslo and Chief Justice of the Norwegian Supreme Court from 1991 to 2002. Envisioning the Supreme Court as a more prominent political player in society, Carsten Smith was instrumental in transforming the Norwegian Supreme Court from a reactive court of appeal to a proactive court of precedent. Smith realized the power of clerks and he worked continuously to develop the clerk unit at the Court.

Gunnar Grendstad, William R. Shaffer, Jørn Øyrehagen Sunde and Eric N. Waltenburg
August 2019,
Bergen, Santa Cruz, Bergen, and West Lafayette

1 A Master Plan

On Friday afternoon, 28 June 1974, in the northern city of Tromsø, University of Oslo law professor Carsten Smith confidently stepped up to the podium and prepared to deliver his well-crafted address to the annual meeting of the Norwegian Association of Judges. Roughly 200 judges were in attendance, along with representatives of judges' associations from the other Nordic countries. Invited guests from the Ministry of Justice and the Office of the Government Advocate were also present.

Before lunch, a number of speakers had already addressed predictable and uncontroversial issues. Minister of Justice, Inger Louise Valle, underscored the primary role of the courts as resolving conflicts and urged the courts to improve this honourable service to their citizens. Chief Justice of the Supreme Court and chairman of the Norwegian Association of Judges, Rolv Ryssdal, appropriately responded to the Minister of Justice's request by underscoring the necessity of appointing more judges to the courts. To wit, improved judicial service should be obtained by more judges (Sunde 2015a).

Smith had titled his speech 'The courts and the development of the law', and he knew that some of his remarks were and would be controversial. But little did he know that his address would cause confusion and uproar among the judges, ruin what everybody expected would be an enjoyable conference dinner and force his wife, Assistant Professor Lucy Smith, to withdraw to her hotel room early because she had become so upset by the hostile atmosphere around the dinner table.[1]

Carsten Smith was a prodigy. Born in 1932 in Oslo, he decided early to embark on a legal career. By the age of 32, he had published several books, been appointed to full professor and was soon to take on the editorship of the Nordic flagship law journal *Tidsskrift for Rettsvitenskap*. In an address to the meeting of the Norwegian Association of Judges in 1969, he had called for more boldness and determination on the part of the Supreme Court in developing the law. Justice Ryssdal, who became chief justice in 1969, was present at this meeting. When he invited Smith to give the address in Tromsø, Ryssdal must have had a sense as to what was coming.

Many of Smith's 'theses' – that is what he called them in a footnote when the address was published the following year – had already been circulated before the address at Tromsø as "a basis for discussions" (Smith 1975:319). He summarized his address in eight theses (Smith 1975:318), the first being his most central one: that the nation's highest court should

1 In no way a timid person, Lucy Smith holds three significant firsts in Norway: first female with a law degree (dr.juris, 1981), first female law professor (1987) and first female rector (1993-1998), all at the University of Oslo.

take the lead in "developing the law" and acknowledge that its most important task is not to resolve concrete and individual cases, but to "lay down guidelines for the future" – thereby effectively contradicting the position of the Minister of Justice who had spoken only a few hours earlier. Another thesis was that the development of the law and the practice of judicial review must lead to a greater and more open acknowledgement of the political function of the courts. Smith also called for a profound change in the appeals process so that the Supreme Court could both get rid of most of the automatic criminal case appeals it received from the appellate courts and increase its denial of civil cases, thereby positioning the Supreme Court to more fully control its own docket. It was Smith's perception and plan that the reduced caseload would permit the Court to concentrate on more complex and consequential cases. This reform, Smith argued, would necessitate a dramatic increase in the number of aides to assist the justices' decision-making.[2] He called for greater 'judicial legislation' and for lower courts' decisions to be acknowledged as legitimate legal forces. Smith advocated greater transparency in that all Supreme Court decisions, without exception, should be published in full. The fact that the courts should participate in the development of the law, Smith argued, ought to lead to appointing justices who in addition to their legal qualifications could demonstrate social understanding and knowledge, and that one should also acknowledge that justices' political experience can be valuable.[3]

To sweeten his agenda, which in the view of many judges was quite subversive, Smith offered greater standing and distinction on the part of the courts. He anticipated that the implementation of his agenda would increase the social influence of the Court, which in turn would attract greater respect for it among the other governmental institutions and the mass public because the Court would be contributing something of value and importance to an open democracy.

Smith's address was not well received by the judges present in the audience (Sunde 2015a:38). Trial court judge Hans Fredrik Marthinussen, who had received Smith's theses in advance in order to offer some prepared remarks, stated that he disagreed even more strongly with Smith after the address due to Smith's forceful delivery. Other judges openly distanced themselves from Smith's position. They specifically underscored that the main task of the courts was to resolve individual cases. Any deviation from such a task would smack of politics and would irreversibly cut the umbilical cord to 'the law'. The buzz and debate that suffused the annual meeting of judges throughout the day after Smith's address was unfriendly to the point of hostility. Smith took the debate and the uncompromising

2 In his address Smith only once referred to clerks, using the term 'aides' (Smith 1975:319).

3 A final and more superficial point, which Smith later recanted, was to get rid of the outdated robes, which had no more 'right to life' than the old uniforms of civil servants.

responses in stride. He thanked his colleagues for taking him seriously and drily noted, according to the minutes that were later published, that "I am still alive" (Sunde 2015a:39).

Smith wanted the Supreme Court to take on a more active role in shaping Norway's policies. He envisioned a merits docket less cluttered with appeals of individual and legally petty cases. He wanted to take his battle out of the ivory tower and engage the courts, the third branch of government, in a larger debate on law and politics. Smith was profoundly inspired by the U.S. Supreme Court under the leadership of Chief Justice Earl Warren and its high-profile civil rights decisions in the 1950s and 1960s. Smith saw himself as a torchbearer; he wanted to engage the Supreme Court where the battles could be fought with the dedicated involvement of the justices. However, in order to fully embark on policymaking and the development of the law, Smith also needed an army. He needed officers and soldiers in the Supreme Court. The justices were his officers and their positions had been in existence since 1815. However, he also needed clerks as his soldiers. Smith wanted clerks to help the justices in the demanding work of separating the wheat from the chaff, thereby allowing the justices to devote more of their time and effort in deciding more salient cases that promised greater legal and policy implications.

1.1 Hit the Ground Running

The 1974 Tromsø address was Carsten Smith's master plan. As he noted, after its delivery he was still alive. In a sense, he was not going anywhere, nor was his plan; time would work in favour of his project. In 1991, from his secure base at the University of Oslo Law School, the Social Democratic Labour government headhunted Smith as Chief Justice of the Supreme Court over the Court's own preferred candidate, the 65-year-old Arne Christiansen (Grendstad, Shaffer, and Waltenburg 2015:54-55). Smith became the first chief justice since 1909 not to have been appointed to the chief justiceship from the bench. A drawback to Smith's unique route of appointment was that he was less familiar with the inner workings of the Court, despite having served three short stints as an interim justice on the Court in the late 1980s and early 1990s. Smith was actually the first chief justice since 1854 never to have served on the bench at all, apart from three brief stints as interim justice in the late 1980s (Sunde 2015a:314). A more looming drawback was that Smith never acquired sufficient seniority to chair a panel of justices through deliberations of a case and therefore had not been able to demonstrate his legal acumen as a presiding justice. Without having chaired a panel, long considered by Supreme Court justices to be a crucial test of judging, Smith never had the chance to establish his judicial bona fides to his colleagues on the High Bench. Therefore, the expectation was that his associate justices would withhold any nods of approval until Smith had been sufficiently tested. In 1991, Smith was an untested judge and already a controversial freshman chief.

Shortly after his appointment as chief justice and prior to a meeting of the justices on what can be labelled Smith's Court, Smith circulated a memo emphasizing that his views on the position and development of the Court were unchanged and were the same as he had repeatedly advocated in his addresses over the previous two decades. Again, justices demurred. This time, however, his agenda had the full backing of the Social Democratic government that had appointed him.[4] And although there would never be full agreement among the associate justices on his agenda of the Court heading towards the promised land of developing the law, Smith knew that the tide had turned.

The tide may have turned, but it could turn again. Smith still had to fight for his agenda throughout his 11 years as chief justice. First, he hit the ground running. In spring 1990, the government had already appointed a white-paper commission that was addressing the question of eliminating the automatic appeal of trivial criminal cases to the Supreme Court. The commission, which already had on board Associate Justice Gunnar Aasland whose leave of absence from the Court Smith immediately extended, delivered its report in fall 1992. The Parliament followed the commission's recommendations. Implemented in 1995, the 'two-step' reform significantly reduced the Court's caseload and also permitted the Court to use its full discretion to select criminal cases for review.

In 1996 Smith proudly welcomed the King and Queen to the grand reopening of the fully renovated Supreme Court building, a project that Smith initiated shortly after having taken the helm of the Court in 1991. And in spring 1999 Smith gave Associate Justice Tore Schei leave of absence to chair a government white-paper commission on the revision of civil dispute legislation. The commission delivered its report in 2001. Again, Parliament passed the commission's recommendation. Implemented in 2008, the revised statute empowered the Court with full discretion to select civil cases for review, thereby enabling it to control its own docket in this area of law too.[5] In 2002, Smith's ally in Court reform, Tore Schei, became the new chief justice. They shared the same understanding of the Court's challenges and the remedies needed to meet them. Schei continued to pursue Smith's agenda until his own retirement in 2016.

In 2016, incoming Chief Justice Toril Marie Øie praised her two predecessors (Øie 2016). She specifically addressed the linchpin of the Court's development: increasing the number of clerks. Without the resources of a clerk pool and its contributions towards assisting the justices in picking the most interesting and consequential cases from a growing number of appeals, the justices would not be able to devote their full attention to the principled cases in order to develop the law. To put it concretely, without the help of

---

4 It is hard to pinpoint Carsten Smith's political views – for what it is worth. In the late 1970s he was an advisor to the Conservative Party in the Storting. Some of his law school colleagues thought he was or had been a member of the Liberal Party. And then he was firmly backed and appointed by the Social Democratic Brundtland government in 1991.

5 NOU(1992), NOU (2001), Ot.prp. nr. 51 (2004-2005), and Ot.prp. nr. (78 1992-1993).

the clerk pool, the justices would never be able to fully transform the Supreme Court from a court that resolved individual cases assembly-line style into a powerful policymaking court of precedent.

Chief Justice Øie praised outgoing Chief Justice Schei for having minimized the backlog problem, for having established efficiency in the Court's handling of cases and for his success in reducing the number of cases decided by the Court so that more of the justices' time and energy could be directed at resolving principled cases and establishing precedents (Øie 2016). During Schei's Court, the number of law clerks had increased from 16 to 23. By 2015, for the first time in the Court's history, the number of clerks surpassed the number of justices. Significantly, the clerks' tasks and contributions were no longer limited only to the *input* side of the Court's gatekeeping duties. During Schei's tenure, the clerks had crossed a procedural Rubicon and began to make increasing contributions to the *output* side of the Court's decision-making. By the end of Schei's chief justiceship, the clerks were on hand for the justices' deliberation of cases and could assist the justices in their final decision-making and opinion writing.

1.2 THE GROWTH OF LAW CLERKS

In 1957, under the leadership of Chief Justice Sverre Grette, the Supreme Court hired its first clerk, Jacob Rosted Suur Walnum, a 1946 graduate of the University of Oslo Law School (Steenstrup 1973:579). A government white paper referred to his position at the Court as "legal secretary" (Justis- og politidepartementet 1962-63:1). Walnum's primary task was to assist the Appeals Selection Committee (ASC) in its screening of cases.[6]

Over the next two decades, the number of legal secretaries remained skimpy, and their numbers did not increase until 1977, when there were two. In 1984 the number of legal secretaries increased again to three, and then to six in 1989, the year the clerk unit was formally organized (Sunde 2015a:149). With Carsten Smith in place as chief justice in 1991, two things happened. The title of legal secretary was changed to clerk ('utreder') and the number of clerks rose dramatically. When Smith retired as chief justice after 11 years, the number of clerks had increased to 16. In other words, during Smith's 11-year tenure as chief from 1991 to 2002, the number of clerks had increased by 10 from 6 to 16 – an increase of almost one clerk per year. When Chief Justice Tore Schei, Smith's successor, passed the gavel to his successor, Toril Marie Øie, in 2016, the number of clerks had increased to 23 – an increase of almost one clerk per two years.

6 The Norwegian Supreme Court annual report 2016:4 (Norges Høyesterett 2017).

Figure 1.1 Chiefs, Clerks and Justices

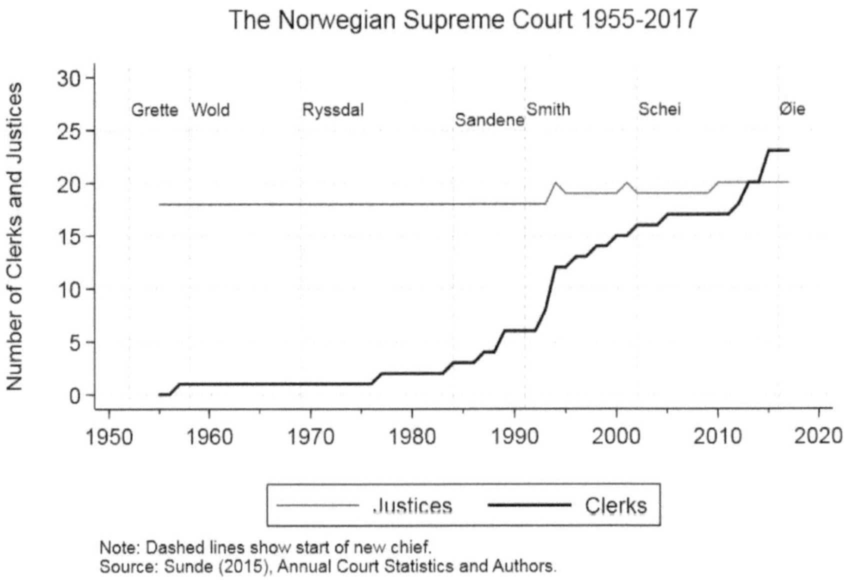

The substantial growth of the number of clerks shown in Figure 1.1 is in stark contrast to the stability in the number of Supreme Court justices.[7] Since 1938, the Norwegian Constitution has stipulated that the Supreme Court shall consist of one chair and at least four other justices.[8] But no constitutional provision, statute or convention prescribes a maximum or optimal number of justices to be appointed to the Court. Since 2010, the Court comprises 20 justices. Because the Court operates with two parallel decisional panels, there is a balance that must be struck between the number of justices on a court of precedent and the degree of unity of the law that such a court is able to secure. Too many justices staffing decisional panels threaten to produce inconsistent legal precedents. As former Chief Justice Tore Schei stated: "[t]he strong development of the clerk unit is based on the fact that the number of justices on a court of precedent like [the Norwegian] Supreme Court must be kept as low as possible" (Schei, in Norges Høyesterett 2017:9). For now, 20 justices seem

7 No continuous public record exists as to the exact number of clerks on the Supreme Court. The clerk numbers in Figure 1.1 rest on a compilation of sources including Sunde (2015a) as well as recent annual reports from the Supreme Court and the National Court Administration. When facing lacunae in our year-by-year time series, our general assumption was that the number of clerks was constant until a newer source reported an updated figure.

8 The 1938 Constitutional amendment of Section 88, second clause, reads: "Høiesterett skal bestaa af en Formand og mindst fire andre Medlemmer" (https://grunnloven.lovdata.no/).

to be the saddle point solution. Mounting pressure on the Court's decision-making capacity will be resolved by increasing the number of clerks, not the number of justices.

1.3 INSTITUTIONALIZATION

Our primary thesis is that a process of institutionalization was necessary for the achievement of Carsten Smith's master plan for the Norwegian Supreme Court. The development of the clerk unit and the evolution of its duties were integral to this institutionalization. According to McGuire, "Institutionalization refers to the development of a regularized system of policy making" (2004:129-130; see also Bumin, Randazzo, and Walker 2009). He identifies three "indicators" of this institutionalizing process – "differentiation, durability, and autonomy" (2004:130). Of particular relevance to our analysis here, these same indicators are present for the Norwegian Supreme Court, and many of McGuire's operationalizations of these indicators have parallels in that Court's context.

McGuire defines *differentiation* as the degree to which an institution is a well-defined entity in the political system. He asserts that the U.S. Supreme Court has experienced several developments – such as the emergence of a distinct federal bench and the end of circuit riding for the Supreme Court justices – that have resulted in it taking on a unique identity with clearly established boundaries that separate it from the other governmental organs (2004:129-130). But, somewhat tongue-in-cheek, McGuire points to the Court's residence in its own building as perhaps the most "concrete measure" of its achievement of differentiation from the other branches of the national government (2004:131). He writes: "Surely the justices' move into their own building in 1935 was evidence of their unique identity and status.... It was tangible recognition that the Court's mission had been institutionalized" (2004:131). A similar development occurred in the case of the Norwegian Supreme Court, when, during Smith's tenure, it took up sole residence in the Palace of Justice in 1996.

The concept of *durability* captures an organization's capacity to persist and pursue its institutional goals even in the face of appreciable environmental change (McGuire 2004:131). An organization's financial resources endow it with a certain degree of durability. Moreover, McGuire avers, inasmuch as the judiciary is dependent on the budgeting decisions of the legislature, the size of its budget is indicative of the broader government's support of the Court's role in the political system (2004:131). In both cases, then, the larger the budget, the more durable the organization. As displayed in Figure 1.2, it is clear that the institutional durability of the Norwegian Supreme Court through its budgets has increased over time.[9] In the 1990s, during Smith's tenure as chief justice, the Court's budget grew dramatically as a consequence of the increase in the number of clerks as well as the remodelling of what was to become the new Supreme Court building.

Figure 1.2 Budget 1955-2017

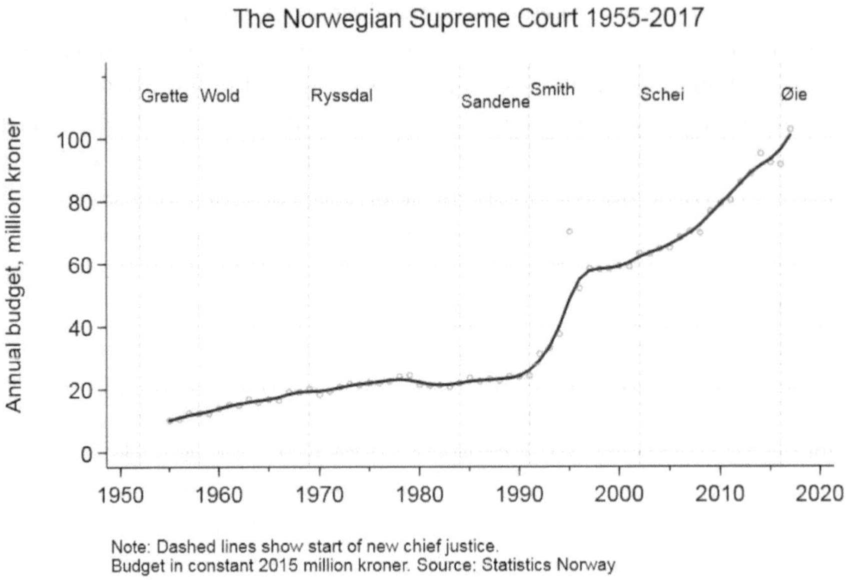

Budgeting, however, is not the only element McGuire points to as evidence of the Supreme Court's degree of institutionalization. He also argues that the rise and integration of the clerk institution has contributed to the U.S. Supreme Court's institutional capacity and its resilience in accomplishing its institutional mission (2004:132). In this regard, too, the Norwegian Supreme Court tracks closely with its American counterpart. As discussed earlier, the number of clerks has grown monotonically since 1957 (review Figure 1.1), while the clerks have taken on more tasks in assisting the justices. Again, the dramatic increase in this development took place during Smith's tenure as chief justice. As a result,

9 The government presents its annual budget, 'Stortingsproposisjon Nr. 1', to the Storting in October every year (Regjeringen (various years)). Figure 1.2 displays the annual budgets for the Norwegian Supreme Court in 2015 constant Kroner (Statistisk Sentralbyrå 2018). On six occasions, during the final budget debate ('Salderingsdebatten') when the budget was balanced in the Storting, there were slight *increases* in the Court's budget (most notably in 1989: 1,739,000; 1992: 6,420,000; 2002: 1,475,000; and 2006: 2,432,000) and on four occasions there were slight *decreases* (most notably in 1993: 3,094,000). (All changes in 2015 kroner.)

the clerks provide essential staff support so that the justices may more efficiently perform their judicial duties.

Finally, McGuire argues that *autonomy* is important because it ensures an organization has "some degree of independence in making its own decisions without dictation from outside actors" (Keohane 1969:862). And in this regard, McGuire points to the Supreme Court's docket control as especially important. He writes that "the Court's ability to construct its own agenda ... gives it the flexibility to focus on the legal and political issues of greatest concern to its members" (2004:132). Between 1984 and 1989 the number of clerks in the Norwegian Supreme Court rose from three to six, and in 1989 the clerk unit became a part of the Court's organizational structure. Hence, things were already moving when Smith started his tenure as chief justice in 1991. The number of clerks increased dramatically, the unlimited ability to filter criminal cases was introduced in 1995 and the clerks started working on the output as well as in the input of the filtering process.

Thus, the adoption of Smith's plan was possible with the institutionalization of the Norwegian Supreme Court, of which docket control and the expansion of the clerk unit were integral components. Fundamental to the Court's transformation was an expansion of its processing capacity, its durability. This would make the Court more efficient in pursuing its mission of clarifying and developing the law. Here, clerks were essential. They would assist the ASC in disposing of appeals and identifying salient cases worthy of the Court's finite decisional attention. Moreover, as the clerk unit expanded, the clerks would assume greater responsibility for identifying the relevant legal foundations to establish precedent. In the process, they would ensure the decision's legal reasoning was sufficiently sound and legitimate. Without enough clerks, this workload and this responsibility would fall on the justices.

How best, then, to secure more clerks? As we discuss in more detail in later chapters, the path the Court seemed to follow was to contrive to paint a picture of institutional need. Simply put, a severe workload and a mounting backlog crisis made for a convincing rationale for an expansion of the clerk unit. That more help was needed was an effective budget strategy that resonated with other key actors in the process – viz. the government and Parliament. And although backlogs and case pressures wax and wane, once the clerk unit expanded, it did not contract as caseload pressures receded. Instead, an expanded clerk unit became an integral component of the Court's institutionalization and transformation to a court of precedent. Caseloads no longer drove the work of the clerks (if they ever fully did). Rather, the clerks were vacuuming legal sources to contribute to the Court's mission of clarifying and developing the law.

This book is an analysis of the linchpin of Smith's agenda of 'judicial legislation'. Without the resources of a large pool of clerks, the Court would have a harder time handling the growing number of appeals. Without the resources of a large pool of clerks, the Court would have fewer resources to confidently pick the most policy-prone and consequential cases. Without the resources of a large pool of clerks, the justices would have less time for thoughtful deliberations. And without the resources of a large pool of clerks, the justices would not be able to fact-check, proofread and assure the quality of the Court's decisions. So, in 2016, after the chief justiceships of Carsten Smith and Tore Schei, the Norwegian Supreme Court was transformed from the somewhat sleepy and overburdened case-by-case-resolving court into a proactive court that cherry-picks cases at its own full discretion in order to 'develop the law'. As a result, the Court has become one of the "most powerful supreme courts in Europe" (Sunde and Ulvund 2014:17).

In her first annual report on the Court, the new Chief Justice Toril Marie Øie asserted that the ever-increasing complexity of legal forces requires that the clerk unit provide even greater support for the justices when they decide a case on its merits. In 2015, the Court was provided budgetary lines for three additional clerks. Chief Justice Øie stated that these new positions gave the Court the opportunity to organize greater support from the clerks in cases that were granted review in panels, Grand Chamber or plenary session. By 2016, for the first time, the clerks were assisting the justices' decisions on the merits. Chief Justice Øie concluded that the Court's experience with the support of clerks at this stage in the decision-making process had been successful and valuable. She stated that it is the Court's wish that the development of assisting the justices' decision-making continues, but that would necessitate increasing the number of clerks on the Court.[10]

As of 2018, the clerk unit is the largest unit on the Court; it includes a total of 26 employees.[11] The section is headed by one leader and two deputies and comprises an additional 20 law clerks. The clerk unit also includes two court clerks ('protocol secretaries') and one student intern.[12] In our discussion we will alternate between using 'clerk' and 'law clerk' when we refer to the conventional use of the clerk ('utreder'), and we will consistently use the term 'court clerk' for the more administrative role of 'protokollsekretær'. The main task of the clerks is working for the ASC, but they may, as is made explicit in the calls for new clerks, receive some additional tasks and assignments from the chief, the associate justices and the Secretary General. But as explicitly stated by the leadership of the Supreme Court, the clerks increasingly assist the justices at the decision-making stages on the merit panels and on the more infrequent decision-making when the justices convene in Grand Chamber and *en banc*.

10 The Norwegian Supreme Court annual report 2016:4 (2017) (Norges Høyesterett 2017).

11 www.domstol.no/no/Enkelt-domstol/-Norges-Hoyesterett/Om-Hoyesterett/Personalia/Juridisk-utredningsenhet1/ (last accessed 1 October 2016).

12 The total number of employees at the Court in 2017 was 75: 20 justices, 26 persons in the clerk unit and 29 persons in various administrative positions (Norges Høyesterett 2018b).

1.4 Plan of the Book

During the time frame we cover here – that is, from the hiring of the first clerk in 1957 to 2018 – we observe a Court that transformed itself from a reactive court of appeal resolving individual cases to a proactive court of precedent that relentlessly searches for appeals to clarify and develop the law. We also observe the transformation of Carsten Smith, from a villain when he gave his speech to a hostile audience in 1974 to a hero, albeit a controversial one, whose successors willingly embraced and further institutionalized the idea of a powerful clerk unit. Key dates in this process are detailed in the Appendix at the end of this chapter. The Supreme Court continues to argue for the expansion of the clerk unit in order to strengthen the Court.

In the next chapter we outline the structure of the Court's decisional process. We identify the four decisional stations: gatekeeping, oral arguments, deliberations and opinion writing. Throughout the 60-odd years since 1957 that we study here, these stations have been constant. Between 1970 (the first year for which we have reliable numbers) and 2017, the Court has processed 104,121 appeals. Considering the Court's decisional process allows us to appreciate how limited the first clerk's activities were at the first, gatekeeping station. Today, clerks are irreplaceable at the first station and increasingly involved in the final three stations.

In Chapter 3 we discuss the increasing presence and participation of clerks on the Court. Some justices wanted more clerks on the Court, but for different reasons, while the old guard of justices argued that additional clerks would militate against the overall legal quality of the Court's decision-making. The chapter is important in understanding the growth of clerks and the institutionalization of the clerk unit on the Court.

In Chapter 4 we demonstrate the intimate involvement of clerks in the important deciding-to-decide process that the justices carry out in the gatekeeping ASC. Here, we draw on a number of interviews with clerks and justices to get a deeper understanding of the processes.

In Chapter 5 we discuss the new roles clerks have taken on beyond the ASC. Since 2010, the clerks have begun to assist the justices in the three subsequent merits stations of decision-making. The chapter discusses how clerks broke new barriers that were insurmountable only a few years earlier.

Chapter 6 examines the demographics of law clerks and compares the law clerks with the applicants for law clerk positions. The chapter draws on the authors' two unique sets of data: the complete list of all 121 individuals who have served as clerks since 1957 through 2017 and the list of applicants for the calls for the clerk unit within the last 11 years.

Chapter 7 analyses the statistical relationships between the number of clerks, the number of backlogs, the number of merits decisions and the number of non-unanimous decisions. The chapter draws on annual data from various sources complied by the authors.

In Chapter 8 we turn to the Supreme Courts in the other four Nordic countries: Iceland, Denmark, Sweden and Finland. Based on interviews with clerks, we compare the recruitment of clerks, their gatekeeping tasks and the organization of the clerk units.

In the final chapter we summarize and discuss our findings. The general process of institutionalizing and empowering the Norwegian Supreme Court was implemented along two paths. One path was to increase the Court's control of its own docket. The other path was to increase staff support by hiring more clerks. Having reduced the backlog problem, which was used as the main argument to introduce docket control and hire more clerks, the increase in the number of clerks took on an unchecked momentum. The unrelenting increase in the number of law clerks was part and parcel of the Norwegian Supreme Court's institutionalization and concomitant transformation into a major political actor.

1.5 Appendix: Timeline – Clerks, Justices and Gatekeeping in the Norwegian Supreme Court

- 1957 – The first 'legal secretary' (clerk) hired at the Supreme Court.
- 1960 – The Civil Dispute Act of 1915 is amended to permit denial of appeals if in 'particular instances' the case is unimportant to the parties or does not have significance beyond the case itself.
- 1974 – Law professor Carsten Smith sparks a heated debate by arguing for the Supreme Court, the highest court in the land, to significantly reduce its case load, boost the number of clerks, select appeals strategically to develop precedents and embark on legal activism.
- 1975 – After close to 20 years, there is still only one 'legal secretary' on the Court.
- 1976 – In the plenary *Kløfta* decision, the Court reactivates the dormant instrument of judicial review and adopts the 'privileged position'.
- 1979 – All justices on the Supreme Court sign a letter to the Ministry of Justice requesting legislative amendments to enact stricter appeals selection procedure in order for the Court to concentrate on its main tasks of unity and development of the law 'in areas where legislation is inadequate'.
- 1981 – The Civil Dispute Act of 1915 is amended again to permit denial of appeals if the case does not have significance beyond the case itself.
- 1987 – The number of legal secretaries increases from three to four, but the Court leadership turns down an offer from the government of two additional clerks due to lack of tasks and office space. Justices are cool to the idea to surrender quality and to assign screening tasks to legal secretaries.
- 1988 – The number of appeals strains the Court's capacity and a sense of 'crisis' emanates.

- 1988 – Ten years after the issue was first addressed, the Court formally reduces its work week from six to five days – justices too take Saturday off. (Justice Liv Gjølstad authors the first Court decision on a computer.)
- 1989 – The government budget appropriates funds to include a leader and a deputy for the pool of legal secretaries. The legal secretaries are organized as a separate unit – a secretariat – within the Court, its primary function being to assist the ASC.
- 1989 – The number of justices allocated to the ASC increases from three to four to improve the screening capacity of the committee. Three-justice gatekeeping panels are nested within the Committee.
- 1990s – Clerks shifted gradually from preparing interlocutory appeals only for the ASC to also include, first, civil case appeals and, later, criminal case appeals.
- 1990 – The white-paper commission on criminal reform is established. The government appoints Associate Justice Gunnar Aasland as one of five members.
- 1991 – The government appoints law professor Carsten Smith as the new chief justice (over the Court's own preferred candidate). Smith quickly relieves Justice Aasland of Court duties to commit fully to writing the white paper on criminal procedural reform. There are six legal secretaries on the Court.
- 1992 – The white-paper commission on criminal procedure reform delivers its report (NOU 1992). It recommends relieving the Supreme Court of automatic criminal appeals from the court of appeal.
- 1992 – Chief Justice Smith changes the title of 'legal secretary' to 'clerk' ('*utreder*').
- 1994 – Discussions on increasing the number of justices allocated to the ASC from four to five to improve the committee's screening capacity came to naught.
- 1994 – The government appoints two justices to the Court as a temporary measure to alleviate backlogs of appeals under the expectation that the next two vacancies on the Court will not be replaced.
- 1995 – Criminal procedure reform is implemented. It relieves the Supreme Court of mandatory criminal appeals, substantially reducing its caseload. Criminal case appeals need the *consent* of ASC to be heard by the Court.
- 1996 – Oslo trial court and Eidsivating court of appeal have moved out of 'the Palace of Justice' and leave a renovated and spacious building to the Supreme Court as its sole occupant.
- 1996 – Chief Justice Carsten Smith chairs the three-year white-paper commission on the reorganization of the courts. The nineteenth justice seat on the Court is made permanent.
- 1997 – Chief Justice Smith's attempt to introduce personalized clerks to justices finally fails. The justices vow not to have clerks in the courtroom.

- 1999 – Chief Justice Smith delivers the white-paper commission's report (NOU 1999). It recommends establishing a Court Administration in the city of Trondheim and that vetting applicants to the Court must take place outside of the Ministry of Justice.
- 1999 – The Dispute Act Commission established and to be chaired by Associate Justice Tore Schei. The Commission delivers its report in 2001 (NOU 2001).
- During the 1990s the clerks' tasks expanded from handling interlocutory appeals only to gradually include more and more civil appeals. At the end of the 1990s the clerks handled both civil and criminal appeals (Aamodt 2017:2).
- Towards the end of the 1990s the Court allocates a senior clerk as mentor to new clerks. The clerk unit introduces spreadsheets to track the clerks' handling of appeals as well as monitoring appeals through the clerk unit.
- 2000 – The Court introduces its case processing and case tracking system '*Høyrett*'. The system links together various internal documents of the Court which can be retrieved when necessary, including the clerk's memo to the ASC. The system also permits the Court to monitor case processing against recommended deadlines (NOU 2001:613).
- 2001 – Clerk contracts were changed from permanent employment to single fixed terms of five years. Realizing that clerks would be looking for the next career move well before the end of their five-year contract, contracts were extended in 2007 and 2011.
- 2001 – The Court briefly counts 20 justices (Ot.prp. nr. 44 2000-2001:2,34).
- 2002 – Associate Justice Tore Schei appointed chief justice. There are 16 law clerks on the Court.
- 2002 – The administration of the courts is removed from the Ministry of Justice and re-established as The Norwegian Courts Administration in the city of Trondheim. The reorganization enunciates the independence of courts and establishes a new procedure for the appointment of justices outside of the Ministry.
- By 2005, new clerks receive a justice mentor to complement the clerk mentor.
- 2006 – The intensity of the clerks' reviews of *all* appeals to the Court peaked. Going forward, appeals clearly not worthy of being heard were treated more summarily while more important cases received closer scrutiny (Aamodt 2017:2).
- 2007 – The Court starts to offer clerks six-year contracts.
- 2008 – The Dispute Act of 2005, replacing the Dispute Act of 1905, is implemented. Civil law case appeals need the *consent* of the ASC to be heard by the Court. (The gatekeeping ASC changes its name from '*Kjæremålsutvalget*' to '*Ankeutvalget*'.) Grand Chamber is institutionalized to handle intermediately important cases.
- 2010 – A barrier is broken when for the first time a clerk is permitted to sit in on the justices' deliberations in order to substantially assist in justices' opinion writing.

- 2010 – The number of justices on the Court increases from 19 to 20. The number of justices on the ASC increases from four to five to enlarge its screening capacity; three-justice gatekeeping panels are nested within the Committee.
- 2011 – The Court starts to offer clerks seven-year contracts.
- 2013 – The ASC starts to summarily reject criminal interlocutory appeals that evidently do not merit closer review, saving time and improving efficiency (Aamodt 2017:4).
- 2015 – The clerk unit is reorganized. An existing clerk position is converted into the second deputy at the clerk unit. Three new clerk positions bring the total number of clerks in the unit to 23. The additional number of clerks shall serve the justices on the Court's decision-making on merits panels during and after oral arguments, including drafting the facts section of the final decision (Aamodt 2017:4). A clerk now sits in on oral arguments and in conference in approximately 25 per cent of the cases, primarily in civil cases. A clerk's participation is obligatory for cases heard in Grand Chamber or *en banc* (Aamodt 2017:4). The Court's two court clerks ('*protokollsekretær*') are moved to the clerk unit in order to improve the clerk unit's support for the merits panels. The two court clerks, each being a liaison between the Court and the parties to a case, are also responsible for the practical operations in the two courtrooms during oral arguments. Including the student intern and the two court clerks, the clerk unit counts 26 persons.
- 2015 – Outgoing Chief Justice Tore Schei (2015c) states that the number of clerks on the Court should be doubled. The year before, Justice Arnfinn Bårdsen (2014), on behalf of the Court, states that the number of clerks should be increased to 40.
- 2016 – Associate Justice Toril Marie Øie replaces Tore Schei as chief justice.
- 2017 – Chief Justice Øie, in her first annual report editorial, states that she wants to recruit more clerks on the Court and have them assist in the full range of the Court's decision-making. In a letter the Court specifies that it wants to increase the number of clerks from 23 to 30 by 2021 to increase the clerks in assisting the justices in the full range of their decision-making (Høyesteretts Kontor 2017).
- 2017 – The government establishes a white-paper commission on the organization, independence, efficiency and cost-effectiveness of the national courts as well as to the increasing number of demanding cases that the courts are handling. The report is due in 2020.
- 2018 – The Supreme Court launches its new case processing system '*Lovisa*' (March 1). It replaces '*Høyrett*' that had been in service since 2000. The clerk unit continues to monitor the case handling and appeals process using spreadsheets.

2 The Structure and Organization of Decision-Making

In this chapter we lay out and discuss the four stations of decision-making in the Supreme Court: the selection of cases for decisional panels by the Court's gatekeeper, the Appeals Selection Committee (ASC); the oral arguments on a case's merits heard in panels; the panel's deliberation behind closed doors; and the opinion writing that is the result of the justices' work in the decisional panels. These four stations are important for our argument in this book. First, the stations identify the various tasks that the Court's justices perform and the challenges that accompany the tasks across the decision-making process. Second, the different stations lay the foundation necessary for the identification and analysis of the 'whats', 'whens' and 'whys' relevant to the clerk institution.

The first step or station in this decision-making process is the most important one: the ASC's screening of appeals and selection of cases for the Court's decisional panels. Between the deluge of appeals to the Court and the smoother sailing that commences with oral arguments stands the ASC as a lock in the canal. Today, the Committee denies review of 85 to 90 per cent of the merits appeals filed with the Court. The remaining 10 to 15 per cent are appeals that contain principled legal and political questions that warrant a claim on the Court's finite time and energies. In 1955, about one-third of all appeals were denied (Sunde 2015a:121). Since 1957, when the first legal secretary, or clerk, was hired, it has been the clerks' primary task to assist the justices in this crucial deciding-to-decide process.

The four stations provide the structure of decision-making, while the justices serving on these stations constitute its manpower. In combination the stations and justices are the organizational basis for the Court's fundamental task: the resolution of legal questions and controversies. In Chapters 3 through 5, we will address how the number of clerks has increased and how the clerks have become increasingly involved in the Court's decision-making process, moving beyond their support role with the ASC to aiding the justices at the oral arguments, deliberations and opinion-writing stations as well. In order to appreciate this development, in this chapter we discuss the details of the four stations of decision-making as they evolved over time.

2.1 Prelude: Four Groups of Five Justices

The Norwegian Supreme Court has complete and final jurisdiction in civil, criminal, administrative and constitutional cases. Such broad jurisdiction is extremely rare for

European Supreme Courts. The broad jurisdiction affects not only the character of the caseload, but also the recruitment of justices to the Norwegian Supreme Court.

The justices have different career paths, areas of expertise and jurisprudential preferences. But when they perform their various duties on the Court, they are assumed to be generalists who will take on whatever appeal or task is before them. Indeed, this presumption of justices as legal generalists is thoroughly reflected in the way the Secretary General of the Court allocates duties among the justices on behalf of the chief justice. With 20 justices on the Court, the Secretary General initially follows a basic procedure where the justices are rotated and divided into four groups of five justices. The assignment to a specific group is made irrespective of the individual justice's background, area of expertise and personal preference. The first group consists of justices on 'office week'. Essentially, this group of five justices is taken out of rotation. Many of them have finished serving on decisional panels and are given the opportunity to write their opinions and catch up on other business. Justices can expect to have an office week once every five weeks. The office-week group also includes justices who have leaves of absence, are on study leave, are on assignment or are on vacation.[1] The Court's remaining 15 justices serve either on the ASC or on one of the two rotating five-justice decisional panels.

Similar to the justices, the clerks are presumed to be generalists. This means that the clerks have to prepare all kinds of cases for the ASC. With the influence of EU law and the European Human Rights on Norwegian law in the 1990s, two clerks were given the task of keeping track of important changes in each of these two systems of law. However, this formalized specialization within the clerk unit was a temporary deviation from the system of clerks expected to be generalists despite the fact that some informal specialization does exist among the clerks.

2.2 The Appeals Selection Committee – The Gatekeeper

As we have noted, the ASC acts as the Court's gatekeeper. It has done so since 1887 for criminal cases and 1915 for civil cases (Sunde 2015a:116). Its task is to determine whether a given appeal raises one or more legal questions or issues that are sufficiently significant to warrant the Court's attention on its merits. It is also fully authorized to pass final judgements on interlocutory appeals.

1 An example of a leave of absence is Justice Bergljot Webster who in 2013 and 2014 chaired the government white-paper commission on rules and regulations for lawyers (NOU 2015). An example of an assignment is Justice Liv Gjølstad who in 1992 became the leader of the 'worker committee' ('brukerutvalget') of the renovation project leading up to the reopening of the Supreme Court building in 1996.

The Secretary General allocates five justices to serve on the ASC for a period of four to six weeks.[2] Over the course of a year, justices serve two to three times on the Committee (Bårdsen 2014:533). Although five justices are assigned to the Committee, only three justices sit together as a group and constitute the actual Committee. Therefore, in practice and at any time, several interwoven three-justice gatekeeping panels exist (Sunde 2015a:136). Each panel's decision is the decision of the ASC and, hence, the Supreme Court. With five justices available for a three-justice panel, a total of 10 different combinations of three justices exist.[3] The most senior justice on the panel leads the panel's work. In no small part due to the number of appeals made to the Court, the Committee's gatekeeping work is hard and demanding,[4] and perhaps reflecting this is an unwritten rule that no justice will be assigned to the Committee before he or she has sat on the Court for half a year (Sunde 2015a:136). The notion is that new justices need to learn the ropes, to become familiar with the Court's routines and to gain a broader institutional understanding of the legal issues that will inform their decision-making on the Committee.

During their four- to six-week stint on the Committee, all five justices will end up serving on the actual gatekeeping committee an equal amount of time. This is achieved through the short-term rotation system among the justices assigned to the ASC. As we noted earlier, the justices are assigned to the Committee without any recognition of their specialty or preferences; nor are any appeals directed to the Committee with a view to the sitting justices' abilities or interests (Bårdsen 2014:533). However, there is nothing preventing a justice involved in the case from asking for expert advice from a non-participating justice. Finally, since the Committee's decisions on appeals are made through the circulation of written documents rather than in face-to-face meetings, sufficient flexibility exists so that a justice from the Committee may be assigned to serve temporarily elsewhere on the Court if a need arises.

If deemed necessary, the chief justice can appoint a separate group of justices to discuss a more complicated case or consider several cases with overlapping legal questions. When the Court is not in session, usually coinciding with general vacations, the ASC consists of three justices who only convene to handle emergency appeals. The most senior justice assigned to the ASC, or the chief justice if he or she is present, always chairs these more specialized gatekeeping committees.[5]

2 In 2010, when the Court received its 20th justice, five justices were allocated to serve on the ASC (Sunde 2015a:136). *See* www.domstol.no/no/Enkelt-domstol/-Norges-Hoyesterett/Saksbehandling-og-ankeforhandling/Forretningsorden/Forretningsorden-for-Hoyesteretts-ankeutvalg/ (last accessed 28 December 2016).

3 The formula for the number of combinations of three justices drawn from a pool of five justices is: C5,3 = 5!/(3!(5-3)!) = (5*4*3)/(3*2*1) = 10.

4 Once one justice noted to one of the authors that the work in panels is ok, but the job on the ASC is hard and demanding.

5 Due to the chief's leadership and other administrative functions on the Court, he or she serves less time on the ASC than do the other justices.

Procedures are set to ensure that appeals are distributed randomly among the justices on the Committee, and random procedures are also used as to which of the three justices on the Committee first receives the appeal for consideration. Written documents are the grist that the ASC mills. The justices on the Committee receive one folder per case. Each folder is kept closed with a rubber band. The folder is then physically circulated among the justices. A justice may access the digital case handling system if additional documents are needed. The justice who receives a case and the clerk's memo first may already have been in touch with the clerk preparing the case for the Committee. The memo is not written by a personal clerk of the justice. Instead, there is a pool of clerks who are assigned cases. Most importantly, the clerks examine if the case indicates a need for law to be unified, clarified or developed. If so, the case is of principled value and hence should be granted leave of appeal. This memo might be long or short depending on the character of the case.

Each justice reads the documents in the folder of the appeal and either makes a handwritten note on the folder itself or writes a note in a document in the digital case handling system.

The senior justice on the Committee can deviate from the random procedures if the Committee's workload or other exigencies so require. The Secretary General also replaces any justices who must recuse themselves due to a conflict of interest. If the Committee is not in session and a delay in the time necessary to process the appeal is impermissible, the chief justice or the senior justice on the Court will appoint a committee to handle the issue.[6]

The ASC is empowered to make final decisions on interlocutory appeals unless a more principled decision needs to be made by a merits panel. Interlocutory appeals are returned to the Court's administration, and the parties are notified of the outcome. If the Committee denies a merits appeal, it too is returned to the Court's administration so that the parties can be notified of the outcome.

When a merits appeal has been granted and is en route to oral arguments for a decision on its merits, the preparatory justice on the Committee – that is, the justice who first received the folder containing the appeal – will be in charge of the appeal moving forward. Outside the Court, no one knows which justice on the Committee received the appeal first, how the individual justices voted or the justice responsible for preparing and directing the appeal to the decisional panel.

An administrative scheduler communicates with the parties' lawyers to set a date for oral arguments (Norges Høyesterett 2013:34). The scheduler also operates as an administrative coordinator among the advocates in the case if any new documents are presented in the case or there is a request for recordings or additional evidentiary materials.

---

6 *See* https://www.domstol.no/no/Enkelt-domstol/-norges-hoyesterett/om-hoyesterett/forretningsorden/Forretningsorden-for-Hoyesteretts-ankeutvalg/ (last accessed 4 November 2018).

After the parties have responded to the scheduler, the Secretary General matches the case with a five-justice panel already assigned on the Court's scheduled calendar. At the same time, the preparatory justice reports his or her decision regarding the amount of time the appeal should be allocated for oral arguments. The justice's decision is based on five elements: the salience or weight of the legal question in the case, the amount of time the intermediate appeals court used on the case, the amount of time the parties requested for oral arguments in their appeals, any additional points of relevance that were addressed in the communication with the parties in the preparations for the oral arguments, and the justice's own experience with the type of case at hand and the uncertainty of the legal field in which the case is embedded. Allocated time for oral arguments can range from one hour to several days; usually an appeal is heard in a single day (Arnesen, Bentsen, and Grendstad 2018).

2.3 Oral Arguments

If no statutory authority directs otherwise, once the Committee has forwarded the appeal to the merits stage, oral argument is the default Supreme Court decisional procedure in both civil and criminal merits cases.[7] The principle of oral arguments rests on the view that it provides transparency and guarantees a thorough and responsible consideration of the cases. Oral arguments are seen as better suited to penetrate the intricacies and subtleties of a case. They also better ensure the legal principle of contradiction where the advocates are positioned to respond to claims by the other party. And finally, oral argument, combined with public access, offers a basis of legitimacy that would more quickly erode if decisions were decided with written documents only (Schei 2015b:8).

Typically, the Court's two rotating five-justice panels hear the relatively few cases that have been screened in for full merits review. These panels are composed of the ten justices who have neither been assigned to office week nor been slated to sit on the ASC. The assignment of the ten justices to the two parallel panels occurs as follows. First, the ten justices are ranked according to their seniority on the Court. (If the chief justice is among the ten justices available for merits panel assignment, he or she is always ranked first.) Then the justices are allocated to each of the two panels in an alternating manner; this maximizes the range of seniority on the two panels. This procedure also ensures that the most experienced or most inexperienced justices do not serve on the same panel. The most senior justice on the panel will be chair. The first group of five justices will serve on the

7 The Dispute Act Section 30-10, first clause, and The Criminal Procedure Act Section 327, first clause. Exception to the rule of oral arguments exists for civil cases (*see* The Dispute Act Section 30-10, fourth clause) but not for criminal cases (Skoghøy 2016:323).

'First Panel' and is allocated to Court Room number one on the third floor. The second group of five justices will serve on the 'Second Panel' and is allocated to the larger Court Room number two on the second floor.

Some lawyers refer to this allocation of justices to the two panels as the 'principle of random assignment', but given the ranking that takes place prior to the allocation, a more appropriate label coined by a Supreme Court justice would be 'controlled lottery'.[8] The panels' composition of justices is reorganized every week as some justices may move into or come from their 'office week'. Approximately every fifth week a greater turnover occurs when the whole ASC changes. Hence, composition of panels changes from one week to the next. Since a five-justice panel is likely to hear between one and two, but never more than three cases per week, we rarely observe the same combination of five justices across more than two cases.[9]

Oral arguments are rarely held on Mondays. This allows the justices assigned to the merits panels to use the first day of the week to prepare for upcoming oral arguments. Justices study the lower courts' decisions, the legal question(s) present in the case, the statements from the two parties and the memo written by a clerk for the ASC. There might also be a need to take a look at the status of the legal field to which the upcoming cases relate.

On the morning of the day or days set for oral arguments, the justices convene in a back room and don their robes. It is an unspoken rule among the justices not to prime each other in any way or to exchange any opinions on the case before them. Each justice is expected to enter the courtroom and hear the parties based on their individual understanding of the case. The court clerk, who is responsible for the final preparations of the courtroom, cracks open the door and signals to the justices that all is ready.

At the stroke of nine, the door opens and all in the courtroom rise as the justices enter in descending order of seniority and fan out on each side of a large U-shaped table facing the lawyers representing the parties in the case.[10] As the justices take their seats and adjust their chairs, almost in choreographic motions, they throw glances across the courtroom to quickly survey the parties in the case and also scan the room to see how many of the seats reserved for the public have been filled.

The most senior justice is referred to as the presiding justice of the case. The chief justice is always the senior justice if he or she is present. The presiding justice will be in charge

8 Justice Arne Christiansen coined the term 'controlled lottery' (*kontrollert loddtrekning*) in a 1981 Supreme Court decision (Rt-1981–673: 679). There are 15,504 combinations of five justices being drawn from a pool of 20 justices: $C20{,}5 = 20!/(5!(20 - 5)!) = (20*19*18*17*16)/(5*4*3*2*1)$.

9 Hence, analysts are mostly deprived of data in which we can hold the panel composition constant and allow cases to vary.

10 Start of oral arguments used to be at 9:15, but was moved up to 9:00 in order to expand the lunch break from 30 to 45 minutes.

of the case on the panel until the Court reaches its final decision. The presiding justice has already been briefed by the preparatory justice of the case in the ASC.[11] There are no clerks in the courtroom listening to the oral arguments (see Figure 2.1).

Figure 2.1 Judging alone. Traditionally, the five justices on the merits panels face the parties alone. There are no law clerks in the courtroom observing the oral arguments and clerks have no role in the decision-making process moving forward. The figure shows five justices during oral arguments in September 2004 (Rt-2004-1457). Photograph and permission Erlend Aas/NTB Scanpix.

The presiding justice sits at the top of the table and directly faces the two litigants and their lawyers. He or she begins the session by quickly moving through any formalities related to the panel's composition or other forms of procedure related to the case. Occasionally, a justice might request to be excused from serving on a panel because he or she needs more time to write an opinion on a case from an earlier panel assignment. If such a request is made and accepted, the Secretary General temporarily assigns one of the five justices allocated to the ASC to fill the vacated seat. This relief justice is referred to as doing 'picket service'. Of course, the procedure is also used if a justice for some reasons is unable to participate on the panel. The procedure of picket service began in the 1980s, but it was not until the tenure of Chief Justice Tore Schei (2002-2016) that it began to be used more systematically (Sunde 2015a:177; Øie 2016). The justification for picket service is to ensure

11 There are no set rules for the briefing of the presiding justice by the preparatory justice. Some justices want to talk things through more than others and some cases may require a more thorough briefing than others.

the opinion-writing justice has enough time to write decisions that meet the standards of quality a court of last resort requires. When such a replacement occurs, at the opening of the case the presiding justice asks the parties' advocates if they have any objections to the change in the line-up of justices assigned to hear the case since it is different from the line-up of justices announced when the date for oral arguments was published.[12]

Finally, the presiding justice quickly identifies the case and the parties before yielding the floor to the lawyer of the appellant party. The associate justices, seated along the two sides of the table, slightly turn their heads in order to fully catch the action from the lawyers' oral arguments – as if the U-shaped table were a horseshoe magnet with two poles creating a legal-magnetic field that allows it to secure the arguments from the lawyers.[13]

Before oral arguments, the litigants and their lawyers are permitted and expected to submit to the justices a brief containing a clear outline with necessary keywords and references for their arguments. As the lawyers carefully go through their well-prepared and rehearsed arguments, they also walk the justices through their briefs so that when a lawyer turns a page on his or her brief, the justices do the same in almost choreographic motion. The justices may interrupt the lawyers with questions and comments, but such exchanges are rare and take up little of the time during oral arguments. The lawyers are already fully informed about the panel's schedule through the Court's guidelines on case preparations and oral arguments. Following these guidelines, the presiding justice may cut the lawyers off when it is time for a small break or for lunch. At a break, the presiding justice leads his or her court out of the courtroom in descending order of seniority.

The small breaks, introduced by Chief Justice Smith, take place at about 10.15, 11.10 and 13.30 (Sunde 2015a:327). During these small breaks, while gathered again in the back room, the justices are still expected not to discuss the case with one another. But it is permitted for the justices to bounce questions off one another that they may ask the litigants after the break. The breaks, however, are not legal practicums or moot courts. More often than not, exchanges among the justices involve small talk about any number of subjects on the justices' minds.[14]

Oral arguments are the most public aspect of the Court's decision-making. In general, oral arguments are also a very important and distinguishable element of the institution of

12 The question on line-up is not merely a formal question. The Government Advocate Fredrik Sejersted noted that during Schei's 14 years as Chief, one of the first things that lawyers look at when a case is docketed is the composition of the panel. This is of course due to the different positions that justices may take or are expected to take on various issues (Sejersted 2016).

13 There is some empirical evidence, at least in the context of the U.S. Supreme Court, that the shape of the courtroom and the organization of the bench influence courtroom behaviour (*see* Black, Johnson, and Owens 2018).

14 It speaks to the underlying informalities behind the strict Court facade that members of the public, who also leave the courtroom and enter the outside corridor to stretch their legs, may run into an unrobed justice hurrying through the corridor to fetch something from his or her office.

conflict resolution in Norway (Nylund 2010). Formally, what has not been presented during the oral arguments at the Supreme Court cannot provide a basis for the Court's final decision.[15] Therefore, oral arguments provide a significant opportunity for the justices to glean important information about the issues and legal questions at bar. If a justice wants to emphasize an argument that the parties may have disregarded, the justice has to ask the parties to take the argument into consideration during the oral arguments. Because of the quasi-random nature of panel composition, the blinded assignment of appeals to the panels and the Court's broad substantive jurisdictional authority, it is very likely that the justices reviewing any given appeal are not experts in the specific area of the law upon which the appeal turns. Accordingly, the justices make use of the oral arguments to develop a fuller understanding of the legal issues. Also indicative of the informational purposes that oral arguments serve, Norway's Supreme Court advocates are not pressed to present their cases within a rigid and tightly compressed time period, unlike their counterparts in the U.S. Supreme Court. The justices and advocates abide by the overall time period allocated to the oral arguments of the case in the courtroom.

2.3.1 Grand Chamber and Plenary Sessions

The growing presence of international law has made the legal field more complicated and generated principled legal questions more frequently (Nadim 2017). Hence, it is expected that the Court will adjudicate an increasing number of cases in Grand Chamber and *en banc* and in so doing increase its authority and influence in the Norwegian constitutional system.[16]

As of this writing, resolving cases in Grand Chamber and *en banc* is still infrequent, and the default mode of operation remains decision-making by way of the two five-justice panels. Grand Chamber and *en banc* hearings occur when an appeal is deemed of 'special importance' or concerns an 'extraordinary case'. Thus, cases heard and decided in Grand Chamber and *en banc* are by nature complicated, principled and even downright 'political' when, for example, they contain contested issues linked to the *ex post facto* or *full compensation* sections of the Constitution (Grendstad, Shaffer, and Waltenburg 2015). A higher proportion of dissents and concurrences also accompany their decisions simply because the number of justices participating in the decisional process is greater (Bentsen 2018b).

15 Some of the following paragraphs are adapted from Grendstad et al. (2015: 65ff).

16 Nadim points out that since 1926, when plenary decisions were instituted, and until 2016, including Grand Chamber decisions that were instituted in 2008, a total of 148 cases were decided in these panels. That amounts to an average of 1.6 cases per year. In years 1996 to 2016 only, the Supreme Court decided 2.55 cases per year (Nadim 2017: 169, 174). In 2010, for instance, the Court resolved three controversial cases en banc using its power of judicial review. Rt-2010-143, Rt-2010-535, Rt-2010-1445 (Nadim 2017; Sunde 2015a).

The 11-justice Grand Chambers are convened to hear cases of 'special importance'. To compose the Grand Chamber, ten justices are drawn at random and join the chief justice. All of the associate justices, other than those permissibly exempted or recused due to a conflict of interest, are eligible for the Grand Chamber lottery. 'Special importance' means *inter alia* that there is a possibility that the outcome of the case deviates from a precedent. It may also mean that the case raises a conflict between statutes, provisional ordinances and parliamentary decisions. Based on the same criteria, but in 'extraordinary cases' which also includes constitutional issues, the Court can hear cases *en banc*. When *en banc* sessions are convened, every justice, other than those with a permissible exemption or a recusal, sits for the case.[17] If an even number of justices is available, the most junior justice will leave his or her seat. But this junior justice will remain in the courtroom during oral arguments and will follow the decision-making process and step in as an ordinary voting justice if any of the other justices is unable to complete participation in the case.

Prior to 2008, and in accordance with the Court Act of 1915, the Court had to convene *en banc* if two or more justices considered a statute used in an appeal to be in violation of the Constitution. After 2008, the Court Act does not contain an equivalent trigger to decide a case in Grand Chamber or *en banc*. But lawmakers assumed that if Parliament had in fact considered a law in light of the Constitution, the competence to review such a consideration should be performed by the Supreme Court in plenary session.[18]

The decisional rules to hear a case in Grand Chamber or *en banc* depend on the case's location in the Court's decision-making process. Basically, the chief justice at any point can decide to move a case to a Grand Chamber or the full Court. A case can also move to a Grand Chamber or *en banc* hearing if two justices on the relevant five-justice panel call for it to be so heard. And a case can move to *en banc* if six justices on the Grand Chamber call for it to be so moved.[19] Grand Chamber sessions were instituted in 2008 in an effort to facilitate more flexible decision-making between the hum of the ordinary five-justice panels and the far more disruptive reorganization of the Court's procedures that plenary decisions bring about.[20]

2.4 Deliberations

When oral arguments have been completed within the time frame that was allocated to the case, the presiding justice thanks the parties, adjourns the Court and leads the associate

17 The Court Act, § 5.4.

18 *See* Skoghøy (2008: 483 and endnote 11, p 499).

19 The Court Act, § 6.

20 A senior member of the Court once referred to the major disruptions of the regular cycle that followed the reorganization of the Court into plenary mode simply as 'hell'.

justices through the back door and out of the courtroom. The justices take off their robes and may exchange a few general comments on the case. The presiding justice communicates with the court clerk to schedule a time for deliberations. If the case is easy and time permits, the deliberation may be carried out the same day as the oral arguments. If the case is hard and oral arguments have lasted the whole day, the justices will meet on one or more of the following days for deliberation.

The preference is always to move to deliberations fairly quickly while the case is fresh in the justices' minds. In the same way as the justices prepared for oral arguments, they prepare individually for deliberations. Thus, when they meet again, there have been no prior, public declarations. Nevertheless, there may be a quiet expectation about the views that the other justices may hold.

Deliberation, or conference, takes place in the same courtroom where oral arguments took place. The rule is that only the justices who served on the panel, Grand Chamber or *en banc* participate during the deliberation and discussion of a case's merits. Traditionally, the court clerk is also present and at hand for any practical or timely issue that may arise. But without any immediate requests from the justices, the court clerk may quietly carry out other duties such as proof reading, or the clerk may even occasionally leave the courtroom for short periods of time to accomplish other tasks. Meanwhile, the justices have retaken the same seats they occupied during oral arguments. Without any members of the public in the courtroom, there is no need for the justices to don their robes. The court clerk may be available for smaller tasks. Since 2015, a law clerk will be present during deliberations if he or she is to assist in writing the majority opinion.

The deliberations are 'formalized discussions'. They start with the presiding justice presenting, without interruptions from the other justices, his or her views on the facts of the case and the relevant statutes in question. The exposition, lasting up to an hour, perhaps more in very difficult cases, usually takes the shape of the final arguments and informs the content and decision of the Court. This exposition is also a demonstration of the skills and knowledge of a justice and contributes to the standing of the justice among his or her peers. Based on this presentation, the presiding justice ends by suggesting, not concluding, how the case should be finally decided.[21]

Then, in strict order of descending seniority, each justice offers his or her views on the case. In larger cases, these deliberations may take some time; second and third rounds of discussion can take place, as individual justices might describe their ratiocination at some length in an effort to convince or persuade their counterparts. No justice is tied to his or her opinion during deliberations, and justices may change their position on the case at a later stage.

21 Some of the following paragraphs are adapted from Grendstad et al. (2015:66ff). *See also* Schei (2010; 2015b).

It is important to note the norm that the justices are expected to speak to the case and not to any of their colleagues with whom they agree or disagree. Combined with the decorum of not interrupting one another and the fact that any given composition of the five-justice panels is almost unique, the norm of speaking to the case and not to the other justices reduces potential for tension that could otherwise develop between strong and self-confident intellects.

Deliberations on Grand Chamber and *en banc* cases follow the same procedure as on panels. The presiding justice – and in these cases the chief justice who by default chairs these procedures – takes the lead when justices meet for deliberations on a day following oral arguments.[22] Because these cases will be more complex and involve thornier legal issues and principles, and since more justices are participating, the formal discussions take longer. Each justice speaks in turn, and several rounds of discussions may take place given the complexity of the issues involved.

The justices complete their deliberations by casting their tentative votes. The vote in conference is preliminary but nevertheless and for all practical purposes is indicative of the final vote. Vote fluidity may occur until the final decision has been authored, or any dissents or concurrences have been completed, at which time a last round of votes is finalized and made public. Before the meeting is adjourned, the justices agree on a tentative timetable for when the decision will be announced (Schei 2015b).

2.5 Opinion Writing

During the tenure of Chief Justice Smith, the Court experimented with a clerk listening in at the deliberations to assist writing the majority opinion. The quality of the clerk's draft was too poor and the Court decided to discontinue the experiment. The Court instead follows a norm of equal division of the opinion-writing workload. The Secretary General keeps track of the justices' opinion writing and has developed a system by which it is imparted to the justices before oral arguments whose turn it is to write the majority opinion. Opinion assignment is not at all communicated to the parties of the case. When the first round of deliberations is completed and before the meeting breaks up, the presiding justice confirms the formal assignments of the opinion writing. Changes in assignment can be made, however, when the justice to whom the opinion would ordinarily be assigned is in the minority. Due to the workload of preparing the case for oral arguments, for chairing the panel during oral arguments and being responsible for presenting the case at the start

22 If, for some reason, the chief justice is unable to carry out these duties, the justice with the highest court seniority takes over.

of the deliberations, the presiding justice will never write the opinion (but may write a dissenting or concurring opinion if he or she so chooses).

There are separate schedules for opinion writing on Grand Chamber and *en banc* decisions. As noted earlier, all justices on the Court, except those who are recused due to conflict of interest, serve in *en banc* cases. Because these cases are more demanding, more time is needed to prepare to compose the opinion. Therefore, the designated opinion author will know his or her assignment well in advance of the oral arguments. Since the ten justices sitting with the chief in Grand Chamber cases are drawn at random, the designated opinion writer is determined by yet another *ad hoc* schedule.

The justice who writes the opinion of the Court will circulate the draft among the other justices on the panel within a week or so. Recall that a justice from the ASC might be performing picket service because a justice assigned to the decisional panel might have been excused from hearing an appeal in order to complete a previously assigned majority opinion. The picket service justice normally will not be assigned any opinion-writing duties; yet, he or she may mount a "pickett's charge" and write a concurring or dissenting opinion if his or her preferences are strong enough. A draft of the Court's decision is presented in a new meeting with all the justices on the panel. If the case is difficult, a final decision may require several meetings.

In a collegial institution like the Norwegian Supreme Court, there is a shared responsibility for the final decision, especially if it is unanimous. Comments on the draft include both grammar and structure, but specific comments on substance are offered in writing. Comments are usually accepted since they are offered by sincere colleagues who have read the first draft with fresh eyes.[23] But the writing style of the author is still respected. A more individualized writing style and a sharper articulation of individual preferences are present when a justice writes a concurrence or a dissent.

A final conference takes place among the justices in roughly one to three weeks following the oral arguments in panels. The presiding justice starts by asking if any of the justices has altered his or her opinion. If not, the justices move on to the final review of the decision. In this final round of dotting the i's and crossing the t's, the deletion or revision of entire sentences is permitted as long as the original intent and substance remain unaltered.[24] This

23 Any disagreement between the justices is first attempted to be resolved by a compromise. On the other hand, too many compromises may lead to decisions providing insufficient guidelines to the lower courts.

24 Former Chief Justice Tore Schei has emphasized that even though justices offer individual votes, the justices invest a lot in maximizing the quality of the decisions, which must be required from the highest court in the land with important societal functions. Schei commended the employees and organization of the whole Court in achieving the required quality levels (Schei 2015a).

procedure is based on the principle that casting votes on the Court is part of an oral procedure and that the final and written decision on the Court must reflect this procedure.[25]

The justice who has been assigned to write the majority opinion is referred to in more technical terms as 'the first voting justice'.[26] When a final decision is reached, the presiding justice asks whether the other justices are ready to cast their votes. The first voting justice is asked to read the final conclusion of the case. The justices who agree with the majority opinion state that they "in substance and outcome agree with the first voting justice", and subsequent justices who agree state "Likewise".[27] A justice who concurs or dissents states his or her own views and is followed by any other justice who agrees with him or her using the same phrase. The decision is completed when the justices cast a new round of votes, and it is finalized when the presiding justice casts his or her vote.[28] The final decision is proofread; ensuring the consistency of its sources and references is the responsibility of the court clerk.

The decision is brought to the public in one of two ways. If the decision is expected to attract public interest, a notice of the time of the decision's announcement is publicized, and the decision itself is conveyed to the parties and the public by the justices convening in the courtroom in robes. A summary of the decision is read by the first voting justice before each justice casts his or her vote. If little public interest in the decision is expected, the public and a more formal presentation is skipped, and the decision is communicated to the parties electronically and published on the Court's home page in full.[29]

2.6 ENTER THE CLERKS

When the Supreme Court in September 1996 moved into the fully renovated Palace of Justice, the Norwegian news agency NTB published a story that tersely stated the following:

25 Supreme Court cases decided by the procedure of oral arguments shall also be decided by the justices casting their votes by voice. The presiding justice always casts the final vote. See The Dispute Act Section 19-4, fourth clause, and The Criminal Procedure Act Section 41, fourth clause, and Section 32 third clause (Skoghøy 2016:324f).

26 The 'first voting justice' ('førstvoterende') is a term that is also conveniently used by media and law text books in order to bypass the actual identification and naming of the justice who penned the Court's majority decision.

27 The phrases occur in two versions of the two Norwegian languages used by justices on the Court: 'Jeg er i det vesentlige og i resultatet enig med førstvoterende' or 'Eg er i det hovudsaklege og i resultatet einig med førstvoterande' and 'Likeså' or 'Det same'.

28 The Dispute Act Section 19-4, fourth clause, and The Criminal Procedure Act Section 32, third clause.

29 The Criminal Procedure Act Section 32, third clause, and The Dispute Act Section 19-4, third clause, second period, require that the voting shall take place in public. Usually the outcome of the decisions is communicated directly to parties and then made public. It may also happen that the Court may notify the parties that the voting will in fact take place in public if the Court is of the opinion that there is a larger public interest in the outcome of the case (Grendstad, Shaffer, and Waltenburg 2017; Skoghøy 2016).

> Ever since the Supreme Court was established in 1815, the country's supreme court has suffered a cramped and homeless fate. Only after more than 180 years, the Supreme Court has finally acquired its own splendid building – without doubt the country's most beautiful workplace for the 18 justices and the Chief Justice (NTB 1996).

The story did not mention the 13 clerks or the administration that also would start working in the building. The news story identifies the most known and conspicuous workforce on the Court. But the quote also illustrates how easy it is to miss the increasingly important workforce behind the walls: the clerks. In the next chapter we discuss more thoroughly key moments in the growth of the clerk unit on the Court. We present the integrated role that the clerks performed for the ASC after the Court had gained full control of its docket in 2008. And we discuss how, starting around 2010, the clerks have become increasingly involved in what historically had been the exclusive domain of the justices: oral arguments, deliberations and opinion writing.

3 "… Like Ordering Soldiers toward a Shower of Bullets"

> My leitmotif is simple: The justices on the Supreme Court are so central in the country's legal life that all the assistance – at all levels – that can help create the most ideal work situation, must be made available. … As a main guideline, I therefore hold that as long as any justice asks for more assistance than the clerk unit can deliver, the unit must expand (Supreme Court Chief Justice Carsten Smith, 1997).[1]

3.1 Caseload and Backlog

A perennial feature of the Supreme Court is that appeals keep arriving. And a recurring challenge for the Supreme Court is that unprocessed cases keep piling up because the number of appeals outstrips the Court's capacity. Above a certain threshold, caseloads and backlogs are two concrete measures of stress on the Court. Caseloads provide the external pressure on the Court at the gate. In the absence of efficient gatekeeping, appeals become mountainous caseloads that can turn into backlogs. Backlogs constitute the internal and congestive bottlenecks of the Court. They are indicators of the accumulation of unperformed tasks. Both caseload and backlog have animated discussions of resources and capacity of the Court – as to the number of justices, the number of clerks and the tools necessary for hewing out from the piles of appeals the gems of legal questions.

In his call-to-arms address to the Norwegian Association of Judges, Carsten Smith was explicit about the Supreme Court's need for assistants to help the justices deal with the increasing incidence of appeals in order to reduce the number of merits cases decided by the Court. In 1974, a total of 1,888 appeals arrived at the Court and 367 cases were decided in decisional panels. In 1991, the year Smith became chief justice, 3,701 appeals arrived at the Court and 334 cases were decided in decisional panels. Whereas the number of merits decisions was fairly stable, the number of appeals the justices first had to wade through doubled.

Figure 3.1 shows the development in the total number of appeals to and the total number of decisions in merits panels on the Norwegian Supreme Court. The figure enables us to appreciate the increasing pressure on the Court's resources and capacity as the total

1 Court internal memo, qtd in Aamodt (2017:1).

number of merits and interlocutory appeals increased from 1,632 appeals in 1970 (the first year for which we have this type of data), passing 2,500 appeals in 1988 for the third time in the 1980s and then reaching its all-time high of 3,701 appeals in 1991. Not until the criminal procedure reform was implemented in 1995 did the number of appeals drop precipitously to an all-time low of 1,316 in 1996. And then, as the figure shows, the number of appeals started to pick up with the new millennium, as if a new tide was building.

Figure 3.1 Caseload

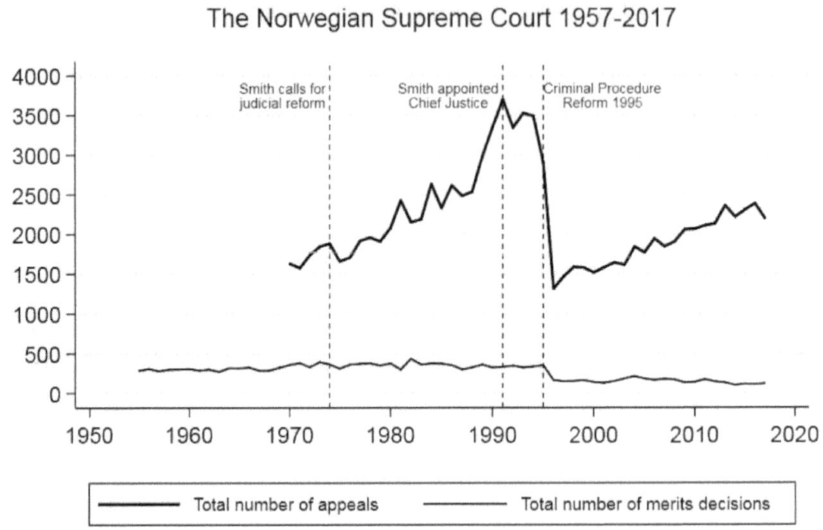

Caseload: Total number of appeals and total number of decisions in merits panels
Source: The Norwegian Supreme Court Annual Statistics

A less dramatic, but no less relevant figure is the total number of decisions handed down in the Court's two parallel five-justice merits panels. In performing their gatekeeping role, the three justices on the Appeals Selection Committee (ASC) do not need to convene to make their decisions. The decisional panels, however, need more coordination inasmuch as they require a much larger degree of collective behaviour involving advocates for the parties, the litigants themselves and public presentations of the oral arguments. In the 41 years between 1955 and 1995, the year that reform in criminal procedures was implemented, an average of 336 decisions per year were handed down in the merits panels. In the 22 years between 1996 and 2017, an average of 153 decisions were handed down in the two merits panels. This indicates that the workload and output of the Court decreased at the same time as the number of clerks increased.

The congestion on the Court can be measured in its number of backlogs. One type of backlogs is appeals that have been granted review by the ASC and are waiting to be decided in decisional panels. Figure 3.2 shows the dramatic change in the number of backlogs of decisional panels in the 1955-1965 decade. Evidently, the Court was only slowly reducing its backlog from 438 cases in 1955 to the more steady rate of 100-200 backlogs between 1963 and 1997. Shortly after the 1995 criminal procedure reform, backlogs fell to a new lower level.[2] For all years since 2008, the number of backlogs has been below 50 (data are missing for 2000-2006). Although the clerks are not involved in handling cases in the merits panels, their contribution to keeping the backlogs of the ASC low helps to reduce the Court's work pressure and sense of crisis on the Court. To put it simply, backlogs anywhere hurt the Court everywhere.

Figure 3.2 Backlogs

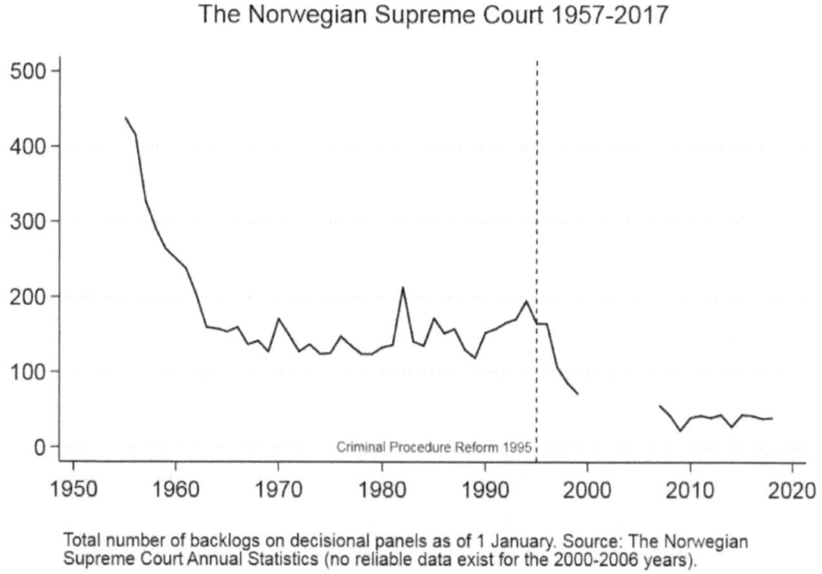

Figures 3.1 and 3.2 depict the context of the overall workload of the Court from 1955 to 2017, the time period we are analysing in this book. During this time period, the Court hired its first clerk in 1957, the justices disagreed about the number of clerks to be employed

2 The Norwegian Supreme Court publishes annual workload and backlog statistics. Their data on backlogs since 2000, except for the total of panel backlogs for the years 2006-2017, are unreliable and are not included in our figures and analyses. Because of the inconsistencies of the two tracking systems used by the Court, we cannot be certain of the validity of the numbers.

in the clerk pool, the Court transformed from a court of appeal to a court of precedent and the clerks' role slowly evolved beyond providing assistance to the justices on the ASC to encompass support for the justices across the Court's full decisional process.

3.2 Demonstrating the Potential

The basic task of the first clerk in 1957 was to assist the ASC. That essential task has remained unchanged even as the number of clerks slowly grew through the 1980s. In 1965, at least on paper, a clerk's duties were increased. Clerks were also given the responsibility of assisting the justices in finding relevant legal sources linked to the appeals that were to be decided in the ASC.[3] In 1965, with only one clerk and the Court receiving 1,404 appeals, it was clear that most of the job of reviewing legal sources and handling appeals was still done by the justices themselves (Sunde 2015a:148).

In the 1977 government budget, the Court received funds for hiring a second clerk. Operationally, however, the number of clerks did not double; the clerk who was already in place was on a long-term sick leave. Fortunately, the Court had hired Karenanne Gussgard for the newly created second position. Gussgard showed a strong commitment to her new job and in many ways demonstrated the institutional potential of hiring clerks. During her time as a clerk, the justices started receiving memos for a few of the appeals they were to consider, and they also received drafts of final decisions for selected appeals (Sunde 2015a:149).

A strong legacy of Gussgard's clerkship was her contribution towards uniformity of decisions across similar cases. She initiated a filing system of index cards that grew over time into an extensive archive. She composed index cards of decisions and filed them according to the clause that had been used for the Court's decision in the case. A strength of the Gussgard archive is that it was more up to date than printed conventional legal sources, which would necessarily omit decisions that were made after the printed volumes went to press. In the early 1980s Gussgard was still the only clerk on the Court. Given the time-bounded and rotating nature of the 18 justices' assignment to the ASC, even a single clerk could be a force of continuity. Yet, the daunting number of appeals that flooded the Committee made equal treatment of equal cases over time an elusive aspiration. In 1983 Gussgard left the Court to serve as a trial court judge in Oslo (1983-1990) only to return to the Supreme Court in 1990 when the government appointed her as a justice (1990-2010).[4]

3 Legal secretary ('juridisk sekretær') was the official title until Chief Justice Carsten Smith changed it to clerk ('utreder') in 1992.

4 The only other justice with a background as clerk to serve on the Court is Cecilie Østensen Berglund. Very much a Court insider, Berglund clerked on the Court during 2002-2005, became a deputy on the clerk unit

3.3 Demands for Efficiency, Sacrificing Saturdays

During the 1980s, the reverberations of the liberal-conservative business era's demand for greater efficiency were also felt on the Court. In its budget proposal of 1984, the government required the courts to demonstrate greater speed and efficiency as measured by the time it took a case to move through the judicial system to final resolution (Sunde 2015a:152; Stortingsproposisjon nr. 1 1983-1984:31). Additionally, Sunde (2015a:153) notes that the 1980s was a decade in which 'management by objectives' took hold in Norwegian society and that the Supreme Court, as was true for other secular governmental bodies, increasingly had to document and report its activities.[5]

Demands for greater efficiency and requirements that activities be documented were (not unreasonably) perceived as bureaucratic burdens that aggravated some of the justices. They saw these governmental requirements as improper and unwarranted impositions on the Court's autonomy that would also reduce their own authority. One of these justices was Elisabeth Schweigaard Selmer.

Associate Justice Selmer had been recruited to the Supreme Court in 1971 almost straight out of her job as Minister of Justice for the centre-conservative Borten government. In 1978, after having served on the Court for seven years, Justice Schweigaard Selmer proposed that the Court implement the five-day work week that was common in other areas of society. The problem, obviously, was Court capacity. The justices were already strained by the gruelling and growing workload on the ASC and lack of staff support. Giving up Saturday as a working day and expanding the weekend would mean that the Court would give up a total of 'two worker-labour years'.[6]

Evidently, removing Saturday from the workweek had to be compensated in one way or another. In the absence of efficient tools and mechanisms for screening appeals, the loss of Saturdays could be compensated by increasing the number of justices, increasing the number of clerks and/or expanding oral arguments on decisional panels to include Mondays, which the justices by tradition had reserved for preparing for the week ahead. None of the options seemed possible or attractive. But, in a sense, officially removing Saturday from the workweek could be seen as the thin end of a wedge that opened up new ways of rethinking change.

---

in 2005-2007, served as the deputy secretary general on the Court during 2007-2009 before returning from an appeal court judgeship in 2017 when she was appointed Supreme Court Justice.

5 Management by objectives (MBO) is a process whereby the management or the principal defines the main objectives of the organization and includes the members of the organization in deciding how to reach the objectives. The various tasks and sequences of work can be measured so that efficiency, performance and achievements can be monitored. The MBO concept was first popularized by Peter Drucker (1954).

6 'Worker-labour year' is a technical, administrative term for the amount of work one person is expected to carry out if employed for a full year. Effectively, the Court would lose the equivalent of two justices if it gave up Saturday as a work day.

In the 1980s, the Supreme Court was still committed to the twin goals of "ensuring unity of the law" and "taking the lead in the development of the law in areas where legislation fails to reach".[7] But the goal of unity of the law was easier said than achieved as long as the Court operated in two panels and not in one panel only. Ever since 1905 the Court had been operating under a 'temporary' regime of resolving cases in two parallel five-justice decisional panels. Chief Justice Erling Sandene, who served as chief from 1984 to 1991, was very reluctant to request the addition of justices in order to add a third merits panel to the Court, however temporary this adjustment would turn out to be, for fear of its deleterious effect on the unity of the law.

Comparatively, the fact that in the 1980s the high courts of Sweden and Finland reduced their panels from three to two was considered a boon to their achievement of the unity of the law. Moreover, Sandene believed that unity of the law was already being compromised by the Supreme Court; thus, going against the grain and dividing itself into three parallel panels would make unity of law even more elusive, if not an outright impossibility.[8] Hiring more clerks to improve the division of labour on the Court had still not taken hold in the minds of the justices. Thus, the only viable way forward was to implement a more rigid, Taylorism-styled work-week calendar.[9]

By the end of the 1980s, the justices did get Saturday off. Without tangible compensation for the loss of a workday and without further ado, Chief Justice Erling Sandene simply removed Saturday from the weekly calendar when allocating justices to the various tasks on the Court.

3.4 The Court Turns Down an Offer for More Clerks – 'A Year of Crisis'

In the 1980s, the Court's leadership still did not fully grasp the institutional opportunities a larger number of clerks would afford. The number of clerks increased to four in 1987, but their number could in fact have risen to six. The Ministry of Justice offered the Court a total of six clerks to assist in processing the appeals that had accumulated following the new Criminal Procedure Act (passed in 1981 but taking effect in 1986). Chief Justice Sandene and Director Sophie Solheim, however, failed to see what tasks all these clerks could perform. Additionally, they were worried that they did not have office space to

---

7 A letter from all the Supreme Court justices to the Ministry of Justice, 18 July 1979 (Ot.prp. nr. 41 1980-1981:4).

8 In the immediate post-Second World War years, the Court was temporarily divided into three panels in order to handle the large number of war crime trials (Sandmo 2005).

9 Sunde (2015a:151) claims that the 1988 implementation of the five-day work week was as profound for the organization of the Court as the implementation of the two-step criminal reform of 1995.

accommodate so many clerks in the 'Palace of Justice', which the Court shared with the Oslo area's trial and appeal courts. (It would do so until 1994.) The Court already used offices in the adjacent building in Grubbegata for some of its personnel.[10]

The justices sided with the Court's leadership on the matter of adding more clerks. In a meeting of the justices, it was decided to turn down the full offer from the Ministry and accept only four clerks (Sunde 2015a:149). The justices' view reflected a deep sentiment among them illustrated by an unwavering Associate Justice Jens Bugge (1982-2000). He argued that the quality of the Court's work deteriorated when clerks were recruited and assigned tasks the justices previously handled. According to Justice Bugge, the Court was much better off when the whole process – from deciding to decide on the ASC to the final vote on the merits – was the exclusive responsibility of the justices themselves. An alternative view is that the justices preferred a heavier caseload as a means to burnish the Court's institutional prestige.

Meanwhile, as Figure 3.1 demonstrated and Figure 3.3 details, the number of appeals kept coming to the ASC. From 1985 to 1994, the ASC handled a total of 30,360 appeals, of which 7,272 (24 per cent) were civil appeals and 23,088 (76 per cent) were criminal appeals. During that same period, 3,333 cases were decided in the ordinary five-justice merits panels, with similar distributions between criminal (2676, 80 per cent) and civil (657, 20 per cent) cases.[11] A justice recalls this period as "a deluge of criminal cases".[12]

10 Sandene and Solheim's resistance to change also delayed the introduction of computers. In many ways, it was gentle requests from clerks that hastened the introduction of computers. The Supreme Court was the last of the three courts based in Oslo, all located in the same building, to modernize their offices with up-to-date equipment.

11 Associate Justice Wilhelm Matheson points out that of the criminal cases, 400 cases (15 per cent) dealt with driving under the influence of alcohol (Matheson 2016:599). The numbers in the text are the authors' own data.

12 Justice interview 17 November 2017, start page 100, p. 100.

Figure 3.3 Civil and Criminal Appeals

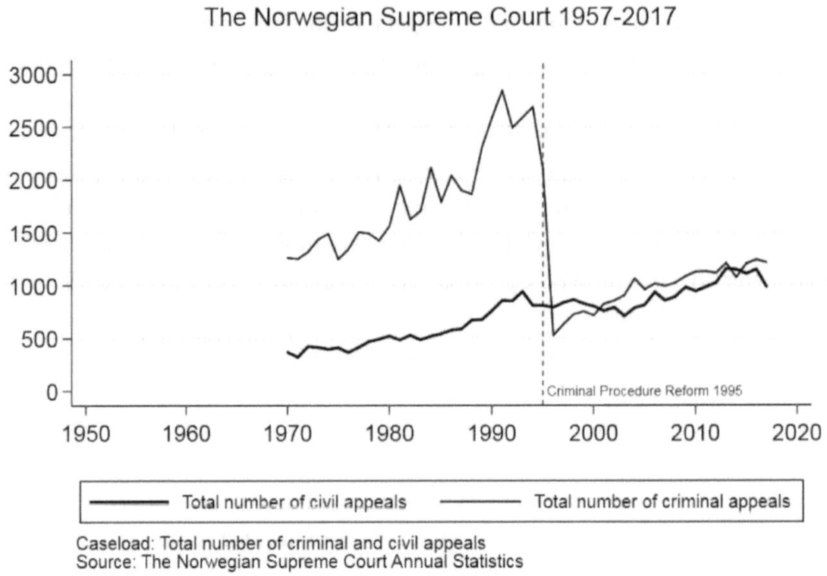

Whereas clerks sometimes would prepare civil law merits appeals for the Committee, the justices themselves handled all criminal law merits appeals. With the appeal courts being courts of original jurisdiction in severe criminal cases until 1995, a right to appeal to the Supreme Court as the second and last instance always existed. An advantage of the justices handling the criminal cases was that they accumulated a general understanding of the field and therefore could process the petty criminal appeals fairly efficiently. Yet, the sheer volume of criminal appeals was a burden for which the clerks could offer some minor assistance – viz. for many of the criminal appeals, the clerks would go through the documents and insert small slips of paper to aid the justices' own navigation through the documents.

The Court calendar was tight but with lacunas occasionally opening up, which acted as safety valves. Criminal case lawyers, dispersed in their law firms around the city of Oslo, could be summoned on short notice when suddenly a slot on the calendar became available to expedite an appeal (Grendstad, Shaffer, and Waltenburg 2015). But these were random opportunities and could not be counted on to occur at especially propitious moments. Thus, there were unassailable signs that the nation's highest court was mired in problems of capacity. The year 1988 would be remembered as "a year of crisis" (Sunde 2015a:149).

But the dark cloud had a silver lining. In many ways the trial and errors of handling the daunting number of cases that were appealed to the Court, the gruelling workload of the ASC, the inexperience and reluctance of the Court's leadership to draw upon the service of clerks to facilitate the operations and workflow of the Court, as well as the physical limitations of the Court itself laid open a new understanding of changes that could be sought and implemented.

The expansion of the clerk pool in 1984 from two to three clerks was a result of an external initiative by the Ministry of Justice. The unit's next expansion three years later was also pushed from outside and somewhat reluctantly accepted by the Court. After 1987, the drive for expansion of the clerk pool was a result of an internal initiative. If 1988 was a year of crisis, something was about to change.

3.5 Something Has Got to Give

Both Justice Elisabeth Schweigaard Selmer and Justice Tore Schei hailed from influential legal families and, true to tradition, they both had married lawyers.[13] It so happened that they found themselves working together on the ASC in December 1988. This was the Committee's dreaded December. Joining them as the third member on the Committee was Justice Vera Holmøy, who had been on the Court for 12 years, having been appointed in 1976. At the age of 65, Justice Schweigaard Selmer (granddaughter of Supreme Court Justice Herman Reimers) had served as Minister of Justice and already had 18 years of service on the Court. Of this trio, Justice Tore Schei (son of Supreme Court Justice Andreas Olai Schei and later chief justice himself) was very much the junior member, possessing less than two years' experience on the Court. Schei also bore substantial responsibility for two small children since his wife was a business lawyer.

Impeccable legal credentials, membership in prominent legal families and pressing family commitments, however, could not exempt these justices from their demanding Committee duties. Screening cases on the ASC was hard work, and the appeals kept coming. Despite working late as usual, they still found themselves screening appeals on Sunday, 18 December 1988, which, as far as family commitments and final Christmas preparations go, was the hallowed fourth Sunday of Advent. During a break in the screening of appeals, the three justices agreed that enough was enough. Things could not go on with an unending river of petty cases that first flooded the ASC and then swamped the Court.

Something had to give. The solution was docket control.

13 Hjellbrekke and Korsnes have studied data indicating that lawyers are among the professions whose children's social retention through education is the highest. Four out of five children of lawyers complete higher education (2010:48,52). They also point out that propensity towards establishing dynasties is most conspicuously found among lawyers, physicians and engineers (2014).

3.6 "... Ordered toward a Shower of Bullets"

Between 1971 and 1991, the number of appeals handled in the ASC more than doubled from 1,575 to 3,701. Several justices, Justice Bugge for one, said that they had to prepare their families for their long absences when they were heading for the Committee; in the late 1980s and early 1990s justices on the Committee anticipated 18-hour working days that would continue through the weekends (Sunde 2015a:148).

By 1989, shortly after the Sunday of the Advent burnout in 1988, then-Justice Schei initiated a committee that was to offer solutions to the backlog of appeals and the heavy workload of the ASC. One suggestion was to bring a fourth justice onto the Committee. A fourth justice would allow the Committee to have several nested three-justice screening panels working at the same time (Sunde 2015a:148). By 1994, it was suggested that a fifth justice be added to the Committee. The five-justice ambition did not materialize until 2010 when the number of Supreme Court justices increased to 20.

Rather than increasing the number of justices on the Committee, however, an alternative solution was to increase the number of clerks available to assist the justices on the Committee. At least since his 1974 speech, Carsten Smith had promoted the idea that the Supreme Court ought to have discretionary jurisdiction, and for at least that long, the idea had no support. But the justices' experiences during the 1980s – the 'year of crisis' in 1988 and its December burnout – indicated that discretionary jurisdiction and docket control were in the offing.

Of course, law professor Carsten Smith was not oblivious to the challenges on the Court. As dean of the University of Oslo Law School – one leg of the legal triangle in the nation's capital (the Supreme Court and the Ministry of Justice being the other two) – Smith was well aware of the wheels that needed grease. In addition, he had already served three stints as an interim justice on the Court – November and December 1987, November and December 1989, and January 1990 – so he knew first-hand of the ASC's challenging situation, although he had not accumulated the required six months of justice apprenticeship deemed essential to sit on the ASC.

It was not too long after the 'year of crisis' in 1988 that the government airlifted law professor Carsten Smith and parachuted him into the Supreme Court as chief justice over the objection of the Court itself, which had preferred to elevate 65-year-old Associate Justice Arne Christiansen to chief. The government was not interested in the Court's personnel preferences. The government supported Smith's agenda, and he took the helm of the Court in 1991 (Grendstad, Shaffer, and Waltenburg 2015).

Of the many things Smith wanted to achieve, docket control and judicial legislation had top priority. If the Court could get a firm hand on the spigot to control the inflow of appeals, it would be able to be more selective in processing cases. Fewer appeals would be granted review; the Court would significantly lighten its workload on merits decisions, and the justices could spend more time deliberating principled cases of their own choosing. Although it would be wrong to characterize strongly independent justices as a 'huddled mass', they still yearned to be free from their workload. Chief Justice Carsten Smith later stated that he felt like a general ordering soldiers towards the shower of bullets when the justices were heading for their five-week service on the Committee.[14]

Justices Schweigaard, Selmer and Schei were already convinced that docket control was the answer. Associate Justice Gunnar Aasland agreed with them. With an overburdened ASC, an understaffed clerk unit and Justice Aasland already doing 'God's work' on a consequential white-paper committee, Smith could not believe his good fortune when he arrived as chief justice on the Court in May 1991.

In March 1990, the government had established a white-paper committee on criminal procedure reform. Justice Aasland had been appointed to the committee along with four lawyers. One of the problems was that the courts of appeal had original jurisdiction of major criminal cases so that meaningful appeals by default had to be heard by the next level in the legal hierarchy – namely, the Supreme Court. One of the committee's mandates was to re-examine this default appeals process. When Smith understood how well the mandate of the white-paper committee dovetailed with his own agenda, he eagerly seized the opportunity for the discretionary jurisdiction that he saw coming. Smith quickly relieved Justice Aasland from his remaining Court duties. Being fully relieved from duties on the Court two times for a total of seven months, Aasland could commit himself fully to work on the committee.[15] In the executive summary of its report, the committee acknowledged that Justice Aasland wrote important parts of the report himself. The committee also concluded that without Aasland's leave from the Court, it would not have been possible to complete the committee's mandate within a time frame of roughly two years (NOU 1992:11).

The committee received its name from one of the most important of its assignments: the two-step reform (NOU 1992). After the reform, trial courts were to have original jurisdiction over all criminal cases so that appeals now could be heard by the appeal courts. This reform provided great relief to the Supreme Court; no longer would it act as the second instance court of appeal for severe criminal cases. But in addition to policing all appeals at the gate, the second recommendation of the committee was equally important. It recom-

14 Leading from behind and avoiding most of the bullets himself, Chief Justice Carsten Smith had very few stints on the drudging ASC. During his tenure as chief justice between 1991 and 2002, Smith participated in only 113 decisions on the ASC, an average of nine or ten decisions per year (Source: https://lovdata.no/pro/). Somehow, wading through appeals was not his calling on the Court.

15 The white paper committee was established on 23 March 1990, with five members and a secretary. A sixth member was added in fall 1990. It delivered its 200-page report in September 1992 after having had 22 one-day meetings and two meetings that took place over several days. It reports two international trips and has commissioned several reports. Justice Aasland was on two leaves from the Court: 23 September 1991 to 16 February 1992 and from 21 April to 30 June 1992 (NOU 1992).

mended giving the Supreme Court itself the necessary legal instruments to select those criminal cases it found significantly interesting to review (NOU 1992:28).[16] Both the great reduction in automatic appeals and the Court's mandate to select the criminal appeals that it decided to hear were implemented in August 1995 and took full effect in the Court's 1996 term (Matningsdal 1996).

Chief Justice Carsten Smith must have been very pleased with this dual outcome. In retrospect, it is hard to overstate the importance of these two changes. They were in full compliance with Smith's vision for the Court to transform from a court of appeal to a court of precedent. The next step was to unleash the clerks to take advantage of the momentum.

3.7 'No Clerks in the Courtroom'

Smith's vision went beyond simply eliminating mundane cases from the Court's docket. He also called for the Court to be in a position to fully select its own cases and achieve complete control over its own docket. Finally, Smith envisioned the clerks doing most of the heavy legal lifting. They would scrutinize the appeals and write memos to help the justices on the ASC to decide on interlocutory appeals and to grant or deny merits appeals. At least for now.

After his inauguration as chief justice on 1 May 1991, Smith summoned the justices to a first meeting in June 1991, where he presented his to-do list of 18 items. Expanding the clerk unit was one of the items on the agenda, although this item was not addressed until the next meeting in August 1991. Smith's to-do list was far too long for a single meeting. So, if 1988 had been a workload crisis that started to change the justices' minds about docket control, 1991 became the turning point for expanding the number of clerks and putting them to work for organizational and strategic purposes.

With the formal institutionalization of a clerk unit in 1989, with Chief Justice Smith at the Court's helm in 1991 and with the government's budgetary blessings, the number of clerks started to increase. Smith's goal was to have the same number of clerks as there were justices on the Court.[17] At the beginning of Smith's chief justiceship in 1991, there were 18 justices and 6 clerks. The number of clerks increased to 8 in 1993 and to 12 in 1994. In 1996 the number of clerks increased to 13, and it kept growing until it reached 16 in 2002 when Chief Justice Smith retired. Although Smith had not reached his goal of matching the number of clerks to the number of justices – he fell three clerks short – the momentum for expansion of the clerk unit was in place.

16 The Criminal Process Act, Section 323.

17 Clerk interview 9 November 2017, start page 84, p. 85.

An important aspect of the 1989 organization of the clerk unit was that the leader and deputy of the newly established clerk unit also attended the meetings of justices. Until this point, the meeting of justices meant a meeting of justices only. But starting in 1992, the leadership of the clerk unit was present when the meeting of justices discussed topics related to the clerks. This change signalled that the clerks had become an integrated and important part of the operations of the Supreme Court. They had contributed to the elimination of the sense of crisis that dominated the Court at the end of the 1980s and had now gained a place at the larger table (Sunde 2015a:156).

Smith's goal was to make sure that the justices got all the assistance they needed. In a 1997 internal memo, he argued that because of the national legal importance of their work, the justices' working conditions should be as optimal as possible. He stated that "as long as any justice asks for more assistance than the clerk unit can deliver, the clerk unit must expand". Indicative of how strongly Smith believed in this goal, he even visited the Norwegian Parliament ('Stortinget') to make his case to the Justice Committee on the need to hire more clerks (Smith's 1997 memo is quoted in Aamodt 2017:1).

Smith's vision for the role of clerks, however, was not restricted to their support of the justices screening cases on the ASC. Smith was used to having research and teaching assistants available to him as a law professor and dean of the University of Oslo Law School.[18] Justices with a background from powerful law firms were also used to having assistants working for them. Smith also drew inspiration from the U.S. Supreme Court. During a visit to it in the 1960s, he observed that clerks there were not organized in a pool but worked directly for the individual justices and performed a variety of judicial tasks, including work on merits opinions. Accordingly, Smith nourished the idea of the justices having personal clerks who could play a significant role in the drafting of the Supreme Court justices' opinions.

The idea of clerks writing the opinion of a case challenged the justices' self-image of the proper duties and responsibilities of a justice. Ever since 1864, when the justices' individual votes became publicized, justices did in fact take full responsibility for their own opinions. But Smith argued that it was a waste of time and precious resources for a justice to compose what was effectively legal boilerplate – namely, the facts and history of the case, the arguments of the parties and the legal introduction to the Court's final decision. This information was already available in the lower courts' documents, in the appeals from the parties and increasingly in the clerks' memos.

Conventionally, the justices had always taken notes during oral arguments, and the justices were prepared to organize the law and facts of the case as a necessary exercise

18 At the German Federal Constitutional Court, the legal assistants could be "closely compared to that of teaching and research assistants at universities", Wieland, himself a legal assistant on that Court during 1984-1988, argued (2002:205).

before deciding on the case's merits. Their job was also aided by the parties' submission of their factual and legal briefs as well as their disquisition during oral arguments. To break this pattern and have the clerks write the facts part of the final decision would not only indicate that the strict sequence of judicial decision-making from putting the facts of the case next to the laws and then logically arriving at an outcome would be challenged, but also mean that the clerks would need to be present in the courtroom during oral arguments and when justices met in conference to deliberate the case afterwards.

In 1997, there was an attempt to have a clerk in the courtroom to take notes during oral arguments in order to draft what could be the *introduction* of the decision. But Smith's idea of the justices having personal clerks who would be present during oral arguments and assist in drafting the opinion was a bridge too far for the other justices. The 1997 attempt was deemed a failure and was not repeated. The justices, according to the minutes of a meeting, agreed that "having clerks in the courtroom during oral arguments is put away for a long time" (Sunde 2015a:148,160). The basic ideal and self-image of a justice was to take full responsibility for all the writing of decision-making. This conclusion also underscored the prevailing practice that clerks were to shore up and continue to assist the ASC. They were not to veer into the three subsequent stations of decision-making, which were best understood as the sole province of the justices: oral arguments, deliberations and opinion writing.

3.8 Flaunting Power: The New Palace of Justice

The institutional changes that Carsten Smith envisioned for the Supreme Court in his 1974 address would, he argued, necessarily *increase* the social influence of courts. When taking the helm in 1991, a manifestation of the social influence that he anticipated following his proactive programme was a renovated Palace of Justice. But the reverse would also be true – an imposing Supreme Court building would contribute to the social standing of the Supreme Court and reflect its elevation and influence in society.

For most of the twentieth century, the Supreme Court had shared 'the Palace of Justice' building in Oslo with the Oslo trial court, which occupied the first floor, and the Eidsivating court of appeal, which occupied the second floor. The Supreme Court occupied the third floor and the attic. Supreme Court justices, the Court's administration and the clerks were sitting all over the place. Some clerks had offices in Grensen 3, half a block away. When they were picking up new appeals to prepare for the Committee or returning those that they had prepared, they had to carry stacks of documents along the sidewalk of Grubbegata between the Court and Grensen 3. Some clerks and justices were located in a neighbouring government building on Grubbegata that was mostly occupied by the Ministry of Fisheries. There were doors from the Palace of Justice directly into this building, and they provided convenient access between the justices' offices. But justices complained about their cramped offices and referred to them as pencil cases or pencil boxes. The narrow stairs from the third floor to the attic of the Palace of Justice was referred to as the 'chicken coop ladder' or the 'chicken runway'. The stairs lead up to offices and the growing Gussgard archive.

When visiting courts in other countries, the justices became ashamed of the poor conditions of their own Supreme Court. The Supreme Court building was crammed full and falling apart. Plywood had been placed on walls to effect temporary repairs. Cheap white paint covered the walls throughout the building, and in some places the paint was peeling off. The conditions were miserable and wretched. On the first floor of the building, a Pepsi Cola vending machine looked totally out of place; it certainly did not contribute to the majesty of a court.

Upon becoming chief justice, Smith launched an ambitious plan with the government for an exclusive Supreme Court building. Receiving approval, in 1992 he engaged the Director General for Cultural Heritage,[19] Stephan Tschudi-Madsen, as advisor for the renovation. Justice Liv Gjølstad became leader of the renovation project's 'worker committee'.[20] In 1994, after a few years of planning, the renovation commenced. Clerks, justices and administrative personnel had to vacate the building – whose address at this point was *Apotekergata* – and were temporarily placed in neighbouring government buildings. The Treasury Department, for instance, located across the street, offered a makeshift courtroom. The whole Palace of Justice was emptied, the old Pepsi vending machine had dispensed its last soda, the building was gutted and slowly but surely brought back to its splendid and original qualities from 1903.[21]

In September 1996, Chief Justice Smith welcomed the King and Queen of Norway to the official opening of the fully renovated Supreme Court building, which, for good measure, now had *Supreme Court Square* as its official address. With the Oslo trial court and the Eidsivating court of appeal having been relocated, the Court was now the building's sole occupant. Evidently, restoring the Palace of Justice to its original 1903 grandeur did elevate and embolden the Supreme Court. It also had an effect on clerks who reported that they were awestruck when first entering the renovated Court building either for a job interview or as newly hired clerks.

The large courtroom on the first floor had been converted to serve as a new meeting room for all the justices; it could also accommodate receptions and larger meetings with visitors. The Eidsivating court of appeal's main courtroom on the second floor was totally redone. After the renovations, it would be used as a courtroom for one of the Supreme

19 (*'riksantikvar'*).

20 (*'brukerutvalget'*).

21 We are in no position to gauge the effects on collegial decision-making on the Supreme Court following the complete overhaul of the building. But we are reminded that even small adjustments in existing structures can have an effect on the collegiality of a court (Black, Johnson, and Owens 2018).

Court's two rotating merits panels and for oral arguments in *en banc* cases. One of the Supreme Court's pair of courtrooms on the third floor was restored and reserved for the Court's other rotating panel. And what had been other small courtrooms for the trial and courts of appeal courts were converted into spacious offices for the justices with the largest office reserved for the chief justice. Associate justices could choose their offices based on their descending order of seniority (which is the same practice today when a justice's office becomes vacant). With justices given new offices, administrative staff was concentrated in offices next to one another, while clerks were occupying new and for most of the time individual offices either in the basement or in the attic.

The renovation also gave the once dark basement a new lease on life. In addition to offices for clerks and retired justices, the basement also included a spacious and, for the time being, foodless canteen. But the basement canteen still invited justices, clerks and administrative staff to bring their brown bags or food bought in nearby shops for a somewhat more social lunch. On Mondays, when justices were not sitting in oral arguments, they were more likely to join their non-justice colleagues for lunch. Retired justices who held emeritus offices sometimes showed up when clerks made waffles on Fridays. The new offices and the opportunities to kick back socially during lunch made the clerks become a part of the Court in a quite different way in a very short period of time.

3.9 The Purge and the Soft Backlash

The hiring of clerks during the 1990s followed the standard government practice of offering permanent contracts. Tacitly, however, it was understood that a clerkship was a temporary position and that it was expected that after some years on the Court, clerks would move on to other jobs for which the clerkship had offered valuable experience. This system worked well, as clerks did in fact move on to other employment opportunities. But in the mid-1990s, as we have discussed, two forces took effect. One was the critical change in criminal procedures in 1995 and the secular change in civil procedures starting in 1981, both enabling the Court to be increasingly selective in the composition of its own docket. The other was the slow but persistent and increasing influence of international law.

Consequently, as the nature of decision-making and the pace at the Court changed in the 1990s – a result of its transformation from a reactive court of appeal to a proactive court of precedent – the Court understood that the quality of its clerk pool needed to change too. There was a concern that with the Court's goal of developing the law, it would necessarily need to rely on a more dynamic and preferably younger workforce than what the older justices would be able to offer the Court alone. A greater rate of turnover among the clerks would militate for a more current Court. Moreover, hiring clerks on a limited contract would make obvious the fact that, although it provided important assistance to the justices, a clerkship was ultimately an apprentice position. Limited contracts would also guarantee that clerks would not develop into entrenched bureaucrats or a 'second tier of justices' who would forget that their main function was to facilitate the work of the justices.

Backed by the necessary statutory provision, in 2002 the Court implemented the new policy and offered new clerks fixed five-year contracts only. Clerks already hired on permanent contracts were well aware that the new type of contracts could not be enforced retroactively. On the other hand, now that each new clerk's contract was linked to a countdown clock, there was an even stronger expectation that it was time for veteran clerks to move on. The clerk leadership and deputy leadership positions, however, would still be offered permanent contracts. No matter how valid the intent, though, the policy change produced an effect on the rate of clerk turnover that went too far. Clerks, now knowing that the clock was running, began looking for new job opportunities long before the end of their formal contracts rather than risk conspicuous lacunas in their legal resumes. And when clerks started to leave the Court after only a couple of years into their clerkship, the Court knew that it would be unable to benefit fully from the skills and competence that they were investing in the clerks. Adjusting its recruitment policy, the Court extended its fixed-year contract first to six years in 2007 and then to seven years in 2011. Still, there is some thought that the clerks are not providing the Court with a sufficient return on its investment in human capital. Accordingly, if any additional changes to a clerkship's tenure are to be considered, it is likely that the short-term contracts will be extended to eight or even nine years in order to discourage the clerks from leaving the Court too early.

The legal foundation in the Court Act, Section 61, that enables the Court to hire clerks on short-term contracts may run afoul of the Working Environment Act, Section 14-9(1), requiring that when the type of work that employees are doing is permanent, they must be appointed permanently as well. But who are we to claim that the Supreme Court is breaking the law? Suffice it to say that hiring clerks on short-term contracts for permanent institutional tasks would perhaps operate, as one well-positioned justice phrased it, "in the grey area of law".[22]

3.10 MENTORING CLERKS – FROM BUDDY TO FRONT-LOADING

Sometime during the mid-1990s, the Court established a mentor or 'buddy system' for new clerks. Up to this time, there was no standardized procedure of introducing the clerks to the other personnel on the Court. In the late 1980s, the process of hiring clerks was very informal; even a job interview was not necessarily carried out. Clerks hired in the beginning

22 Justice interview 6 November 2017, start page 42, p. 44.

of the 1990s were rarely introduced to Court personnel either. In the late 1990s, on one of the first days on the job, one clerk recalled, he had been brought to the justices' lunchroom. There, standing in the doorway while the justices were eating their lunch, the Director General introduced him to the room. Not surprisingly, the new clerk felt the situation a bit awkward. However, the story is very telling. Since 1995 clerks and justices were located in the same building, the clerks socialized with retired justices and the leader of the clerk unit attended the meeting of justices. Still, the clerks kept their distance from the justices.[23]

Clerks who were recruited during the 1990s recall the apprentice system as more of a buddy programme than as a mentor programme. The buddy would read some of the novice clerk's first memos; then the clerk leadership would read a few. Fairly quickly, however, new clerks would be on their own. Any feedback from the justices would be limited to a few words in the left-hand column of the memo that was reserved for their notes. It would be fair to say that the mentor programme in the late 1990s was less institutionalized and did not constitute a significant element of the clerk's training.

The clerk mentor system the Court has today was established around the year 2000 with each new clerk receiving a mentor; by around 2005 each new clerk was also assigned a justice mentor. The clerk mentor programme starts on day one with new clerks being introduced to their personal mentors, clerks who had served on the Court for a while. The mentors take the new clerks on a tour of the Supreme Court building and introduce them to the different units and their employees, including the justices. The mentors also bring the novice clerks up to speed on the Court's computer system and introduce them to documents that describe the various procedures of the job. New clerks also are introduced to the specific and current 100-page guidelines for the preparation of appeals for the ASC. Following this break-in period, the review of a few completed memo examples and some discussion with the mentor, new clerks are given a couple of civil law appeals to work on. The mentors read and comment upon the novice clerks' draft memos. Once these drafts pass muster with the clerk mentors, they are passed on to the leader of the clerk unit who also offers feedback.

Starting around 2005, the Court also institutionalized the assignment of justice mentors to new clerks. The allocation of justice mentors took place in a meeting with the leader of the clerk unit and the chair of the ASC. The justice mentors are drawn from one of the most senior of the five justices allocated to the ASC. Formally, the new clerk is assigned a justice mentor for up to ten weeks. This means that a new clerk would be mentored by two different justices, as justices only serve five-week stints on the ASC. The justice mentor would not only read and comment on memos themselves, but also have individual meetings

23 With the start of the annual Christmas party in 2005 including all justices, clerks and staff, the social distance between the various groups in the Court diminished considerably (Sunde 2015a:336).

with the clerk for closer discussions. One justice noted that she would take notes on the clerk's memo and strive to get in touch with the clerk to give personal feedback.

Although the mentor system is semi-formalized to last anywhere between four and ten weeks, there is no formal ending to the mentorship programme for individual clerks. Only when the clerk leadership signals to the clerk that he or she may send the memos directly to the Committee does the mentorship programme come to an end. Although the work of a clerk is very independent, it does not mean that the clerk is completely on his or her own. Several clerks emphasized that the doors are open to the offices of other clerks so that dropping by to discuss an appeal is both encouraged and welcomed. The clerk leadership can also be approached if needed, and clerks are also welcome to address appeals during the general meetings of clerks that take place every other Monday. Finally, several justices are understood to be approachable and would also appreciate a clerk's knock on their door to discuss a legal matter.[24]

The clerk mentor system has existed since the late 1990s. What started out as a buddy programme to steer new clerks in the right direction has developed into an organized but informal mentor programme. There is no document that describes the process for how the clerk or justice mentors are to meet the new clerk or what the mentors shall do. But all clerks and justices involved are familiar with and informed about the programme, since all clerks now were socialized into it. The specific and identifiable change over the last decade is a greater degree of front-loading. There are much closer follow-ups with new clerks during the first month or two than when the programme first began.

Although the main task for clerks is to prepare appeals for the ASC, the formal job description also includes being available for the chief and associate justices as well as the Secretary General for jobs and smaller tasks that are routed through the clerk leadership. For example, clerks may be requested to substitute for court clerks, guide visiting groups around the Court building, assist in writing speeches and lectures, and provide background material and research for publications that justices are writing. Occasionally the Court receives national and international surveys or requests for information, and a clerk is usually tasked to draft responses to these requests. If the Court's annual visit to one of the country's counties happens to be an area from which the clerk comes, then the clerk can be asked to do research for the Court's excursion. When a former justice passes away, a clerk may draft the obituary.

24 Clerk interview 8 November 2017, start page 67, p. 68.

3.11 New Chief, New Broom

When Chief Justice Carsten Smith left the Court in 2002, he could take pride in several achievements, among them the Court being the sole occupant of the modernized and rehabilitated Supreme Court building, the development of the clerk unit and steering the Court from a court of appeal towards a court of precedent. But during his chief justiceship, the Court fell behind when it came to keeping the number of backlogs down. Appeals were stored in boxes and cases in odd places throughout the Court building. There was a widespread impression that the appeals process was slow and that the number of backlogs was uncomfortably high. Appellants made a perverse adaptation to the situation. They submitted an appeal without complete documentation and expected the process to take long enough for them to submit the rest of the documents later. They were caught off-guard when Smith passed the Court's leadership to Tore Schei.

The new chief had two major tasks for the clerk unit. The first was that clerks shall ensure *quality* in that a Court decision shall rest upon the most complete and exhaustive use of relevant legal factors. The other was that clerks shall ensure *efficiency* in that there should be no backlog of appeals at the ASC. When Schei became chief in August 2002, he wanted to reduce the number of backlogs, and he quickly impressed upon all who worked in the Supreme Court that there was a new sheriff in town. He quickly mobilized the whole Court – clerks and justices alike – to start reducing the number of backlogs, and everyone was to make an effort to reach this goal.[25] This mobilization cost Schei whatever honeymoon he might have had as the Court's new chief, as it quickly made him an unpopular man. Had it not been for the fact that Schei himself contributed no less an effort than the others, he may not have been able to pull off the effort.[26]

The law clerks were integral to Schei's backlog project. Some were given specific tasks; for example, one clerk was specifically dedicated to handle old appeals. And all the clerks were asked to put in significant overtime to wind down the outstanding cases. Using a time clock, the clerks could bank their extra hours and use them for additional time off when family and/or childcare needs required.[27]

Once the backlog was brought under control, Schei instituted a new regime for case processing. Clerks were expected to work on three to five appeals at the same time, at a pace where a typical appeal could be handled in about two weeks. After a clerk processed the appeal, it was left for the ASC to make a decision in another two weeks. And if an

25 One of our interviewees referred to Schei's backlog-reducing mobilization as "dugnad" (Clerk interview 7 November 2017, start page 82, p. 83), for which 'barn raising' perhaps is the best translation into English.

26 Justice interview 6 November 2017, start page 42, p. 43.

27 Clerk interview 9 November 2017, start page 84, p. 86; Clerk interview 7 November 2017, start page 62, p. 63.

appeal was granted review, a final decision on the merits panel could be expected within the next five months.

During the clerk unit's meetings every other Monday, the clerks could discuss the processing of appeals and backlogs, the nature of cases and also bring attention to more difficult cases. Since the clerk leadership entered all appeals into a spreadsheet in order to track the processing of appeals, the clerk leadership knew full well how fast or slow each clerk was processing the appeals. Since the clerks knew that their processing of appeals was monitored, they were prepared to report on appeals for which they exceeded the two-week norm for completing the memo for the Committee. The clerks approved of Schei's orderliness and his organizational contributions to the Court for which he earned the nickname 'boy scout' from some of the clerks.

3.12 A Momentum for Clerks

In 1995, with the elimination of automatic appeal of criminal cases to the Supreme Court and with the introduction of discretionary reform for criminal cases in which clerks were hired to assist justices on the ASC in case selection, one should expect an overall lighter workload and smoother sailing. Not so. Two factors account for the still heavy and increasing workload on the Court.

3.12.1 Forward-Looking – The Development of the Law

The first factor was, to a large degree, self-imposed. Carsten Smith's call in 1974 for the Supreme Court to become a proactive court of precedent was actually a call for the Supreme Court to turn its attention towards cherry-picking certain appeals in order to be a force in the law's development rather than adhere to its historical role of resolving individual cases. With respect to an allegedly staid national institution, this would result in a rather dramatic change, as the Court would pivot from being a reactive and backward-looking institution to a proactive and forward-looking one. The discussion of the reorientation took place mostly within the legal community, but not without fights. Yet, the change in the Court's orientation gained traction in the 1990s. And it affected the Court's and the justices' place in the larger political system. A proactive forward-looking Supreme Court requires a greater willingness among the justices to act like legislators, as they were no longer constrained by codified laws and manoeuvred into unchartered waters of policy-making.

In a letter to the Ministry of Justice as far back as in 1979, the justices explained that the two main tasks of the Supreme Court were to ensure the unity of the law and to take the lead in developing the law in areas where legislation is insufficient. The letter was incorporated in a government proposition in 1981 on revision of legal procedures (Ot.prp. nr. 41 1980-1981:4). In 1979, taking such a lead was obviously a very modest and timid goal, since there were no statutory laws that could provide the justices with instruments of such proactive nature. It was evident that courts occasionally had to pick up where elected politicians left off. Justices would have to interpret clauses that legislators sometimes left behind in haste or in compromised confusion or simply left intentionally vague in order not to disrupt the legislative policy coalition. New facts and new times could also challenge enacted legislation so that statutes needed fresh interpretations.

In the beginning of the 1990s, the Supreme Court's goals expanded to three: the unity of the law, clarification of the law and development of the law. The goals were penned by Chief Justice Smith himself and appeared for the first time in print in 1994. With the discretionary criminal process reform in the mid-1990s, it was evident that the goal of development of the law suddenly had much greater potential. After all, the goals' architect, Carsten Smith, was positioned at the Court's helm and had rooted for this opportunity.

When Chief Justice Tore Schei became the Court's torchbearer in 2002, the three goals were still in place, but towards the end of Schei's tenure on the Court in 2016, something had changed; 'unity of the law' had fallen completely out of favour. The term was silently dropped from documents, official statements and – conspicuous by its absence – ultimately from the Court's home page. Just as Schei stepped down from the Court in 2016, so too did the term 'unity of the law', but with much less fanfare. The Court, however, argued that no substantial change had taken place when 'unity of the law' was removed. At some point the Court discovered that the phrase was simply redundant, since its substance followed from the term 'clarification of the law'.

An argument in the 1980s and 1990s for increasing the number of clerks instead of the number of justices and panels was that the ability to secure unity of law lessened when the number of justices and panels grew. In the 2010s, the crucial importance of legal unity was publically referred to, and the task itself was tucked away as a part of the clarification of law. Still, there are examples where clarification of the law does not contribute to legal unity. Yet, this was an argument that did not interest the Court. The growth in the clerk unit had enabled the Court to cherry-pick cases to make precedent. The Court was now more forward-looking than ever, focusing mainly on developing the law.[28] And it was not looking back.

---

28 In this period some Supreme Court justices increasingly started to refer to the Court as a Constitutional Court, *e.g.* Bårdsen (2015). Even though the Court undisputedly addresses constitutional issues, it is still a court of general jurisdiction and should not be referred to as a Constitutional Court (Smith 2016).

3.12.2 Outward-Looking – The Internationalization of the Law

Whereas the goal of the 'development of the law' by design was following Smith's domestic vision and agenda for the Supreme Court, the second factor – the internationalization of the law – effectively was an accident of history. It also had a more profound impact. Following the fall of the Berlin Wall and the end of the Cold War, a deluge of international laws was implemented into Norwegian law during the 1990s. The development was spearheaded by the introduction and implementation into Norwegian law of the *European Economic Area* (EEA/'EØS') agreement in 1994, and it was consolidated with the incorporation of the *Convention for the Protection of Human Rights and Fundamental Freedoms*, or *the European Convention on Human Rights* (ECHR/'EMK') into Norwegian human rights law in 1999. This legal and politically earthshaking development took place without any drumrolls and was aptly referred to as the 'silent revolution' of Norwegian law (Arnesen and Stenvik 2009:11). The default position in the field of laws and legislation was that in any conflict among laws and statutes, it was to a great extent presumed in the 1990s and 2000s that international laws were to take precedence over Norwegian law. The internationalization of Norwegian laws did not take full effect until the beginning of the twenty-first century.[29]

An immediate and lasting concern of the internationalization of law was that it ushered in a much more complicated legal field. International law introduced new authors and creators of law who practised their craft far beyond Norway's national borders. Legal principles often were articulated in languages that were not always translated into Norwegian, using terms, translated or not, that were vague, ambiguous or both. Oftentimes, then, translations and interpretations from outside were a balancing act for a Norwegian legal discipline that primarily had been inward-looking and reared in the local vernacular.[30]

It is not unusual for new legislation to be adjudicated in order to clarify the new law, modify or adapt the new law to a specific context and to give direction to the new law. This need for judicial interpretation and clarification is even more necessary as a law grows in complexity and/or ambiguity (see Gilmore 1977). Now, as noted earlier, complexity and ambiguity are part and parcel of the internationalization of Norwegian law. Yet, when called upon to clarify, adapt and direct the implementation of international law into Norway's legal system, the Supreme Court was at a severe disadvantage. Endowed with sharp legal minds and thoroughly trained in Norway's legal system, the justices were not neces-

29 Justice interview 6 November 2017, start page 47, p. 48.

30 In 2016, Karin Bruzelius, a former Supreme Court justice (1997-2011), bemoaned the complicated state of the legal field as to sources of laws, the language of laws and the lack of standardization of laws and legal sources. The situation, she claimed, was a challenge to the rule of law. Justice Bruzelius asked for a government committee that could bring clarity to the field and establish what in fact was Norwegian law in force (Bruzelius 2016).

sarily facile when it came to making sense of international law. It was evident, then, that in the short run the international challenge could best be met by clerks fresh out of law school. However, not only was there a need for clerks with specialization in international law, there was a need for *more* clerks.

3.13 STILL A SHORTAGE OF CLERKS

Under a heavy workload throughout the 1980s and during the first half of the 1990s, some justices reluctantly understood that they were better off using the clerks to prepare appeals for the ASC. Although the justices' negative attitude about the clerks' involvement in the process of selecting cases for merits review was stated as a matter of principle, the principles could be adjusted when confronted with the unrelenting workload of the real world.[31] And for those justices unwilling to allow the gravity of the real world to bend their principles, retirement did the rest. Justice Jens Bugge, for example, never fully accepted the expanded role of the clerks on the Committee. Bugge, however, was a member of the old guard, and when he retired in 2000 a new generation of justices, including professors from the nation's law schools, had started to take seats on the Supreme Court.

During the 1990s, all interlocutory civil and criminal appeals were handled and accounted for by the clerks before the cases and accompanying memos were passed on to the justices on the ASC. In addition, some civil law case appeals were also handled and accounted for by the clerks during this decade. Gradually, more and more civil case appeals were handled by the clerks, and this development also started to include criminal case appeals. After the turn of the century, the clerks handled and accounted for all types of appeals to the Court (Aamodt 2017:2, based on Sunde).

In the first decade of the millennium the modus vivendi was that the clerks should assist in preparing all appeals and identifying principled legal questions to present to the ASC. In this process they should supply comprehensive memos of the facts of the case and the legal questions in the manner demonstrated by Gussgard's able clerkship in the early 1980s. With this division of labour, the justices maintained the personal responsibility for the Court's decisions and their votes by taking charge of the opinion writing while making good use of the clerks' memos and the parties' dispositions.

Having tracked the development of the Supreme Court clerk unit, we shall now turn to an in-depth account of the vital role it performs in the gatekeeping function of the ASC. In Chapter 4 we examine the impact of the preparatory work of the clerks, who craft memos outlining the legal issues in a case and recommending whether or not to grant review.

31 Sunde (2015a:161). Justices did give way to more clerks on the ASC when the five-day week was within reach.

Since the ASC almost always follows the clerk's recommendation, there can be little doubt that clerks are crucial to effective gatekeeping.

4 The Court's Gatekeepers

Every workday, the justices in the Appeals Selection Committee (ASC) decide between nine and ten appeals. This filtering process – deciding to decide – is the very prerequisite for the Norwegian Supreme Court being a court of precedent. The Norwegian Supreme Court would not be able to operate as a court of precedent if justices on the Committee were not served by clerks who had thoroughly screened the appeals before they reached the Committee. In short: no clerks, no filtering, not a court of precedent. In this chapter we will examine how the clerks have contributed to this transformation of the Norwegian Supreme Court over the last decades.

By 2008 – with the major procedural change in 1995 in the appeals of criminal cases and the gradual procedural changes between 1981 and 2008 concerning the appeals of civil cases – the Court had secured control of its own docket and finally reached Chief Justice Carsten Smith's goal of being transformed from a court committed to the resolution of individual cases to a court dedicated to the strategic selection of appeals to establish precedents. As both Norway's highest appellate court and a court of general jurisdiction, the Supreme Court has many opportunities to act, in Carsten Smith's words, as a "super legislature" (Smith 1975:300). It bears noting that the Court's extensive discretionary jurisdiction, exercised through the ASC, its broad subject matter jurisdiction and its ambitions to operate as a court of precedent, would quickly overwhelm the High Court's decisional resources, thereby appreciably reducing its capacity to shape and direct Norwegian law and policy.

In Chapter 2 we divided the decision-making process into four distinct stages: the ASC, oral arguments, deliberations and opinion writing. Of these four stages, action at the ASC is most critical because this is where the Court's gatekeeping occurs. The ASC culls the precedential wheat from the perfunctory case chaff, thereby facilitating the Court's capacity to clarify and develop the law. In this chapter we examine how the clerk unit is organized and how it supports the Committee in its crucial gatekeeping role. The basic function of the Committee is to screen all appeals and decide which are worthy of the Court's full merits attention, denying review to the rest. (The Committee also makes final decisions on interlocutory appeals.) As we suggested at the conclusion of Chapter 3, the worker bees in these gatekeeping and deciding-to-decide processes are the clerks. Before any appeal reaches the ASC, a clerk has inspected it and written a memo with a specific recommendation regarding its outcome to the ASC. As to the merits appeals, without a decision to grant review from the Committee, there will be no decision on the merits. As we have noted, only 10 to 15 per cent of the appeals to the Court survive the Committee's scrutiny, and the clerks loom large in this winnowing process. According to both justices and clerks, the ASC adopts the clerk's recommendation about 90 per cent of the time.[1]

4.1 The Supreme Court's Processing of Appeals

Appeals coming from the lower courts to the Supreme Court are categorized into three different types. A *decision* ('dom') is a judgement (in a civil case) or a sentence (in a criminal case) and concerns the merits or the substance of the case. An *order* ('kjennelse' or 'orskurd') does not concern the merits, but the form of procedure and applies to both civil and criminal cases. A *resolution* ('beslutning') is neither a decision nor an order. It is an administrative decision that concerns a case. It can simply be an act of passing an appeal forward without judgment on its merits or procedures. Incoming orders and resolutions are sometimes referred to as interlocutory appeals. Although a clear distinction between a decision and an order, or between an order and a resolution, may not always be obvious, the Dispute Act conveniently saves the uncertain lawyer: one section pithily states that an outcome that is incorrectly categorized as a decision, order or resolution has no bearing on its legal effect or its possibilities for appeal.[2]

Prior to the 2008 civil law reform, the ASC was referred to as *Kjæremålsutvalget* and in certain respects was considered to be a separate court within the Court. Both before and after the 2008 reform, the Committee had the competence to make final decisions on incoming interlocutory appeals that were categorized as either 'orders' or 'resolutions'.[3] The Committee may decide that some orders and resolutions raise a procedural question where a clarification or guidance is needed or that they contain more principled questions, in which case the Committee grants review and passes them on to the five-justice decisional panels for review. Only about 1 per cent of orders and resolutions appealed to the Court are forwarded to five-justice decisional panels.[4] Of more profound consequence to the Court's development of the law, the Committee has the competence to decide which merits decisions appealed from the lower courts should be granted review and forwarded

1 Clerk interview 23 May 2012, start page 2, p. 2. Justice interview 7 July 2017, start page 6, p. 7. Clerk interview 7 November 2017, start page 23, p. 26.

2 *See* the Dispute Act Section 19-1 on the formal definition applying for civil cases, and fourth clause on the negligibility of misclassification. http://jusinfo.no/index.php?site=default/721/1802/1803/1805 (last accessed 27 November 2016).

3 The Dispute Act Section 30-1, second clause, and The Criminal Process Act Section 7. Orders or resolutions were referred to as *interlocutory appeals* ('kjæremål'), hence the Committee's original name *Kjæremålsutvalget* (Skoghøy 2008).

4 A rate of grant substantially below that for normal appeals on the merits. Occasionally, orders and resolutions are decided in the Grand Chamber or in plenary session, *e.g.* Rt-2008-1764 (Schei 2015b:6-7).

to oral argument in decisional panels. (In those instances where the ASC has denied review, the lower court decision stands.)

The ASC has since 1887 in criminal cases and 1915 in civil cases been fully integrated into the overall operations of the Court, and all the justices on the Court have served on the ASC on a rotating basis. Formalities concerning the distinction in the three types of appeals are still in place.

The Committee has competence to rule on orders and resolutions, which for the most part consist of procedural questions or questions relevant for procedure. The point of deciding on procedural questions is to establish standards or clarify ambiguities so that a material and substantial question can be firmly decided. Interlocutory appeals amount to slightly more than half of all appeals handled by the Committee. Interlocutory appeals are denied if all the justices sitting on the ASC agree that the lower court's decision was correctly decided.[5]

The Committee still has full competence to decide which merits appeals are to be denied or granted review. A 'rule of one' operates in this screening decision. That is, the decision of a single ASC-justice may place an appeal on the Court's docket. When the Committee decides to pass an appeal on to a decisional panel for review and oral arguments, its decision is technically an 'order' since the Committee basically has forwarded an appeal, with accompanying arguments, to a merits panel without taking any position on the appeal's outcome. By no means is this an insignificant action. After all, what the ASC has done is to decide what to decide. In other words, it has pulled the policymaking trigger for an apex court with wide discretionary jurisdiction.

4.1.1 An Appeal Arrives at the Court

Traditionally, appeals to the Supreme Court were delivered either by regular mail or by courier to its doorstep. Appeals arrived in boxes and cases. Upon arrival, the Court Administration gave each incoming appeal a unique serial or identification number. The appeal kept this serial number while the ASC processed it. Those relatively few appeals that were deemed worthy of the Court's attention on their merits were forwarded to decisional panels and assigned a new serial number. In January 2000, the Supreme Court introduced *Høyrett*, a new internal data system for organizing and managing the Court's case flow. With the introduction of the *Høyrett* system, each appeal was assigned a unique identifier at its point of entry,[6] just as had been the case prior to the adoption of the *Høyrett* system. Now, however, that identification number remained with the appeal even if the

5 The Court Act, Sections 30-9.

6 Saksbehandlingsenheten – www.domstol.no/no/Enkelt-domstol/-Norges-Hoyesterett/Om-Hoyesterett/Personalia/Saksbehandlingsseksjon/ (last accessed 19 November 2016).

ASC forwarded it to a decisional panel (Sunde 2015a:136). The new common identifier was a harbinger of the ASC being fully integrated into the Supreme Court in 2008.

The *Høyrett* system included documents and information generated within the Supreme Court only, such as the names of parties, a list of documents pertaining to the case and deadlines for handling the appeal. It also included various document templates. The internal documents that the Court generated as it processed an appeal – for instance, the law clerks' notes to the ASC and the Committee's decisions to grant or deny – were also added and could quickly be retrieved when needed later in the decision-making process. But the *Høyrett* system did not include any documents from the lower courts. Nor could the system be accessed from outside the Court. In short, the system was an entirely closed and court-internal system (NOU 2001:613).[7] At the end of the year, *Høyrett* generated the annual statistics of the different types and numbers of appealed cases, decided cases and backlogs.

Once the appeal was formally registered in the Court's case processing system, the appeal moved on to the clerk unit. Here the appeal was also registered in the unit's own spreadsheet before being assigned to a clerk.[8]

4.1.2 Prioritizing the Appeals

Ever since the first clerk was hired in 1957, a clerk's basic task has been to assist the justices on the ASC as they carried out their gatekeeping mandate for the Court. At first, the clerks assisted the justices only on appeals of civil cases. During the 1980s, the clerks started to handle appeals of criminal cases as well (Sunde 2015a:156). In 1989 the clerk unit was formally established, and throughout the 1990s, the number of clerks increased monotonically.[9] As the clerk unit grew in size and therefore processing capacity, the justices concluded that the clerks' processing of appeals being screened at the ASC should be formalized. Specifically, the justices agreed that the clerk unit should process the civil and criminal interlocutory appeals first and then turn its attention to the criminal merits appeals. Organizing their workflow in this manner did not exempt the clerks from processing civil

7 Documents in *Høyrett*, including documents that the clerks prepare for the ASC, are considered court-internal documents and cannot be made available to others.

8 Even though the case processing system *Høyrett* de facto integrated the gatekeeping ASC with the decisional functions of the Court, the Committee did not change its name from *Kjæremålsutvalget* to *Ankeutvalget* until 2008. *Høyrett* was replaced by the new national courtwide case processing system, *Lovisa*, in March 2018. Again, the case numbering system changed to a new format.

9 Also see discussions in Chapters 1, 3, 5 and 7.

merits appeals.[10] By early 2000, the clerks handled *all* interlocutory and *all* merits appeals that came to the Court.

Ebbs and flows in appeals to the Court could occur, and if the capacity of the clerk unit was in danger of being overwhelmed, the clerks were to prioritize criminal merits appeals according to the principle that criminal punishment should result in equal penalties for equal crimes and that punishments should be meted out in a timely fashion rather than being held hostage to the vagaries of caseload pressures. Processing criminal merits appeals required the clerks to check older decisions and make sure that the cases were comparable and the sentences were equal.[11]

4.2 Six Principles of Deciding to Decide

It is important to keep in mind that when the Norwegian Supreme Court transformed from a court of appeal to a court of precedent, the transformation required resources for thoroughly reviewing the appeals as well as mechanisms for strategically selecting appeals to be used as vehicles for establishing precedents. Significantly, one of the rationales for the expansion of the number of clerks is to assist the ASC's identification and selection of specific appeals to be used as vehicles for establishing precedents. In other words, the clerks were a key resource, enabling the Court to more thoroughly seek out appeals for their precedent-setting capacity.

But for the clerks to be effective as they pursued this function, the Supreme Court also needed a mechanism to rationalize its selection of appeals. First, it was important and necessary to eliminate the traditional presumption that aggrieved parties had a right to have their case heard by the Supreme Court. To operate as a court of precedent, it was essential that the Court should exercise complete docket control. The Court's finite decisional resources should not be consumed (wasted) on obvious, run-of-the mill appeals. The aggrieved parties had a right to appeal, but their 'rights' stopped at the threshold of the ASC. The Court's gatekeeper would decide whether their appeals would be heard. Second, it was also important to establish a selection mechanism that was both strategic and that secured necessary discretion. The two-step criminal law reform implemented in 1995 and the civil law reform implemented in 2008 secured all of these requirements.

Today, the basic appeals selection mechanisms for civil merits cases in the Dispute Act and the basic appeals selection mechanisms for criminal merits cases in the Criminal Procedure Act are almost identical as to their statements of purpose. The criminal proce-

10 «at sekretariatet skulle prioritere kjæremål, både sivile kjæremål og straffekjæremål, deretter fornyet behandling av straffesaker, men ikke frita sekretariatet for behandling av sivile anker»(in Sunde 2015a:156,554 n76). *Also see* Aamodt (2017).

11 Justice interview 6 November 2017, start page 42, p. 43.

dures section is longer since it contains special provisions to secure the rights of the defendant.

Section 30-4 of the Dispute Act, titled 'Leave to appeal against judgment', reads as follows:[12]

> 1. Judgments cannot be appealed without leave. Leave can only be granted if the appeal concerns issues that are of significance beyond the scope of the current case or if it is important for other reasons that the case is decided by the Supreme Court.
> 2. The issue of leave shall be determined for each appeal. Leave may be limited to specific claims and to specific grounds of appeal, including to specifically invoked errors in the application of law, procedure or the factual basis for the ruling.
> 3. The issue of leave shall be determined by the Appeals Selection Committee of the Supreme Court by way of decision. A decision to refuse leave or to grant limited leave requires unanimity.

Section 323 of the Criminal Procedure Act states:[13]

> An appeal to the Supreme Court may not proceed without the consent of the Appeals Selection Committee of the Supreme Court. Such consent shall only be given when the appeal is concerned with issues whose significance extends beyond the current case, or it is for other reasons particularly important to have the case tried in the Supreme Court.
>
> The matter shall be decided by a court decision. Consent may be limited to part of the case. A decision to refuse consent shall be unanimous. It may be reversed in favor of the person charged if there are special reasons for doing so.

These two sections provide the mechanisms and rationale for the Court's gatekeeping functions and set the stage for the clerks to act as the Court's 'first responders' when con-

12 https://lovdata.no/dokument/NLE/lov/2005-06-17-90/*#* (last accessed 19 February 2019). A handful of Norwegian laws are translated to English for information purposes only. In the event of any inconsistencies, the Norwegian versions shall prevail. *See* https://lovdata.no/register/loverEngelsk (last accessed 19 February 2019).

13 https://app.uio.no/ub/ujur/oversatte-lover/data/lov-19810522-025-eng.pdf (last accessed 19 February 2019). This English translation of the Criminal Procedure Act at the University of Oslo is an abbreviation of the full Section 323 in Norwegian. The complete section in Norwegian can be found at https://lovdata.no/pro/#document/NL/lov/1981-05-22-25/%C2%A7323 (last accessed 19 February 2019).

sidering an appeal's utility to establish precedent. We briefly discuss the joint features of these two important sections by way of the six operational clauses or principles that can be extracted from the statutes. We also bring to bear on our brief discussion the larger understanding of these principles as presented and argued by the writings of Jens Edvin Skoghøy and Arnfinn Bårdsen, two former law professors who have served as Supreme Court justices.[14]

The first two principles relate to procedures, while the four latter principles relate to substance.

1. For both sections, the *consent principle* states that no appeal will be reviewed by the Court unless the ASC gives its consent to grant review. This means that if the three justices simply sit on their hands, no appeal will be granted. Fundamentally, this principle reversed the 'burden of proof' regarding the processing of an appeal. Prior to the criminal and civil law reforms, the ASC had the burden of proof as to why an appeal should *not* be reviewed; since the reform, the appellant bears the burden of proof as to why the appeal should be reviewed. In other words, there is no longer a presumption of a 'right' to review.
2. For both sections, the *unanimity* clause states that a denial of an appeal requires unanimity among the three justices on the Committee. Again, if no one of the justices takes any action as to the appeal, the appeal will be denied, and it will be denied unanimously.
3. Consent for review can only be granted if the question or questions in the appeal have *significance beyond* the appeal itself. The 'significance beyond' principle means that an appeal worthy of the Court's decisional resources can be used to clarify or develop the law. A legal question may be of great interest, value or significance to the litigants – indeed, almost by definition the appeal will be of salience to them – but if the appeal has implications for only the parties directly involved in the case, or has very limited implications beyond any of them, then the appeal is of no interest to the Court as a court of precedent. Accordingly, the appeal should not be heard on the merits.
4. The *particular important* clause provides a safety valve for quality assurance in the event that an appeal fails to meet the 'significance beyond' clause. If the court of appeal has committed an error, the ASC can quash the decision and return the appeal and ask the court of appeal to reconsider its decisions. Alternatively, if an error has been committed at the court of appeal, the Committee can grant review and the Supreme Court can correct the error. The Committee can grant review if it disagrees with the court of appeal's interpretation of a statute or a constitutional clause. A well-argued appeal concerning something of great value to the appellant or the appeal concerning principles

14 Bårdsen(2014), Skoghøy (2008) and Skoghøy (2016). Bårdsen's article must also be understood as a message from the whole Court to the legal community on the procedures of appealing cases to the Supreme Court. Later Bårdsen also regularly gave seminars on appeals procedures to potential litigating lawyers.

of welfare, employment or human rights is more likely to be granted review. If there is a suspicion that a criminal defendant has been wrongly convicted, the ASC may grant review on the basis of procedural questions or interpretation of the law since the Supreme Court is barred from reviewing evidence of guilt. The Committee can also grant review if the defendant has received an exceedingly severe sentence. Review is not granted, however, if the sentence is perceived as too mild (Bårdsen 2014:540-542).

5. The *carving clause* empowers the ASC to grant review to a limited part of the appeal. The initial appeal can be too broad or too vague to meet the above criteria. But a smaller part of the appeal can contain a question or issue of interest to the Court. This is something the clerks ought to identify. If the Committee agrees, it will carve out this part of the appeal and direct the parties to only address this question during review.
6. The *overall assessment* clause does not emerge from a textual or literal reading of the two sections but can be used to further restrict access to the Court's merits panels. Skoghøy claims that even if the statutory conditions for granting an appeal are met, they are 'not sufficient' for the ASC to grant appeal. 'In addition', Skoghøy argues, granting appeal also depends on a 'broad overall assessment'.[15] The underlying rationale of Skoghøy's argument is that each decision to grant or deny requires the Court to consider a trade-off between the significance of the appeal beyond the appeal itself, on the one hand, and the reach of the decision and the costs and resources involved to render the decision, on the other. If the costs of deciding a case outweigh its significance, the appeal should not be granted review. Skoghøy (2016:311) lists the following seven points, or questions, that 'must' be considered before deciding to deny or grant an appeal.
   - *What is the probability of the appellant party winning the case?* The additional consideration of this point is who the appellant is. If the appellant party is a public party, a bank or an insurance company where the implications of the outcome may exceed the immediate self-interest of the party, then the Committee may grant review to establish a precedent even if there was nothing wrong with the appeal court's decision in the first place.
   - *What is the practical implication of the appeal?* Not every principled legal question calls for a day in court.

15 Skoghøy's original term – *en bred helhetsvurdering* – is a somewhat tricky term to translate from Norwegian to English. One dictionary (ordnett.no) suggests 'a broad overall assessment'. Using the term '*helhetsvurdering*' ('overall assessment') alone without the amplifier '*bred*' ('broad') would also suggest translations like 'in light of the broader circumstances' or 'in light of the bigger picture'. To the best of our knowledge, a precise English term does not exist for this rather vague term that indicates a final weighing and harmonization of the various elements that have entered the decisional calculus. *See* Qvigstad and Schei (2018) for a discussion of 'Criteria for good justifications' where they are very critical of the use of, in their translation, a 'general assessment'.

- *How much precedence already exists in the legal field in question?*
- *How much clarification of the law is there to be achieved by granting review to the appeal?*
- *How much time and resources are needed to decide the appeal in question?* A better use of the Court's resources may be to have several smaller questions decided rather than one big question.
- *Does the respondent really need the Supreme Court to reach closure in the case?* Especially in cases where the respondent is a private person there must be a limit as for how long one should require him or her to go another round in the court system in order to settle a principled question.
- Is the case moot? If the appeal court decision is reasonable and defensible, then the case has received sufficient attention even though it raises a principled legal question.

These seven questions also accentuate the conventional wisdom that justices are humans and judging is not math. They also underscore the substantial element of discretion, or margin of appreciation, that exists in this decision-making process and that ultimately influences the fate of an appeal.

4.2.1 Two Statutory Revisions

Based on United Nations' conventions on civil and political rights and following initiatives from the Supreme Court, the *Storting* amended the Criminal Procedures Act, effective as of 2010. The revision concerned the rights of a criminal defendant who had been found not guilty in a district court but found guilty in the appeal court. The revised statute instructed the Committee to thoroughly justify its decision that the appeal court's decision on the defendant's guilt had no chance of being reversed if the ASC denied the appeal.

The Supreme Court also initiated the second statutory revision, which became effective in 2012. This revision applied to both civil and criminal procedure laws. It authorized the three-justice ASC to rely upon written documents to quash lower court decisions in cases of procedural errors rather than the convention of a full review on the merits with oral arguments heard in a five-justice decisional panel. The Committee's decisions require unanimity, and the new statutory practice moves the Supreme Court towards a court of cassation. A justification for the revision was that action in a conventional five-justice decisional panel to consider whether procedural errors should quash a lower court decision required far more resources than could be justified by the non-precedential nature of the case itself. The overall resources of the Supreme Court would be put to better use if the ASC made such decisions.[16]

4.3 The Appeal Arrives at the Clerk Unit

From the registration office the leadership of the clerk unit receives a list of the incoming appeals. The leadership is also informed of the composition of the ASC and maintains close contact with the senior justice on the Committee. As part of overseeing the workload of individual clerks and monitoring the flow of appeals through the clerk unit, the clerk leadership enters the incoming appeals into a spreadsheet that is maintained and updated parallel to the Court's *Høyrett* case processing system.[17] The standard operating procedure is limited arbitrary assignment so that the clerks' workloads are roughly equal in quantity and substance. However, other considerations – namely workload and legal background or experience – can come in to play and result in more targeted assignments. For instance, if a clerk has gained some experience with a certain area of law or is well versed with respect to a particular body of criminal sentencing, it is more likely that this clerk will receive an appeal that taps into this area. Also, if a clerk has gained experience in international law or has returned from an internship at a European court, the clerk is also more likely to have an appeal relevant to this area of law land on his or her desk.

The clerks will find a physical folder secured with a rubber band in their mailboxes. The folder contains the most important documents of the appeal – that is, the appellant's and the appellee's briefs and the case's record in the lower courts. Additional documents linked to the appeal could be brought up from the registration office or downloaded from the Court's internal servers. Legal sources like statutes, precedent, white papers, preparatory reports and documents from parliamentary committees are found in external online databases like the Norwegian *Lovdata.no*. Sources of international law would be retrievable from the same Norwegian database or from the databases of the international institutions and courts.

---

16 *See* Bårdsen (2014:543-548) who refers to the 2010 revision of justifying denials as establishing 'mini-precedents' and the 2012 revision nullifying lower court decisions as 'semi-precedents'. *See also* Skoghøy (2016:311). The changes dated back to a meeting of justices on the Court in 2011 where it was decided to approach the Ministry of Justice to request changes in the statutes to empower the ASC to make final decisions in civil law procedures and criminal law procedures so as not needing to mobilize the full five-justice merits panels to resolve minor issues with obvious outcomes. The two new procedures were baptized "Lex Skoghøy" and "Lex Matningsdal" (Sunde 2015a:145-146, 352). In 2017 Justice Magnus Matningsdal gently reminded readers of the *Lawyer's Monthly* ("Advokatbladet") that the 2012 revision of the criminal procedures was called "Lex Matningsdal" (Schmidt 2017:5).

17 The spreadsheet system at the clerk unit continued even as the new case handling system *Lovisa* replaced the old case handling system *Høyrett* in March 2018. *Lovisa* did not offer the special monitoring features that the small-scale and flexible spreadsheet system had developed over the years.

The main task of the clerk in reviewing appeals is to advise the Committee regarding final decision on interlocutory appeals and whether to grant or deny merits appeals. In fulfilling this task on the merits appeals, the clerk seeks to determine if the appeal in question has the potential to be used for clarifying or developing the law. Over the years the clerk unit has developed an internal document of approximately 100 pages that aids the clerks carrying out their responsibilities for the Committee. The document is updated twice a year.

4.4 THE CLERK SCRUTINIZES THE APPEAL

As the clerks review the materials in the folder, they consult the internal document that details the tasks and procedures they must follow when handling the appeal. In general terms, the clerks must summarize the appeal, address the facts of the appealed case, pinpoint what the appeal is about, what issue or legal question is addressed and whether the appeal either invokes or has a potential for creating a precedent. In fulfilling these tasks, the clerk addresses all procedural and material aspects of the appeal in light of all relevant legal sources.

This work can be broken down into four steps that correspond to the sections of the memo that the clerk writes for the ASC. Each page of the memo is divided into two columns (see Figure 4.1). The right-hand column covers two-thirds of the page and is where the clerks write the memo's text. The left-hand column is left blank and is reserved for the justices' notes when they study the memo. This format corresponds to the standard sheets of paper used at desk exams at the Norwegian law schools. Hence, both clerks and justices alike are well familiar with the style format from their law school years. The expectation is that the length of the memo should reflect the significance of the case. Following the Mies van der Rohe maxim that 'less is more', the clerks design a memo on the disposition of an appeal that typically is about four pages long.

Figure 4.1 The format of the clerk's memo to the ASC. Illustration only

4.4.1 The Formalities

The clerk's first step is to check that all the formal requirements for submitting an appeal to the Court are met. The Dispute Act and The Criminal Procedure Act lay down explicit formal criteria with which the parties' appeals and responses must comply when submitted to the Supreme Court. The clerk must check these criteria critically. The Dispute Act states that an appeal must be submitted orally or in writing to the court that made the decision that is appealed. The declaration of appeal must contain the following information: the identity of the court of appeal; the parties and their lawyers; the case that is appealed; whether the appeal includes the case in whole or in part; the claim that is raised and a statement indicating the result the appellant seeks; the error that was committed in the decision; the actual and legal justifications that an error has been committed; the evidence that will be presented; the basis for the appeal to counter doubts regarding its merits; and the appellant party's view on the subsequent processing of the appeal. To summarize, the declaration of appeal provides a basis for the sound processing of the case for both the parties and the Court. It identifies what is challenged in the case being appealed and emphasizes, if relevant, any new actual or legal justification of new evidence.[18]

The Criminal Procedure Act establishes similar requirements for the format of criminal appeals, but the criteria here are more detailed due to the greater variation in criminal law. Criminal appeals regarding evidentiary errors under the question of guilt cannot be appealed to the Supreme Court.[19] The basis for this condition is the institutional confidence that this question already has been sufficiently addressed by the two lower courts: the trial court of original jurisdiction and the court of appeal. The declaration of appeal of a criminal case must address the decision that is challenged; whether the appeal concerns the decision in whole or only parts; and whether it includes decisions on confiscation of items or profits linked to the crime. It must address if the decision concerns procedural matters; the assessment or weighing of evidence under the question of guilt; the application of the law under the question of guilt or the question on punishment or sanction. It must also identify the error that has been committed if the appeal concerns procedural questions. Further, the declaration of appeal must identify the errors, if any, on the application of the law; any new evidence that is invoked; and the amendment that is claimed. If the appeal concerns a petition for a new hearing, the declaration of appeal must also identify whether the appeal concerns the whole case; the outcome that is demanded; the errors that have been committed; the actual and legal justifications that errors have been committed; and any new evidence that will be offered.[20]

One of the first issues the clerks confront is whether the appeal has been declared in time and if it meets the formal requirement of an appeal. But this technical question also contains an element of discretion. The clerk will consider exceptions to the expiration of the deadline if, for example, the appellant is not to blame for the delay or other reasons should require that the convicted party should have its case heard again. An appeal shall also be denied if it fails to meet the above requirements or contains other errors that preclude it from being considered. There is a possibility, however, that the Committee will offer the appellant a grace period in order to correct the errors of the appeal.[21]

In addition to checking all the formal requirements of the appeal itself, the clerk must also run the lawyers and companies related to the appealed case against an internal list of the Court's justices and their families to determine whether any real or perceived conflicts

18 The Dispute Act, Section 29-9.
19 The Criminal Procedure Act, Section 306.
20 The Criminal Procedure Act, Section 314.
21 The Criminal Procedure Act, Sections 318a and b.

of interest may arise. Justices or justices with family members who have business relations or own stock in companies that are parties to the appeal may be seen as having a conflict of interest and will recuse themselves. Likewise, justices who are related to the judge who presided over the case in the lower court run the risk of having their impartiality questioned and thus will not hear the appeal. Finally, it bears noting that efforts to avoid the appearance of any conflict of interest extend to the clerks as well. Accordingly, a clerk who has been recruited from a firm that is arguing a case before the Court will not be permitted to prepare the appeal for the Committee. Concerning decisions on conflicts of interest, the general rule on the Committee has been to err on the side of caution.

Checking for internal conflicts of interest is routine procedure on a court where independence, impartiality and integrity are paramount objectives. For example, for several years when the Court heard cases where the government was a party, the Court's three female justices – Kirsti Coward, Liv Gjølstad and Karin M. Bruzelius – recused themselves because their spouses held prominent positions in high government offices. A newspaper headline read 'Married to the Government' (Kristjánsson 2010), and the articles noted that Justice Kirsti Coward had a conflict of interest in 30 of 60 civil cases that the Court handled in 2009. Family members in the government did not bear upon the propriety to hear an appeal of only the Court's female justices, however. In 2013 Chief Justice Schei was prevented from chairing a plenary case on fishing rights between the government and a private party because his daughter had been the judge on the case in the Oslo trial court. Interestingly, Schei's daughter ruled against the government in the trial court, and the Borgarting Court of Appeal upheld the lower court's decision. Before the Supreme Court sitting *en banc*, the government won the case 9-8, reversing the lower courts' decisions (*Voldstaddommen*, Rt-2013-1345). Given Schei's history of supporting the private party against the government party in *en banc* decisions (Grendstad, Shaffer, and Waltenburg 2015:185-187), it is not unreasonable to expect that Schei's strong position on the Court would have swayed the justices and upheld the lower court's decision in the narrowly decided case.

If a justice with a conflict of interest is seated on the ASC, another of the four justices allocated to the ASC will take his or her place on the three-justice panel. If a justice with a conflict of interest has been assigned to one of the scheduled five-justice decisional panels, then the Director General will replace him or her with another justice pending approval of the parties of the case at the beginning of oral arguments. Prior to finalizing the roster of justices for Grand Chamber or *en banc* cases, the chief or the most senior justice on the Court will chair a procedural session with the justices who are safely outside any issues of conflict of interest to decide which justice(s) to exclude or include for oral arguments.

4.4.2 *The History of the Case*

The second section of the memo consists of a brief summary of the appeal's history. This section states the legal question of the appeal, identifies the court in which the case originated and the intermediate appellate court that heard the first appeal, and lays out the facts of the case.

4.4.3 *The Parties' Arguments and the Legal Forces*

The third section details the appellant's arguments as to why the Court should review the case and what the outcome should be, as well as the respondent's arguments presumably as to why the case should not be reviewed, and what part of it should be the object of review. As a court of precedent, the Court cannot rely on the litigants' documents to provide a complete account of the legal field of the case. The Court has an independent responsibility for establishing the status of the legal field.

The general understanding among clerks is that the appellant is likely to overstate the significance of the appeal, while the appellee is likely to understate the significance of the appeal. While the appellant is likely to mention principles and impact, the appellee is likely to accentuate the concreteness and limited practicality of the case in an attempt to shoot the appeal down. The clerk is required to expose the appellant's hyperboles and the appellee's understatements in order to arrive at a balanced understanding of the case.

Seen from the Norwegian Supreme Court, there is a large variation in the quality of the appeals and responses. During the interviews, some clerks would stress that a sign of poor quality of an appeal is when the appellant only claims that there is a principled value of the case or completely fails to mention either Section 30-4 of the Dispute Act in a civil appeal or Section 323 of the Criminal Procedure Act in a criminal appeal.[22] One justice stated bluntly that many appeals should never have come to the Supreme Court.[23] To be sure, some lawyers may have been instructed by their clients to file an appeal despite the lawyer's argument against doing so. And then there are those lawyers who may have encouraged their clients to appeal to the Court knowing full well that the case would not be accepted while in the meantime pocketing the legal fees.

One has to keep in mind that if the clerks found that all appeals were well drafted, the justices on the ASC would not need any assistance in their decision-making and the clerk unit would be closed down. The inevitable variation in the quality of the appeals mobilizes the necessary scepticism towards any appeal. On the other hand, the clerks may not show

22 Clerk interview 8 November 2017, start page 76, p. 77. Clerk interview 8 November 2017, start page 81, p. 82.

23 Justice interview 7 July 2017, start page 6, p. 7.

sufficient scepticism. The Office of the Government Advocate, or Attorney General, is the Norwegian government's legal office in civil lawsuits. The Office acts as counsel for ministries in lawsuits and advises the government and ministries on legal issues. Administratively, the Office of the Government Advocate is subordinate to the Prime Minister's Office. The resourceful and influential Office of the Government Advocate has a reputation among clerks for delivering solid and coherent arguments when acting as either the petitioner or the respondent in the case.[24] It is also understood among clerks that appeals from larger law firms with litigation departments of their own submit appeals of better quality than do smaller law firms.

Working through the litigants' briefs, the clerk compiles an exhaustive list on how the relevant legal sources speak to both sides of the legal question in the case. Several of the clerks we interviewed told us of how their work in this process emphasized the legal method they were taught in law school and how they followed the hierarchy of legal forces from international, constitutional and statutory law, through legislative intent, precedents, legal practice and, if necessary, down to equitable considerations.[25]

4.4.4 The Clerk's Recommendation

The clerk addresses and expounds upon all relevant legal questions and the legal sources germane to these legal questions. This includes the legal questions that the clerk thinks the appeal raises and thus may include legal questions that the litigants either failed to identify or did not understand the value of (Sunde 2015a:156). The importance of the clerk's investigation here is that the Court is not committed to the litigants' understanding of the law of the case since the Court as a court of precedent is mandated to have an independent responsibility to clarify the legal conditions that are relevant and that can be applied to the case. Given the gravity of the clerk's task here, he or she can seek individual advice from other clerks or have the appeal submitted to a discussion by all the clerks during their regular Monday meetings.

The clerk advises the Committee on whether the appeal at hand has a material basis and a sufficient potential to be used as a vehicle for clarifying or developing the law. It is

24 Despite the high legal quality of the Government Advocate's briefs to the Court and its overall 'repeat player' status (*see* Galanter 1974), it does not necessarily prevail in Court at the rate one might expect. This is because, as a nationwide legal player and sometimes in the role of the respondent, the Government Advocate may want the appeal to go forward so as to achieve a final national resolution to the legal and/or constitutional question even if the outcome of the case was not the one favoured by the Government Advocate. *Also see* Black and Owens (2012; 2013).

25 The classic book on legal method in Norwegian law is still Torstein Eckhoff's *Rettskildelære* in its various editions since 1971. Eckhoff (1916-1993) was an early advocate of legal realism. For an assessment of the status of the legal method, *see* Askeland (2018).

important to acknowledge an important distinction here. Being of sufficient material basis for clarification and development of the law means that although the appeal itself may not be interesting, it does possess the potential to be used as a vehicle for addressing or pushing forward a principled legal question, or a policy issue framed as a legal question. The identification of a principled question contained within or being ascribed to the appeal is the result of an analytic process that the clerk is the first person to undertake. The principal focus of the clerk is to make a recommendation to the justices on the Committee about whether to docket the case for a review on its merits and the arguments for doing so. And a key consideration for the clerk in making this recommendation is whether the appeal has the capacity to carry a principled legal question forward.

If the appeal concerns an order or a resolution (*kjennelse* or *beslutning*), the ASC can render a final decision. If that decision, in turn, requires a justification (i.e. when the ASC denies a criminal appeal in those instances where the appeal court finds the defendant guilty after the district court makes a ruling of not guilty), the clerk prepares an additional document that includes the introduction of the justification and a summary of the parties' claims. Because many decisions amount to boilerplate, the clerk can draw on various templates available in the *Høyrett* case processing system. The clerk's draft does not include the outcome of the appeal nor the full justification for the outcome. The unfinished draft is handed over to the justices for them to make the decision on the outcome, which then is appended to the clerk's draft.

If the appeal concerns a decision (*dom*) from a lower court, the clerk specifically addresses whether the appeal contains a question of legal principal that ought to be decided by the Court. If the ASC denies the appeal, the administration notifies the parties and ushers the appeal out of the system. From a legal point of view, if the ASC decides to give a reasoning for the denial and create a mini precedent, the memo of the clerk might be used as a basis of the decision and the clerk might continue to be involved in the case, for example, with proofreading. If the Committee grants the appeal to be decided by the Court, the clerk may later assist in the preparatory process as the appeal heads towards oral arguments.

When the clerk has finished the review of the appeal and completed the memo, the appeal folder is then placed in one of the mailboxes reserved for the justices on the Committee.[26] A justice recalls that the mailboxes were enumerated and clerks were instructed to place the folder with the memo in one of the mailboxes following a certain system. If a particular issue was considered necessary to be brought to the justices' attention, clerks could also attach copies of additional documents concerning that issue to the appeal. Sometimes the clerk could bring the folder directly to the office of a justice serving on the Committee.

26 Justice interview 17 November 2017, start page 100, p. 101.

The basic elements and procedures of writing the memo to the justices on the Committee have been in place for many years. After the number of justices on the Committee increased from three to four in 1989 and from four to five in 2010, the clerks could never be certain which three of the four or five justices would actually handle the appeal. Before the procedures and deadlines for preparing memos were tightened at the end of the 1990s, clerks could strategically procrastinate so as to avoid specific justice on the Committee. Later, when justices with publication records, such as former law professors, were recruited to the Court, a clerk could make a reference or two in the memo to legal sources found in the publications of a justice on the Committee in order to play to that justice's pride.[27]

4.5 Deciding to Decide

At any time, the ASC consists of several overlapping three-justice panels with alternating and rotating collections of justices. The most senior of the three justices chairs the panel. A randomized procedure assigns the order in which the justices on the panel will receive the folder from the clerk. The Committee's work is primarily organized by way of written procedures. The default process is decentralized in that the justices do not convene for deliberations on the appeals; instead, they work individually. The documents to be reviewed are physically or electronically circulated among the three justices.

Obviously, the clerk's memo greatly facilitates the justices' decision making on the Committee. The processing style of an appeal varies from one justice to another. One justice may start with the clerk's memo and then continue with the parties' documents and end up with the lower courts' decisions. Another justice may read the documents in the reverse order. The justice who reads the appeal first may add notes to the clerk memo in the left-hand column of the pages. This justice may also open the clerk's memo in *Høyrett* and write notes directly in the file. Then the justice will add some notes and a tentative conclusion on the outside of the folder as to the preferred outcome of the appeal. Before 2012 the two outcomes were grant or deny. Since 2012 the outcomes were grant, deny or quash, or affirm with new reasoning to create 'mini-precedents'. The folder continues to the next two justices in line who will go through the same procedures.

Sometimes a justice will take advantage of the standing desk that is located in the Court's mail room. Here, the justice can do a quick reading to see if the appeal requires closer attention. If the clerk's recommendation on the interlocutory or the merits appeal is obvious, the justice can write agreement on the folder and quickly pass the folder to the mailbox of the next justice. The justices bring those appeals that require closer study back to his or her chambers.

27 Clerk interview 14 August 2017, start page 18, p. 20.

The ASC's default decision is to deny an appeal. That decision requires unanimity among the three justices – an outcome that occurs between 85 and 90 per cent of the time for merits appeals.[28] If any one of the three justices on the Committee agrees to hear the appeal, it is granted and forwarded to the decisional panels for oral arguments. This means that any single justice on the Committee has a "right to veto", which, according to Justice Bårdsen, underscores each justice's individual responsibility for granting review and the justice's individual contribution to the content and variation of the docket (Bårdsen 2014:533). Hence, this procedure and this rule yield significant influence to each justice on the Committee. Acting alone, each justice is an architect of the evolving docket.

The Supreme Court takes pride in efficient procedures. The goal of the Court is for the ASC to decide on an appeal within one month of its arrival at the Court. Some appeals have to be decided very quickly – within a day or two. The urgency of these appeals typically arises as a result of the loss of personal liberty associated with criminal charges. To respond to these appeals, an 'emergency unit' is formed. When clerks assigned to this group receive an appeal concerning the loss of personal liberty (an order of custody), they put aside any other tasks, notify the Committee that an appeal of an order of custody is underway and work on the appeal immediately. Decisions on such appeals usually are completed on the day that they arrive at the Court.

That decisions on custody are taken at the level of courts of appeal, that the Supreme Court therefore is the court of appeal, that the ASC has been given the authority to rule on these appeals and that the law requires swift decisions mean that the Committee has to be operative every day of the workweek throughout the year (Schei 2015b:8). When the Court closes for business during vacations, the number of justices allocated to the Committee, constituting the 'emergency unit', drops to only three. These periods are the only times of the year when it is possible to predict exactly which three justices serve on the Committee.

In 2017, the Court received about 2,200 appeals – a substantial increase from the approximately 1,300 appeals it received in 1996, the year after the criminal procedure reform went into effect (see Figure 3.1). We can get a sense of the individual workload by dividing the number of appeals per clerk and per the three justices on the Committee panels. Figure 4.2 shows that since 1996, justices have increased their workload on the Committee. Whereas each justice participated in screening 207 appeals in 1996, this number increased to 330 in 2017 (a rate of growth of nearly 60 per cent). Another way to look at this is to use working days per year. If we assume that there are approximately 230 working days in a year, a three-justice panel on the ASC in 2017 screened on average 5.74

28 Justice Skoghøy (2016:323) once stated that "in my experience it is an astonishing large degree of agreement on whether to grant appeal".

cases per day, up from an average of 4.24 cases per day in 1996.[29] Of course, the complexity of appeals varies appreciably; consequently, the amount of time necessary to screen one appeal versus another can vary a lot too – an observation confirmed by Chief Justice Tore Schei. He has stated that each justice may use as little as 15 minutes on an appeal but may also spend several days on a more complex appeal if so required (Schei 2015b:8).

Figure 4.2 Workload – Justice and Clerks

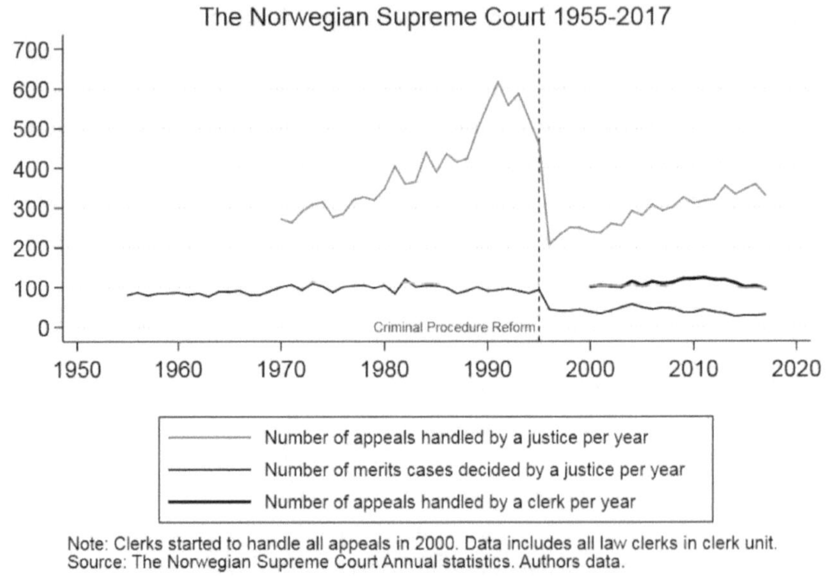

It was not until 2000 that the Court took full advantage of the law clerks and had them handle all incoming appeals to the Court.[30] Hence, the data for clerks in Figure 4.2 start in 2000. The figure shows that in 2017 each clerk handled on average 95.6 appeals, a number that has been fairly stable since 2000 but with a peak year in 2011 with 124 appeals per clerk per year. Again, if we consider workload from the perspective of working days, in 2017 each clerk handled on average 0.42 appeals per day.

These numbers suggest that the clerks are great time savers for the justices on the Committee. The clerks' primary job is to separate the wheat from the chaff. That explains why a justice may only need as little as 15 minutes to decide. And the clerks' identification

29 Norwegian tax authorities state that there are 230 working days in a calendar year. https://www.skatteetaten.no/person/skatt/skattemelding/finn-post/3/2/8/ (last accessed 7 June 2018).

30 Since the clerk unit is responsible for preparing appeals for the Committee, we use all law clerks on the clerk unit, including the clerk leadership, in these calculations.

of the wheat, or needles in the haystack, if you prefer, permits the justices to concentrate their efforts on the more consequential and complex cases that require closer scrutiny.

When the appeal with the clerk's memo has completed its round among the three justices, the justice who received the memo first takes stock of the situation. If all the justices agree, the decision-making has been completed. If the justices fail to agree, the memo goes another round among the justices. Occasionally, a justice on the Committee could call on the clerk and ask for a minor follow-up or clarification on the memo. If necessary to iron out differences or if the complexity of the case requires some clarification, the justices might convene to discuss the appeal. Finally, the decision to grant or deny is signed and noted on folder, which is then returned to the mail room. Prior to 2010 or so, other than receiving the folder and completing any immediate paperwork (as well as availing themselves of the opportunity to check whether the Committee's conclusion deviated from their recommendations), the clerks' work on a given appeal was complete, and there were no more interactions with the Committee regarding that appeal.

4.6 The Appeal Is Granted Review and Prepared for Oral Arguments

Ten to fifteen per cent of merits appeals and approximately a dozen interlocutory appeals are granted review by the ASC and sent to the decisional panels. In the 2000-2009 decade, the number of granted appeals averaged 167 cases per year. The justice who first considered the appeal on the Committee was also assigned to escort the appeal through any procedural steps towards oral arguments on the decisional panel.

As the Court established itself as a court of precedent in the first decade of the twenty-first century, a procedural novelty materialized in which the preparatory justice oversaw any preparation of the appeal in the event procedural decisions had to be made. Currently, the preparatory justice holds a meeting, sometimes by phone and sometimes in person, with the parties' advocates. The clerk who prepared the appeal to the Committee could also participate in these meetings. These procedural meetings took place with increasing frequency throughout the first decade of the 2000s (Sunde 2015a:138). The purpose of the meetings was to clarify to parties the legal question or questions that the Court identified and to underscore that the parties' arguments must be directed towards this legal question and the disputed claim in civil cases or the contested issue in criminal cases (Schei 2015b:8). The meetings also underscored and accentuated the new status of the appeal to be decided by a court of precedent. Namely, the parties may have appealed the case, but they no longer 'own' it. The specific case is now serving a broader legal purpose beyond the direct interests of the parties involved. Indeed, by granting the appeal, the Court has taken ownership of the appeal and put it to use for the Court's own strategic goals. Whatever the immediate outcome of the case may be for the parties, the parties' interests are secondary to the Court, merely a side effect of the need for a vehicle to establish a precedent.

After the ASC granted the appeal and placed it on the Court's agenda for oral arguments, the parties are not permitted to add any new claims or offer new evidence.[31] If the parties ask for exceptions to this rule, the request is brought back to the Committee. As far as is practicable, any procedural decisions made after the Committee granted review and before the oral arguments are heard in the merits panel will be decided by the original three justices on the Committee who originally granted review.

When oral arguments in the five-justice decisional panel commence, the preparatory justice of the ASC and the law clerk who handled the appeal are dismissed from the appeal and return to their desks. It is now the task of the five justices to carry the appeal through the next three stations – that is, oral arguments, deliberations and opinion writing. As the law clerk returns to the clerk unit, the court clerk, already permanently stationed as the courtroom aide, steps up to be on hand for the decisional panel. The court clerk assists with the procedures of oral arguments, stays in the courtroom for the duration of the arguments and is available if any administrative issues arise. The court clerk also will follow the case and be present in the back of the room during the justices' deliberations. The court clerk may be called upon to check references and proofread the final decision. If the court clerk is unavailable to perform these duties, a law clerk may substitute for the court clerk and also contribute to proofreading if required.

4.7 INCHING TOWARDS THE NEXT LEVEL

That the ASC can instruct the parties on what legal question they must address during oral arguments is an institutional change and a procedural novelty that overlaps with the formal transition of the one-time 'court within the court' (*Kjæremålsutvalget*) into the new, streamlined and fully integrated ASC. The procedural novelty also overlaps with the significant transition of having civil cases fall in line with criminal cases so that the justices have discretion to cherry-pick both types of cases in order to focus only on the most important and interesting appeals for precedential purposes. This significant change has transformed the ASC from the Court's antechamber (*forkammer*) to its chancellery (*kanselli*) (Sunde 2015a:138).

During our research on the development of the clerk unit and the greater involvement of clerks in the decision-making on the Court, the Supreme Court justices have been extremely careful to point out that they carefully read the documents of the case and that they make up their own minds as to grant or deny an appeal. To cast a vote is a personal

31 The Dispute Act, Section 30-7.

responsibility that the justices take seriously. Therefore, it was difficult to get the justices to afford the clerks so much influence in the preparatory and procedural stages of the ASC. This influence would not have happened if it was not for the growing sense of crisis following the heavy workload that beset the Court towards the end of the 1980s. And the influence would not have happened if it was not for the expanding international legal field that developed in the 1990s and early 2000s. That the justices consider their votes as a personal responsibility is also the reason why the clerks have been allowed up to but not to move beyond the Committee.

But there is a wrinkle that could affect the clerks' carefully circumscribed role. Since a clerk may have been given an appeal because it matched the clerk's specialty and since documents and the memo prepared by the clerk for the Committee follow the case to the decisional five-justice panels when an appeal has been granted, the influence of the clerks also points beyond the ASC as the Court's first decision-making station. Up to approximately 2010, the preparatory justice occasionally could request additional clarification from the clerk before the appeal was dispatched to the decisional panel. More rarely, such consultations with the clerk could be taken by the five-justice decisional panel before oral arguments, and perhaps later during deliberation and opinion writing.

Accordingly, up to around 2010, the memo the clerk wrote for the Committee and that followed the appeal to the three subsequent decision-making stages operated as something of a soft influence on the latter three stages of decision-making on the Court. But in 2010 something changed. And in 2015 something changed even more. The clerks were heading towards greater involvement in the Court's overall decision-making, a journey that is the focus of the next chapter.

5 "A Weakness of the System"

Late in 2009, the Supreme Court's operating schedule of opinion assignments informed Justice Karl Arne Utgård that he soon would have his work cut out for him. The Social Democratic government had changed the nation's tax regime, and shipowners feared that strategic investments made in earlier years could be subject to heavy taxes once the new tax regime took effect. Three separate cases pitting the government against the shipowners were filed in the Sunnmøre, Aust-Agder and Oslo district courts. The government won in the Aust-Agder district court, but lost in the Oslo district court. (The decision had consolidated the case from the Sunnmøre district court.) The losing parties appealed the district court decisions. The Supreme Court's Appeals Selection Committee (ASC) permitted the cases to be fast tracked, using the 'leapfrog mechanism', thereby bypassing the courts of appeal.[1] Upon their arrival at the Supreme Court, the cases were consolidated, and Chief Justice Tore Schei quickly decided that they should be heard *en banc*. Although it would be easy to get lost in the technical details of the tax legislation that the cases raised, there was a single looming constitutional issue – namely Section 97's prohibition of *ex post facto* laws. *The Ship Owner* case was scheduled for five days of oral arguments starting Monday 11 January 2010, and Justice Karl Arne Utgård was in line to write the Court's opinion (NTB 2010; Sunde 2015a:161).[2]

In a meeting of the justices on 10 December 2009, Justice Utgård alluded to the complexities of the case, and he asked the justices for their permission to use a clerk as he wrote the Court's opinion. If the justices acceded to Utgård's request, the clerk would not only sit in on the case during the five days of oral arguments, he or she also would sit in on the justices' conference deliberation and be on hand during opinion writing. The other justices conceded, and Utgård was allowed to use a clerk (Sunde 2015a:161, p. 554, note 82). It was a fair and eminently logical concession. Were Utgård to find himself in the minority of the *Ship Owner* case, another justice would have to step up to the plate and write the majority opinion; the case's complexities would not change and this justice too would find the assistance of a clerk of great help. Moreover, a reduced Court was hearing this legally complex and constitutionally potent case. Despite being heard *en banc*, for various reasons, only 11 of the 19 justices would have the final say on the landmark decision.[3] Fortuitously

1 The Dispute Act, Section 30-2 permits the Supreme Court to fast track appeals if the case raises 'especially important principle questions' or if time is of the essence.

2 The official case number of the *Ship Owner* case is Rt-2010-143.

3 Out of the 19 justices on the Court, 5 justices were found to have a conflict of interest in the case (Justices Liv Gjølstad, Kirsti Coward and Karin Bruzelius had conflicts of interest due to their partnerships with leading legal bureaucrats in the government, while Justices Bergljot Webster and William Matheson had

or strategically, the clerk leadership had already given the responsibility of the complicated case to a clerk with five years of tax law experience prior to being hired as clerk. With the presence of a law clerk in the justices' deliberations during the *Ship Owner* case, 'a barrier was broken'.[4]

From 1957, when the first clerk was hired, through the appreciable addition of clerks in the 1990s and into the first decade of the twenty-first century, the clerks' primary (near exclusive) responsibility had been to assist the ASC. To be sure, law clerks performed occasional tasks for the chief justice and the Secretary General; they sometimes covered for the court clerks, and they also provided fact-checking and proofreading services on the final draft opinions of Court decisions. However, for the institution of the Court, having a clerk purposefully attending five days of oral arguments and actually sitting in on the justices' deliberations – 'the deliberative moment' inside the 'black box' of decision-making – was truly unprecedented.[5]

5.1 FINE-TUNING THE CLERK UNIT

Since being brought into the Court in 1957, clerks were hired to review appeals and assist the justices on the ASC. To be sure, the nature of their review and assistance evolved over time. Prior to the early 1990s, the clerks only prepared interlocutory appeals for the Committee. Appeals on merits bypassed the clerk unit and were handled directly by the three justices on the Committee panels. Beginning in the mid-1990s, the clerks started to handle appeals on the merits, first appeals of civil cases and later criminal cases. By the turn of the millennium, the clerks handled *all* types of appeals as they prepared memos to be forwarded to the Committee.[6]

As more clerks handled more appeals involving more legal questions and more areas of the law, greater variation in the scope of the clerks' memos ensued. The general tendency,

conflicts of interest due to family or professional ties to legal firms involved in the case, Rt-2009-1617). Two other justices had leaves of absence (Justices Ole Bjørn Støle and Erik Møse), and Justice Arnfinn Bårdsen, the most junior justice on the Court, had to withdraw from the case in order to reduce the number of justices from 12 to 11, so as to effect an odd number of justices (Rt-2010-143). Justice Bårdsen sat in on the oral arguments and the deliberation as a backup in case of illnesses among the 11 justices, but Bårdsen did not cast his vote on the outcome of the case.

4 *See* Sunde (2015a:161).

5 Phrases quoted in Dyevre (2010:303). *See also* Stone (1992:116). Around 1996 and 1997, several attempts were made to have a clerk sit in during oral arguments and then to draft an introduction to the Court's decision. Because the justices were not impressed by the clerks' drafts and also because they were unwilling to have non-justices chip away at the craft of judging, any organized attempts of having clerks in the courtroom were put aside for a long time (Sunde 2015a:160). The formal discontinuation of the attempts did not rule out occasional requests for clerical assistance.

6 Information in this paragraph and the next draws on Aamodt (2017) and Sunde (2015a:156).

however, was that each memo became more encompassing. The clerks' capacity to fully process each appeal reached its high-water mark in 2006. In that year, all appeals were completely accounted for, few stones were left unturned and few if any questions were left unanswered. Yet, as the number of appeals made to the Court kept increasing (see Figure 3.1), a complete account for every appeal was no longer a viable strategy. Indeed, Justice Steinar Tjomsland once drily noted that a clerk's memo would receive the highest grade were it to be submitted as an exam paper. But the effort would be in vain if it was evident that the appeal should never have reached the Supreme Court in the first place. Consequently, the clerk unit started to change the way it handled the appeals.

The shift led to appeals that were perceived as having little or no chance of success, being given short shrift by the clerks so that the justices on the Committee could quickly reject them without further ado. At the same time, clerks dug deeper into the principled, hard or indeterminate appeals where the justices needed a larger degree of assistance from the clerks. Additional efforts were also given to appeals where the facts were complicated, where the appeals were extensive or where the appeals themselves were disorganized and needed tidying up. Therefore, a fundamental element of a clerk's memo was to put the appeal in order so that the legal questions and the facts of the case became clear and manifest (Aamodt 2017:2). Increasingly, the clerks were expected to write more extensive memos for the Committee on those appeals where the outcome was considered indeterminate.

As we discussed in the previous chapter, clerks also could be at hand to assist the preparatory justice while the granted appeal was discussed with the parties to the case and being prepared for oral arguments. Clerks, however, were not expected to follow the case into the courtroom during oral arguments. This is not to say that clerks did not attend oral arguments under any circumstances; oral arguments are public events, and clerks may have a professional interest in observing the legal proceedings. Moreover, it was accepted among the justices that clerks could attend oral arguments, sitting in the public section in order to gain a greater appreciation of their workplace. But prohibitively, the law clerks could not attend the justices' deliberations or be at hand during opinion writing except when substituting for a court clerk, and then only as a wallflower. The two final stations were beyond the clerks' duties and, in the view of some justices, also appreciably beyond their responsibility and perhaps even their competencies.

The clerks' traditional job description did permit them to be on hand for justices at the conclusion of the Court's decision-making process in order to check and verify legal sources, but these tasks were done in coordination with the court clerk whose basic job was to provide administrative assistance to the five-justice panels. The law clerks might occasionally reenter the decision-making process and proofread the Court's final opinions, although this task also was part of the formal job description of the court clerks. Indeed, proofreading final opinions continued to be among the court clerks' tasks even after their formal place in the organizational structure was moved to the clerk unit in 2015.

5.1.1 *Complementing the Litigants Only*

Traditionally, the parties' advocates had the responsibility of ensuring their briefs contained all the relevant legal materials for the Court's consideration. It was the clerks' responsibility to process the appeals, write a memo and bring the appeals to the ASC. In criminal appeals the clerks had the added responsibility of assuring that the legal rights of the defendant were secured. More recently, as we noted in the previous chapter, the clerk also could assist the justice from the Committee in preparations and interactions with the parties before oral arguments for those appeals that were granted.

As we have already discussed, beginning in the late 1990s the Supreme Court began a gradual transformation from a court of appeal to a court of precedent. Consequently, the stakes associated with identifying the full range of legal sources that would provide the legitimizing foundation for the Court's articulation of precedent rose significantly. At about the same time, the legal field became more complicated and more attentive to international law. And then, of course, there has always been the simple fact that the advocates want to win the case for their clients. Thus, they may have strategic interests to cherry-pick the evidence and arguments that are most conducive to their client's position. For a variety of reasons, then, the burden of presenting all the relevant information for a case could no longer be entrusted to the parties alone. Whatever legal questions, issues and sources the justices or the clerks deemed relevant, but were omitted from the parties' briefs, either had to be provided by the Court itself or simply left unaddressed, to the parties' (and the clarity of the law's) peril.

In a 1997 internal memo, Chief Justice Carsten Smith addressed this inadequacy problem. Specifically, he addressed the justices' work on decisional panels from the point of view of having all relevant documentary sources available. Smith wrote that clerks "could write memos on specific legal questions where the court has failed to receive sufficient documentation from the advocates of the parties" (quoted in Aamodt 2017:3). The basic understanding was that clerks should complement the parties' documentation.

5.2 Legal Complexity Starts to Tax the Justices

By the turn of the century, the new practice and standard on the Court was for a clerk to process each appeal prior to the ASC's consideration. In 2011, Chief Justice Tore Schei became alarmed that there were too few clerks to sufficiently handle the cases for the Committee. Law clerks sometimes were removed from their regular tasks to substitute as court clerks, and whether a direct consequence of this or not, some appeals were being handed directly over to justices on the Committee without the appeals first having been processed in the clerk unit. The time needed to prepare an appeal was also linked to the rising expectation of what the clerks were to address in the appeal and to write in their memos.

Two years later the clerk unit was still behind on processing appeals in a timely manner. Chief Schei had discussed the matter with the Minister of Justice, Grete Faremo, and had asked for more clerks. He pointed out that the justices still needed to consider appeals without the necessary preparations by the clerks, which could undermine the quality of the Court's decision-making. The issue also was discussed in a meeting of the justices; significantly, the clerk leadership participated. Some justices were concerned that the clerks were going too far and addressing legal issues beyond what was raised in the appeal itself. The clerk leadership responded that failure by the clerks to address all aspects of an appeal would only result in more questions coming back to the clerks from the justices (Sunde 2015a:162). Although hiring more clerks would reduce the overall workload on the Court, this was not the only solution. The justices could simply start granting fewer appeals for review in decisional panels, a point of view not unfamiliar to Chief Schei.

In 2014 Schei again discussed workload and staffing with the new Minister of Justice, Anders Anundsen. The number of appeals had increased steadily since Schei became chief, from 1,645 in 2002 to 2,364 in 2013, with an increase in the number of appeals of almost 11 per cent from 2012 to 2013 alone. It was clear that no one was arguing in favour of increasing the number of justices on the Court. On the other hand, the potential for increasing the Court's processing capacity was again located in the clerk unit (Sunde 2015a:161, and notes 83 and 84, p. 554). Schei and other justices had already begun calling for clerks to assist in more tasks and for their greater involvement across all four stages of decision-making. In the 1990s, Chief Justice Smith's attempts to introduce clerks to the service of justices on the merits panels had not gone down well with the other members of the Court, and, as we saw in Chapter 3, Smith's attempt was quickly shelved. But less than two decades later, something was about to change.

As Tore Schei approached the end of his tenure as chief justice in 2016, he grew increasingly concerned with a looming legal development where clerks might come to the rescue (Schei 2015b). Schei had long anticipated that both specialization in law and internationalization of law would make the legal field less transparent and the appeals more complex. This demanding situation was also a challenge to the justices who were expected to be recruited as and to remain legal generalists.

One possible solution to this situation for the Supreme Court was to look to the judicial recruitment process and target groups of lawyers with the needed specializations. When replacing retiring justices, these lawyers would then be allocated to take on the special and complex cases. The snag was that allocating justices to resolve specific cases would violate the stated goal of staffing the Court with generalists. It would also violate the expectation and established procedure of random assignment of justices to the panels irrespective of the cases that the panels were hearing. So Schei averred that recruiting justices with specialized fields of expertise or subdividing the Court into specialized panels would not be a viable route for a general court.[7]

Schei did not support the idea of specialized justices for yet another reason. In many of these special cases, a private party faced a public party. Specialized justices in these public vs. private disputes would more likely be recruited from government bodies and agencies to the exclusion of justices with longer careers in business and private practice. If such a trend in fact emerged, it would violate Schei's preference, in the name of diversity, of hiring justices with a stronger background from private practice (see NTB 2014).

If specialization among the justices was ruled out, an alternative solution to the increasing complexity stemming from the specialization and internationalization of the law was to hire more law clerks. Unlike the Court and the justices, diversification of the clerk unit was not a stated goal of the Court's leadership or a government policy, although attention to diversity is apparent when calls for the recruitment of clerks are made (a point we discuss in greater detail in the next chapter). The procedure of allocating appeals to the clerks based on a rule of randomness was not cast in stone. In fact, the clerk leadership had full discretion to deviate from the rule of randomness and allocate appeals to clerks with the experience and specialization that an appeal required, which may very well have been the case when the clerk leadership gave the *Ship Owner Taxation* appeal to a former tax lawyer. Another element favouring the addition of law clerks boiled down to sheer monetary considerations; in budgetary terms, the Court could get two clerks for the price of one justice. Therefore, strengthening the Court's decision-making process could come about by increasing the number of clerks on the Court and expanding the services that they provided. To put it simply, the clerk pool needed to grow.

But Schei aimed for more. He acknowledged the increased efficiency in the decision-making process that resulted when the clerks assisted the ASC in carving out the substantial and principled part of an appeal so that more marginal issues did not consume the justices' finite resources. Consequently, Schei resurrected Smith's fuller arguments from the 1997 internal Court memo where Smith had stated that

> [j]ustices who requested assistance in writing the introduction to a decision, should receive such assistance, and that clerks also could write memos on spe-

7 In cases on appeal on merits, the Court may appoint specialists who can explain more complicated issues. For example, the Court can request information from experts on forensic medicine on sentencing in criminal cases on drugs.

> cific legal questions where the court has failed to receive sufficient documentation from the advocates of the parties (Smith quoted in Aamodt 2017:3).

To put it simply, Schei perceived the general utility of the clerks and wanted them to participate more actively in the whole gamut of the Court's decision-making process.

Schei addressed instances where justices on the decisional panels needed particular legal sources or legal texts during the decision-making process that were evidently missing or not provided by the parties during oral arguments. Rather than the justices conducting their own legal research, a better use of resources, Schei argued, would be for clerks to provide background documents and the legal sources for the justices on the decisional panels as well as the ASC. Schei asserted that the responsibility the Supreme Court has for the 'correct application of law' is not compatible with justices themselves having to search for legal sources that are missing during oral arguments or needed during deliberations and opinion writing (Schei 2015b:41). The Court, he argued, needs to establish a reliable system that guarantees complete inclusion of all relevant legal documents and legal sources in all cases. The inability of the clerks to support the justices in the Court's decision-making process during and after oral arguments, Schei bluntly stated, was a "weakness of the system" (Schei 2015b:41).

Schei argued that justices who wrote the decisions in larger and more difficult cases should also be able to call upon the clerks to make drafts of the facts of the case, to prepare the legal questions of the case and to take minutes of claims and arguments that were presented in the case. It is especially important in complicated cases that the justices have sufficient time for preparations and sufficient time for deliberations and opinion writing. The support from the clerks in these areas would relieve the justices of some of the burden of writing opinions and also provide useful contributions to the quality of the Court's decisions (Schei 2015b).

Schei's arguments and meetings with the minsters of justice paid off. The evident discrepancy between tasks and manpower in the clerk unit was reduced, but not necessarily fully alleviated, when the Court received its new budget. Starting in the fall of 2015, the Court was able to hire three new clerks.

5.3 Breaking Another Barrier

While one major barrier was broken when a clerk sat in on the justices' full decision-making on the landmark *Ship Owner Taxation* case, another barrier was about to be broken five years later. In November 2015 the Supreme Court had reserved four days for oral arguments in a plenary case that pitted an Afghanistan family against the Norwegian government. The legal question addressed the validity of the government's decision that denied the family asylum in Norway and the degree to which the decision had accounted sufficiently for "the best interests of the child" – the third provision in the United Nations Convention on the Rights of the Child. The family included two girls who were two and six years old at the time asylum was denied. This case was labelled *Internal Displacement* decision.

Back in March 2015, the Court's ASC granted leave to appeal and the preparatory justice scheduled the case for a day and a half of oral arguments before a five-justice decisional panel. Then in August, the time scheduled for oral arguments was expanded to two full days. The panel scheduled for the case consisted of Chief Justice Schei and Associate Justices Utgård, Tønder, Webster and Bergsjø. Oral arguments began as planned, but somewhere in the process there was a snag. The records of the case note that on August 21 the Court decided that the case should be heard by a larger number of justices convening either as a Grand Chamber or *en banc*. The decision to remove the case from its assigned five-justice panel was based on Section 6 of the Court Act that permits two of the justices on a merits panel to demand that such move be taken. The move was based on the case being a complicated if not a principled case, and that Chief Justice Schei understood that the case activated or mobilized competing views among the justices. On the last day of August, Chief Justice Schei decided that the case should be heard *en banc*.[8]

Rescheduling the Court's calendar to accommodate oral arguments in Grand Chamber or *en banc* is a major disruption of the Court's hum of ordinary activities. Typically, litigants and advocates are notified of the scheduled date for their case weeks, if not months, in advance, and the Director General has matched those cases with randomly assigned five-justice panels. Other assignments also have been scheduled – for example, justices' assignments to the ASC and to office week – further locking in the Court's personnel. Grand Chamber or the *en banc* bench are composed from the 20 justices whose calendars the Director General now must reschedule. Rescheduling ensued as the Court decided that four days of oral arguments should commence Monday 9 November.

That the Supreme Court granted the asylum appeal and originally scheduled it to be heard in an ordinary five-justice panel was not surprising, given the case concerned principled legal questions and was appealed to a court that now understood itself to be a court of precedent. More surprising was the turn midstream when the Court decided to elevate the case to an *en banc* hearing.

The parties prepared accordingly for the showdown in the Court. As a party to the case, the government approached the litigation quite seriously; it was to be represented by the Government Advocate himself, Fredrik Sejersted. He was accompanied by Marius Emberland and Marius Stub, both with a PhD in law like Sejersted himself. The family and their third-party interveners (*partshjelpere*) were represented by highly experienced

8 *See* Rt-2015-1388, Section 34. The court-internal reference number of the case is 2015/203.

advocates as well: Christian Hauge, Jan Fougner and law professor Mads Andenæs. Little did the litigants know that another surprise was in store for them!

At the beginning of November, one week before oral arguments, the parties were notified that the Supreme Court itself had gathered information from 17 nations on their interpretation and implementation of the United Nations Convention's provision on the best interest of the child. Marius Stub, representing the government in the case and later publishing a commentary on the plenary decision, stated that the parties in no way were involved in the Court's efforts to gather the information (Stub 2016). The Court's independent effort to gather information on the case and its late delivery of the information to the parties denied the parties the full opportunity to study the new information from the Court. Consequently, they had very little time to adjust and compare the new information with the information that they had collected while preparing for oral arguments. Neither did the time remaining prior to the start of oral arguments permit the parties to present follow-up questions.[9] This inability to probe the Court's added information could prove especially problematic for the appellants: Stub claimed that of the 17 states the Court surveyed, 12 states failed to provide an unambiguous answer to the question that the Court had posed; five states shared the position the government argued; no state in the Court's own survey shared the position of the Afghan family (Stub 2016).[10]

Whereas the clerk sitting in on oral arguments and deliberations in the 2010 *Ship Owner Taxation case* broke a barrier in terms of a clerk's presence and active contributions in the Court's decision-making process in oral arguments, deliberations and opinion writing, the 2015 *Internal Displacement* case broke another barrier – namely the use of the clerk unit to identify and inject information that was distinct from the information the parties were providing in order for the Court to achieve what it perceived as necessary for quality decisions befitting a court of precedent.[11]

The Court's increasing robustness in its case management and administrative procedures that accompanied a growing clerk pool where more functions were geared towards Court's whole decision-making process alarmed some players outside the Court. Anders Ryssdal – son of a former chief justice, an experienced business lawyer, a former president of the Norwegian Bar Association, a member of the Supreme Court bar and one of the eight

9 Conventionally, the parties must submit to the Supreme Court their agenda, briefs and documents no later than 14 days prior to the day of oral arguments. In a revised and updated version of the lawyer's guidelines, the Court states that "[f]or the sake of the justices' preparation, the deadline must be respected" (Norges Høyesterett 2018a:28).

10 The authors contacted the three lawyers for the other party but failed to receive any comments on Stub's article.

11 The *Ship Owner Taxation Case* (Rt-2010-143) and the *Internal Displacement Case* (Rt-2015-1388). The Dispute Act of 2005, Section 11-5, also tersely states that courts have a duty to advise the parties on protecting their interests. It is also primarily the role of the preparatory justice to make sure that the parties fully understand their obligations to the legal question that the Court has defined. *See* Sunde (2015a:174).

contenders for the job of chief justice in 2016 – warned of the potential distortion that reliance on a large unit of clerks could have on the Court.[12] Ryssdal (2015) averred that the clerks, in processing the appeals for the Court, could offer views to the justices that at best supplemented, but at worst did not align with what the parties' lawyers presented during oral arguments. If the materials that the clerks provided the justices contradicted the lawyers' oral arguments made in Court or were not fully aligned with them, unearthing legal issues unaddressed by the parties would require litigants to rethink the way the current Court implemented the principle of adversarial oral arguments. If the clerks were to have a more active role across the Court's decision-making process, the process would need to be organized in a way that the parties would know well in advance of oral arguments what legal sources the Supreme Court sought to address under its guidelines to clarify and develop the law. In such a situation, Ryssdal argued, legal and procedural leadership becomes more important on the Court.

5.4 Securing His Legacy

In 2015, in Chief Justice Schei's final full year at the Court, three new clerk positions were added to the unit. During Schei's 14-year leadership the number of law clerks had increased from 16 to 23. In addition to the increased number of law clerks, the clerk unit was reorganized and expanded in other ways as well. In January of 2015, with the growth of the clerk unit, one of the clerk positions was converted to the second deputy at the unit. In addition, the Court's two court clerks,[13] as well as the student internship position, were transferred into the unit. As of the end of 2015, a total of 26 lawyers belong to the clerk unit.

The added clerks were not to perform only the conventional work of preparing and processing appeals for the ASC. As they were added to the clerk unit, the clerk unit assumed new duties and responsibilities (Aamodt 2017:4). By 2015 clerks also would serve the justices sitting on the Court's merits panels during and after oral arguments, including drafting the facts section of the final decision. These clerks are to be present both during oral arguments and in the justices' conference deliberations (see Figure 5.1). The clerks' primary work efforts in this expanded role concern civil cases, and it is expected that the clerks' assistance will cover approximately 25 per cent of the civil cases decided in merits panels. In addition, a clerk's participation and assistance are obligatory for cases heard in Grand Chamber or *en banc*. As liaisons between the Court and the parties to a case and having administrative responsibility for the operations of the two courtrooms during oral argu-

12 A member of the Supreme Court bar is a lawyer who has passed the test of successfully arguing two cases before the Court in order to qualify for the title *høyesterettsadvokat* (title used until 1978) or *advokat med møterett for høyesterett* (title used since 1978).

13 The Norwegian title for court clerk is *protokollsekretær*.

ments, the Court's two court clerks were transferred to the clerk unit in order to improve the unit's overall support of the merits panels. In the 25 per cent of cases where a law clerk's assistance is required, both a law clerk and a court clerk will be sitting in on the justice's deliberations in conference.

Figure 5.1 A law clerk in the courtroom. In 2015, the Norwegian Supreme Court started to permit law clerks in the courtroom. Typically, a clerk prepares the appeal and writes a memo for the ASC. If the Committee decides to grant review, the clerk may continue to assist the justices of the merits panel during oral arguments. The rationale is that the clerk is better prepared to assist the justices during their decision-making process as well as the writing of the Court's opinion when the clerk has observed the oral arguments. The picture shows the justices about to take their seats for the almost record-breaking eight days of oral arguments in the *Gassled* case in May 2018 (HR-2018-1258-A). Standing while the five justices enter the courtroom, a robed law clerk is waiting to take her seat on a visibly inferior chair at the left end of the justices' horseshoe table. Photograph and permission by Kjetil Kolsrud, Rett24.no.

Law clerks also started to increase their participation on the ASC. When the three justices on a Committee panel fail to agree after having circulated the papers of the appeal among themselves, a meeting in person among the justices is usually required. By 2017, the law clerk usually participates with the three justices in this extra round of discussions (see Figure 5.2). The clerk's participation at this stage makes processing what are obviously more complicated or challenging appeals more efficient. If additional information on the appeal is requested, the clerk is immediately aware of this rather than the request having to be transmitted to the clerk through the ASC panel chair. The clerk's participation is also a preferred human resources policy. Participation in the meetings is also expected to improve the clerk's overall job motivation.[14]

Figure 5.2 A law clerk enters the room and joins the justices on the ASC on whether to grant or deny an appeal. Source: The Norwegian Supreme Court Annual Report 2017.

Schei ended his 2015 plea for improving the organization of the Court and increasing the number of clerks on the Court by requesting more funding, but this time he added a novel twist. Schei pointed out that both the legislative and executive branches had realized the value of developing a competent support and clerk staff for their own operations. Explicitly, Schei argued that it was only by the quality of its decisions, assured by the integrated support of clerks, that the Court could maintain its institutional legitimacy and ensure the public's confidence in the rule of law (Schei 2015b:41).

Implicitly, Schei – self-assured and confidently – compared the functions of the Supreme Court with the functions of the other two branches of government. Traditionally and essentially, the first and second branches of government initiate and implement policymaking. With the expansion of the influential and instrumental clerk unit, the Supreme Court had abandoned its conventional role of resolving individual cases. In its place, it had embarked fully on developing the law and, concomitantly, on making policy – just as Carsten Smith envisioned and promoted in 1974. And with Schei's blunt comparison, the Court wanted to develop the law with an eye to its position vis-à-vis the two traditional policymaking branches of government.

Schei was not circumspect in his ambitions. At a larger conference on Supreme Courts in 2015, he specifically requested that the number of clerks be doubled from its present 23

14 See Norges Høyesterett (2018b:11) for description and further illustration.

and that their duties be expanded (Schei 2015c). And he had at least one ally among the justices. Arnfinn Bårdsen, no stranger to the growing policymaking role of the Court, had argued the Court was not just a court of precedent but that it had in fact fully transformed itself into a 'constitutional court', meaning a court deciding more principled and legal-political questions. Therefore, a more proactive role for the Court was needed and wanted. And to truly realize this, Justice Bårdsen argued that the clerk unit needed 40 clerks to serve the new and expanded Supreme Court (Bårdsen 2014:549).

5.5 The Gavel Has Been Passed

No sooner had the dust settled on the Court's 200-year anniversary celebration in 2015 before all eyes were directed to whom the government would tap as the new chief justice. Tore Schei, after 30 years of service on the Court – 14 as chief justice – prepared to step down at the end of February 2016. The discussions about Schei's successor had quietly animated the legal community for years. Now the discussion entered a more public stage as the government placed the ad for a new chief in newspapers and set 12 November 2015 as the deadline for applications. A record number of eight lawyers, seven men and one woman, submitted their applications. They included two legal unknowns and obviously unqualified candidates, Per Olaf Nordal and Thorbjørn Gaarder, who were quickly rejected. The two outside heavyweights included Hans Petter Graver, law professor and dean of the University of Oslo Law School, and Anders Ryssdal, former director of the Norwegian Bar Association. The four internal candidates were Associate Justices Arnfinn Bårdsen, Jens Edvin Skoghøy, Karl Arne Utgård and Toril Marie Øie.

The Minister of Justice Anders Anundsen appointed a vetting committee consisting of Anne K. Herse, Deputy Secretary General in the Ministry of Justice and Public Security; Erik Keiserud, director of the Norwegian Bar Association; and Yngve Svendsen, trial court judge and head of the National Court Administration's Judicial Appointments Board. The committee delivered its report to the Minister of Justice, and it surprised no one that it considered the well-qualified and uncontroversial Associate Justice Toril Marie Øie as the best candidate. Øie was appointed by the King in Council on 19 February 2016 and assumed the gavel on 1 March 2016.

On 29 February 2016, as the hourglass was about to run out on Tore Schei's term as chief, on the occasion of the government's thank you dinner in honour of Schei, Chief Justice designate Toril Marie Øie (2016) spoke to Schei and highlighted three types of noteworthy developments that had taken place during his tenure. The first type of development related to efficiency. Schei had secured a considerable reduction in the time an appeal required when passing through decision-making stations on the Court. This efficiency also reflected that the Court for practical purposes has eliminated backlogs in all parts of the decision-making process. Efficiency had also reduced the number of appeals granted review in decisional panels. The number of cases decided in merits panels during Schei's tenure as chief had decreased so that more time could be allocated to handle each case. Now that oral arguments and discussions on the case increasingly were concentrated on principled issues, more time became available to the justices for consideration and deliberation.

Figure 5.3 illustrates this development under Chief Schei. The number of decisions on the merits panels peaked in 2004, the second full year of the Schei Court, with 204 decisions, after which there has been a general decline to 117 decisions in 2015 the year before Schei stepped down. The number of decisions was also affected by the formal implementation of the civil procedure reform in 2008 (white-paper commission report that Schei had chaired) and the implementation of 'Lex Matningsdal' and 'Lex Skoghøy', as discussed in Section 4.2.1. Overall, Øie noted, Schei had closely tracked the development of decision-making on the Court and never shied away from implementing measures when he had reasons for concern.

Figure 5.3 Merits decisions on Schei's Court

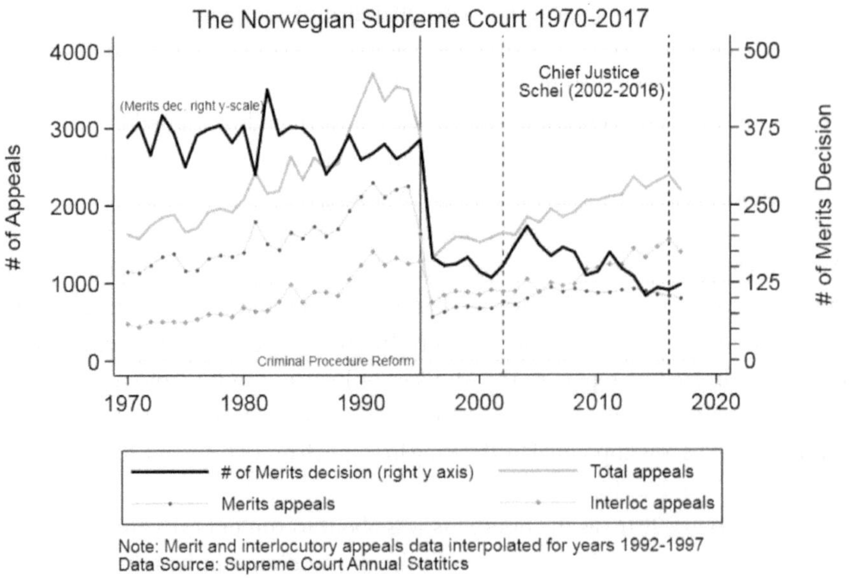

The second development Øie emphasized was the establishment of the so-called 'picket duty'. As we discussed earlier, picket duty involves a justice from the five-justice ASC being used to relieve the majority-opinion author from participating in the oral arguments on the merits panel's next case so that he or she could concentrate on the opinion-writing task. We are unable to track this development as no official statistics for this practice exist. Some workload statistics, however, can be inferred. There are 20 justices on the Court, and in recent years around 120 merits cases per term have been decided in merits panels. Absent the presiding justice, who never writes the majority opinion on the five-justice panel, opinion writing is therefore left to 80 per cent of the justices on the Court. That means that 16 of the Court's justices write about 7.5 opinions every year (i.e. 120 decisions divided by 16 justices), or roughly .67 Court or majority opinions per month.

The third type of development concerns the institutionalization of the clerk unit. During Schei's chief justiceship, the number of clerks had increased from 16 to 23, which provided the clerk unit with the capacity to undertake more tasks, including the opportunity to assist more actively in the preparations of a case moving forward to oral arguments. Øie also alluded to the practice that Schei had initiated in 2015 where the new tasks given to the clerks were "by request to assure the quality of the work of the Supreme Court by confirming sources and offer additional investigations" (Øie 2016:3). As Øie presented this increased institutionalization, the new type of tasks for the clerk unit sounded a bit insignificant. In fact, they were a major additional turn in the development of the Court's clerk unit. Schei's legacy was an empowered Court. He made the Court a more active and visible player in the national policymaking process.

In Chapter 2 we discussed the four stations of decision-making on the Court. Figure 5.4 visualizes the first station of decision-making on the Court at the end of Chief Justice Schei's term and the beginning of Chief Justice Toril Marie Øie's term. The figure shows how the clerks interact with the justices on the ASC in the deciding-to-decide stage.

Figure 5.5 shows the increased interactions between justices and clerks as a case passes through the Court's three final decision-making stations: oral arguments, deliberations and opinion writing. As we discussed earlier, the major change, or break-through, took place when the Court decided the landmark *Ship Owner Taxation* case in 2010. Prior to 2010, the right-hand column in Figure 5.5 would be empty (except for the smaller and administrative roles and tasks of the court clerks). In 2015, with three new clerks added to the Court's budget, the Court had the necessary resources to allocate three clerks to assist the justices on the merits panels in their decision-making.

Figure 5.4 Deciding to decide

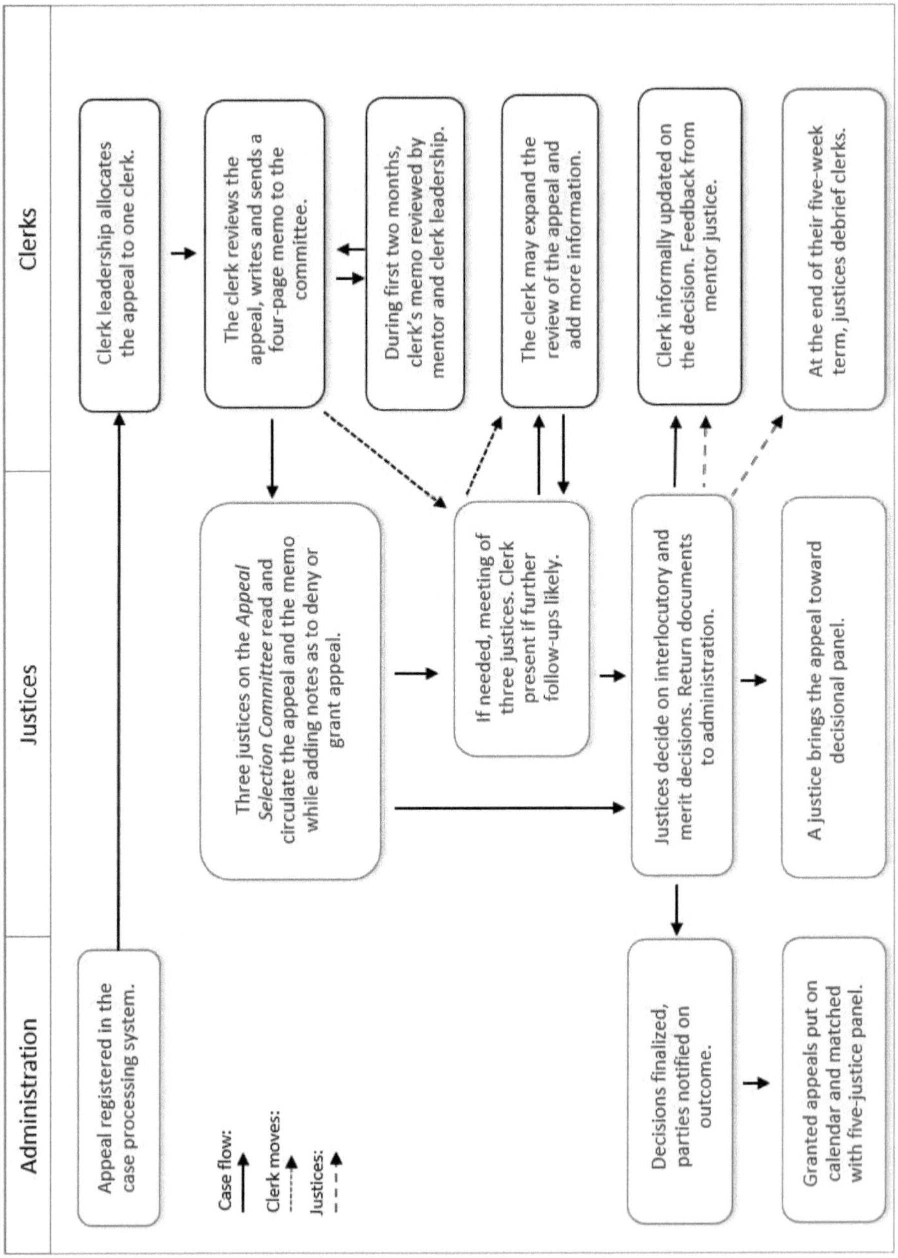

Figure 5.5 Decision-making

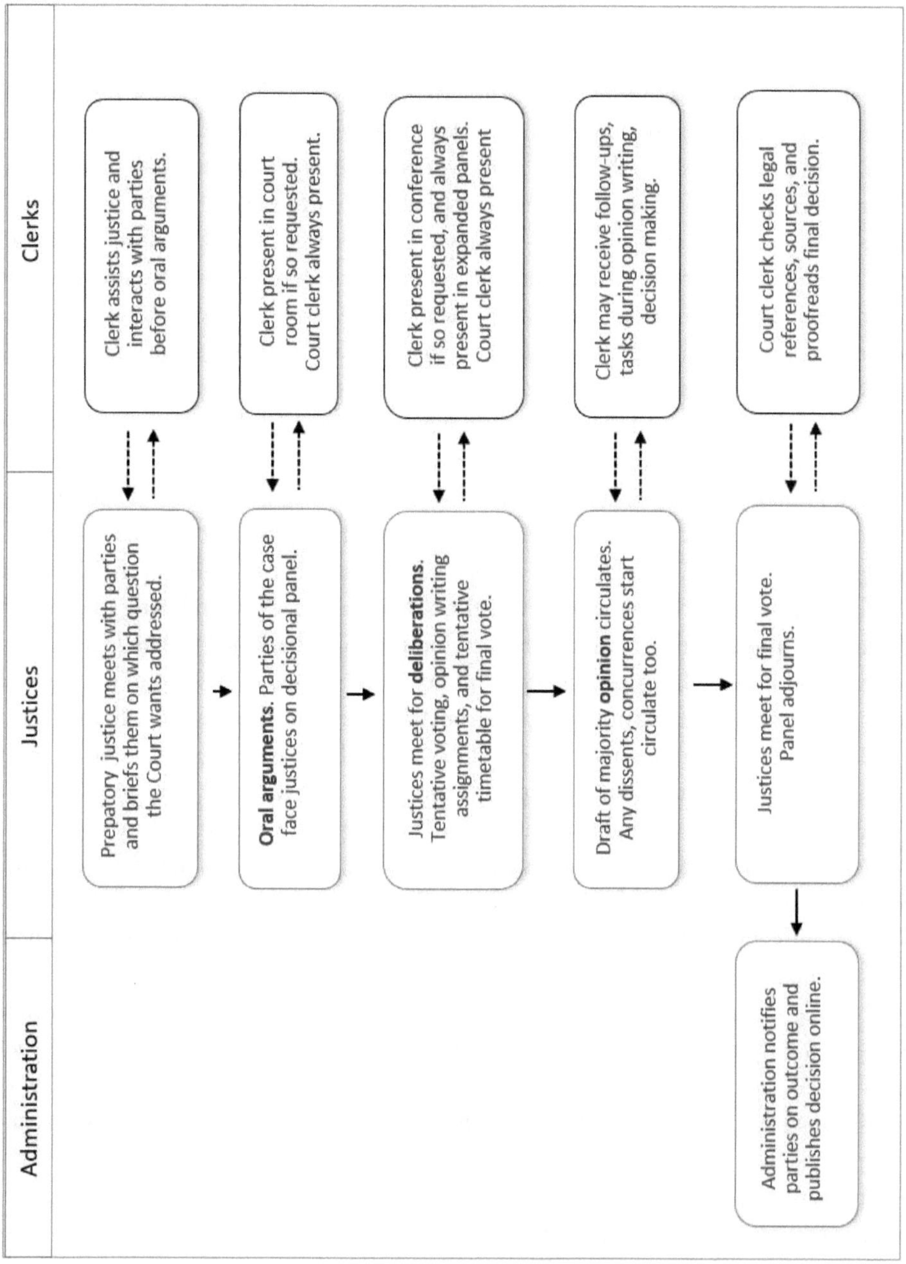

5.6 The Øie Court

In January 2017, Chief Justice Øie had the opportunity to take stock of the first year of the 'Øie court'. In her first remarks in the Court's 2016 annual report, she acknowledged that 60 years had passed since 1957 when the first clerk was hired to assist the ASC. She quickly pointed out that the increasing number of legal sources and the inconsistencies among them prompted a need for the clerk unit to offer significantly greater assistance for the Court's decisional panels. The three new clerks that the Court received in 2015 had provided the resources to systematically offer increased support from the clerk unit for appeals granted and forwarded to oral arguments in the five-justice decisional panels, Grand Chamber or *en banc* hearings. After 2016, the first full year of this new organization, Øie noted that the launch had been a success, and the support from the clerks had been invaluable. Øie expressed the wish that the new practice of clerks supporting the decisional panels would continue and that this development presupposes that the clerk unit would need to be strengthened with the addition of more clerks (Øie 2017:4).

The ground for the expansion of the clerks' duties had been long in the making. Although it was a setback for Chief Justice Smith when he failed to achieve the assignment of clerks to individual justices in the mid-1990s, the number of clerks in the clerk unit continued to expand. Likewise, Chief Justice Schei was successful in hiring more clerks during his 14-year term, expanding the clerk unit from 16 clerks in 2002 to 23 in 2016.

As Chief Justice Øie gained greater confidence in her role as steward of the national legal system, her Court was not exempted from the government's repeated calls for greater efficiency in the operations and services of the national courts. Budgets from one year to the next could be reduced on the explicit expectation that the level of service rendered could be maintained through rationalization and efficiency. As courts are completely funded by the government, it was not surprising that the government's shadow of demands for efficiency would fall on the Øie Court too. The Supreme Court's straightforward reply was that any gains in efficiency would come at the expense of quality in the Court's judicial decision-making.

Digging in its heels in response to the government's calls for budget reductions, in September 2017 the Supreme Court wrote a letter to the Court Administration in which it reiterated and explained more carefully the need for more clerks (Høyesteretts Kontor 2017). One reason the Court offered was the increase in the number of appeals that had to be handled by the ASC. The Court emphasized that the primary task of the clerk unit was to prepare appeals for the Committee and also to assist the justices on the Committee in their preparation of the appeal that had been granted a hearing before the five-justice merits panels.

The other central task that the Court had initiated, secured and was unwilling to give up was expansion of the clerk unit's tasks of assisting the justices in their decision-making on five-justice panels, in Grand Chambers and in plenary sessions. The Court stated that this new practice had been established in the fall of 2015 and that the associate justices had expressed great satisfaction with the support they received from the clerks. The Court argued that the clerk unit's capacity for this type of assistance at present was too limited and the justices' need for support from the clerks was greater than what the clerk unit currently could offer. The letter underscored that to prevent the expanded role of the clerks from faltering immediately after its launch, more clerks should be hired. The letter added that the clerk unit also carried out other occasional tasks for the Court and its justices.

Additionally, the letter offered a slightly veiled warning. If the Court's capacity was not improved, it might negatively influence the quality of the Court's decisions, thereby diminishing the legitimacy upon which the Court depends in order to fulfil its constitutional and societal obligations.[15] The letter then went on to present a plan for increasing the number of clerks. Specifically, the Court requested that six new clerks be hired in 2019 and 2020, and another clerk should be hired in 2021. If implemented, this plan would increase the number of clerks from 23 in 2017 to 30 in 2021. Were this plan to materialize, the number of clerks would increase by 50 per cent in the seven years since 2014.

5.7 Quality

When the justices on the Court decide which appeals to grant review in order to clarify and develop the law, the Supreme Court also takes on a greater and final responsibility of bringing relevant facts, laws and considerations to the whole decision-making process. If the Court were to decide cases like any run-of-the-mill court, then the parties and their lawyers had the responsibility of establishing the facts and the legal basis of a case.

The Court's new role is not merely to resolve legal disputes. It primarily seeks to develop the law, and thus it uses appeals as instruments to cultivate the law and to serve as precedents for other legal actors to follow. In so doing, the Court itself assumes the responsibility of establishing the legal issues and facts that are dispositive in a case. Whereas the parties' advocates primarily are interested in winning the case for their clients, the Court is primarily interested in addressing the precedential potential of the case. The stronger the element of a case's precedential value, the higher the requirement for ensuring overall quality through covering all relevant legal bases of a case.

15 Although no survey has measured trust specifically towards the Supreme Court, in a nationwide survey in 2017, 89 per cent of the respondents said they had very high or high trust in the courts (which, necessarily, includes trust in the Supreme Court). The population had the same level of trust in the parliament and in the police. Over the last two decades, trust in courts has ranged between the mid-60s and mid-80s (Arnstad 2017).

With the Court taking on the mantel of a court of precedent, it necessarily assumes an appreciable responsibility for ensuring that all legal questions and issues are considered and all legal foundations are appropriately addressed. (These points are well illustrated with the Court's use of the clerks to expand the information that it considered in the *Internal Displacement* case, see earlier discussion.) Being a stickler is not without consequence. It requires greater effort and legal expertise on the part of the Court, which in turn places a premium on the role of the clerks. They are to identify significant and relevant legal questions in an appeal. As the clerks consider the legal questions an appeal invokes and the precedential potential of the case, they also will assay the quality of the lawyers of the appeal. If a clerk considers that one or both lawyers of the litigants are not up to the quality that the Court requires, their recommendation to the justices on the Committee may be to deny the appeal rather than having the legal question wasted in the courtroom. Working for a court of precedent, the clerks must thread the legal needle and avoid the prospect of processing the 'right' appeal, but with the 'wrong' advocates.

5.8 Institutionalizing the Clerk Unit – Never a Reversal

The comprehensive legal-historical study of the Supreme Court for the 1965-2015 period presciently observed that it was only a question of time before the clerks became more involved with and integrated in the merits decision-making process in a way similar to the evolution of the clerks' role with the ASC (Sunde 2015a). It was surmised that were such a full integration to develop, then it was likely that it would only be a question of time before the justices give up their ideal of taking full responsibility for all of the writing that goes into the Court's decisions. The justice who writes the majority's decision may initially expect to receive the assistance of a clerk for the part of the decision that covers the history of the case, the facts of the case, the legal sources of the case and the legal principles of the case. Were clerks to pass the critical threshold of contributing or even writing the personal opinions for a justice, it would almost necessarily follow that justices would express a clear preference for which clerk they would like to have as a coauthor. However, the allocation of a dedicated and personal clerk to a justice may not happen any time soon.

The three new clerks that the government granted the Court in the fall of 2015 increased the clerk unit to 23 clerks. The Court had already geared the resources of the clerk unit towards greater assistance in the preparation of the case for the ASC by the clerks' closer scrutiny of principled cases. The institutional contribution the three new clerks effected was the presence of a clerk during oral arguments, the assistance of a clerk during deliberations and the support of a clerk during opinion writing. Typically, the clerk had already suggested the legal questions and studied the legal sources by which quality assurance of the legal material and documents presented in the case could be assured. During opinion writing, by requests from the justices, clerks can now investigate issues, assess or check certain aspects of the case and in part or in whole write the introduction to the case up to the point where the justice in a personalized style writes the opinion of the Court.

The current practice of clerks participating in the whole decision-making process of the Court firmly puts to rest the traditional view that it is the parties' lawyers who are expected to prepare and fully present the case to the justices on the decisional panels. Now, if any of the justices on the decisional panel so require, the clerk who prepared the appeal for the ASC and who now is on hand for the justice during the remainder of the decision-making process can be requested to investigate limited questions related to the case. Although it has been dismissively added that such requests did "not happen very often" (Skoghøy 2016:323-324), a clerk is now present during oral arguments, in conference and at hand to assist the justices in the writing of the decision in approximately 25 per cent of the cases, most of which are civil cases. Moreover, it is now explicitly stated and required that a clerk participates in this manner in all plenary and Grand Chamber cases.

In 1985, not quite 30 years after the first clerk was hired, the Court turned down an offer from the government to add to the four clerks it already had. In 2017, almost 60 years after the first clerk was hired, the Court urged the government to increase, if not double, its number of clerks from the current 23. Today, after its transformation from a court of appeal to a court of precedent, the Court recognizes that assistance from the clerks is essential to ensure its efficiency and the continued high quality of its decisions. The law is also on the move, with a continuous need for the Supreme Court to clarify and develop the law. The Court expects clarification and development of the law to continue to be required in light of the ongoing specialization and internationalization of the law.

By 2000, every appeal that came to the Court was handled by a clerk before it was decided by the ASC. Shortly afterwards, the clerks were instructed to give short shrift to obvious appeals – that is, those appeals that were clear grants or clear denials. The clerks were further instructed to invest more time and use more resources to prepare appeals that were deemed to contain principled questions or could be used as vehicles to clarify or develop the law.

In 2010, a distinct barrier was broken when a clerk moved beyond providing assistance to the ASC only and sat in on the justices' *en banc* deliberation of the 2010 landmark *Ship Owner decision*. In addition, the clerk also contributed to the writing of that landmark decision, although the extent of this 'input' has never been confirmed. In 2015, another distinct barrier was broken when the Court had one of its clerks, unbeknownst to the parties of the case, further investigate the appeal and offer new evidence to the parties in the final week before oral arguments.

Unsurprisingly, the justices are clear on the matter: in addition to the basic service the clerks continue to provide to the ASC, the justices are satisfied with the augmented service they now receive from the designated clerk at oral arguments, deliberation and opinion writing.

Throughout the 60-odd year period of having clerks on the Court, we observe a conspicuous consistency. Once a clerk carries out a new task or breaks a new barrier, a reversal of the task or a backtrack across the barrier does not take place. There was the short-lived attempt during Smith's tenure in the 1990s to have a clerk sit in on oral arguments and the justices' deliberation and write the *introduction* to the Court's decisions. As we noted earlier, this attempt failed. Today the clerks are involved in the decision-making more than ever by working more closely with the justices in approximately 25 per cent of the Court's decisions. With an increased number of clerks on the Court and their increased participation in the decision-writing process, personal clerks might be the next barrier to be broken.

6 Who Are the Law Clerks?

On 15 March 2017, the Norwegian Supreme Court celebrated its clerk unit's diamond jubilee. All 121 current and former clerks were invited; 80 attended. They were met by two former chief justices, Carsten Smith and Tore Schei, as well as the current chief justice, Toril Marie Øie. Øistein Aamodt, the head of the clerk unit and a former clerk himself, warmly welcomed the attendees, and they were treated to an address on the Court's current political and constitutional role by Associate Justice Arnfinn Bårdsen. As might be expected on an occasion such as this, Justice Bårdsen's remarks eventually turned to some stocktaking of the institution of the clerk unit. He discussed the clerks' crucial role in the Court's transformation to a court of precedent and its emphasis on the development of the law; how the clerks were instrumental in reining in the Court's crushing backlog of appeals; the growing need to recruit clerks as legal specialists; and he also contextualized his comments by briefly reviewing the evolution of the clerk unit over its 60-year history. Justice Bårdsen's remarks left little doubt: the clerk unit is integral to the functioning of Norway's highest court. But what sort of individuals compose this highly consequential unit?

In this chapter we present a demographic profile of the clerks who have worked for the Norwegian Supreme Court. We draw on a dataset that spans the clerk unit's full history with the Court. It includes data on the clerks' gender, age at the time of beginning employment with the unit, the identity of the law school from which the clerks took their degrees and the number of years they served as a clerk. Because of the time series nature of these data, we are able to chart the evolution of the clerk unit across these four dimensions over the 60-year period of the unit's existence. To supplement these data, we also have data running from 2007 to 2017 on the pool of applicants from which individual clerks were hired, and we have data on several demographic attributes of the justices themselves. These additional datasets allow us to draw relevant points of comparison between the clerk unit as established and the broader pool from which it is drawn, as well as between the clerk unit and the justices for whom the clerks work.

We show that women have had an enduring and appreciable presence in the clerk unit. There is strong circumstantial evidence that, like their Nordic counterparts in Sweden, Finland and Denmark, clerks are coming to the Norwegian Supreme Court with prior legal experience. Over time, Norway's broader legal academy has been represented in the clerk unit. Clerks serve long enough to provide the unit with an institutional memory; yet, there are mechanisms in place (as well as basic incentives among the clerks) to ensure that the clerks do not become second-tier mandarins in an entrenched bureaucracy. And finally, like the Court, we find that the clerk unit has become more diverse in the lived experiences of its members over time. The question is crucial because when leaving the Court, they bring the institutionalized knowledge of the Court to the wider legal community, and by this they also facilitate the communication between this central institution and the legal system.

6.1 Female Clerks

Norway is notable for its highly egalitarian culture, a consequence of which is the large role women have long played in its politics. By some measure, Norway was among the first nations in the world to grant universal suffrage when it extended the franchise to all its citizens in 1913 (Grendstad, Shaffer, and Waltenburg 2015:121; Heidar 2000:85).[1] By the 1970s, women were being actively recruited to run for seats in the *Storting*, and the nation's major parties began to adopt quota rules that women candidates would account for some minimum percentage of the party's organization (Grendstad, Shaffer, and Waltenburg 2015:121). And these quota rules appear to have borne fruit for the presence of female MPs. Since the 1980s, women consistently have occupied over one-third of the *Storting's* seats.[2] As of 2018, Norway's legislature ranks 13th among national parliaments with respect to the proportion of seats held by women (41.4 per cent), just behind its Scandinavian neighbours Sweden (8th, 43.6 per cent) and Finland (11th, 42 per cent), and well above other established democracies such as Canada (60th, 31 per cent) and the United States (102nd, 20 per cent).[3]

Norway similarly stands tall in terms of women's representation on its highest court. The first woman, Lilly Bølviken, was appointed to the Supreme Court in 1968, and – after 30 years of slow increase – by the early twenty-first century, the proportion of female Supreme Court justices was roughly equal to the proportion of female MPs. A government proclamation has effectively ensured that the proportion of women justices should not drop below 40 per cent (Grendstad, Shaffer, and Waltenburg 2015:122; NTB 2008), all but guaranteeing that Norway will continue to place near the top among the world's apex courts in terms of female representation on the bench (Hoekstra, Kittilson, and Bond 2014; Valdini and Shortell 2016). One would expect, therefore, that the proportion of women composing the clerk unit would be appreciable, and our data do not challenge this expectation. Women have constituted 54.2 per cent of all the clerks and legal secretaries to work

1 Finland permitted near universal suffrage in 1906. In fact, if we only consider *free and independent* countries (Finland, Australia and New Zealand did not qualify as such at the time of their suffrage extension), Norway was the first country in the world to introduce universal suffrage.

2 https://www.statista.com/statistics/741351/share-of-women-in-the-norwegian-parliament/ (last accessed 24 May 2018).

3 http://archive.ipu.org/wmn-e/classif.htm (last accessed 24 May 2018).

for the Court between 1957 and 2017. Indeed, overall, women have accounted for a significantly greater proportion of the clerk unit than have their male counterparts.

One possible explanation for the strong presence of women in the clerk unit is that the applicant pool from which the clerks are drawn comprises appreciably more women. It also is important to note that as the clerk unit grew in size, so too did the presence of women in the population of lawyers, thereby creating the potential to hire more women and increase the diversity of the clerk unit. This certainly seems to be the case, at least between 2007 and 2017, the years for which we have data. Women constituted over three-fifths of the pool of applicants between 2007 and 2017. And in terms of the proportion of women between 2007 and 2017, the clerk unit and the clerk pool are virtually identical.

Of course, this explanation begs the question of why women seem especially likely to apply for positions with the Court's clerk unit in the first place. One possibility for the over-representation of women in the clerk pool is that the Court's clerk unit offers a particularly 'family-friendly' setting for young lawyers. The Court promotes itself as a workplace that promises a healthy work-family balance for career lawyers who are in a process of establishing a family. In interviews, a number of respondents pointed to the clerk unit's generous family leave provisions as a force that drew them to submit applications when calls were put out. It bears noting that women are occupying a greater share of the elite legal positions in Norway, and as indicated by the family-friendly environment presented by the clerk unit, it comes as no surprise that they would appear in greater numbers there first.

We hasten to note, though, that family leave policies resonate not only with women. Several male interview subjects also noted the attractiveness of this employment benefit when making their decision to apply for a position with the clerk unit. Consequently, the family-friendly setting is unlikely the sole explanation for the large share of women pursuing employment in the clerk unit. A second possible explanation is the narrower career path previously open to female lawyers in Norway. According to Menkel-Meadow, women lawyers are "overrepresented in the lower ranks of the central government" (Grendstad, Shaffer, and Waltenburg 2015:125; Menkel-Meadow 1996:237). Accordingly, working in the clerk unit is likely seen as an especially attractive option to women. It is highly consonant with their formal training. In more than a manner of speaking, they are 'practising' law. It is prestigious and affords them the opportunity to develop an even greater understanding of the 'law' rather than develop a specialization in a narrow substantive area. And being an alumna of the clerk unit certainly cannot militate against their future career prospects. Of course, Menkel-Meadow's commentary on the career paths of female lawyers is now about a quarter-century old. Although there can be something of a glacial pace to career trends (dogged as they are by systemic inertia), it seems likely that women are increasingly occupying the higher reaches of the legal profession. For example, a large share of the 'Supreme Court bar' is composed of women.

Submerged in the overall statistics is the long history women have had in the clerk unit. Although the Court's first (and at the time only) clerk was male, he was replaced by a woman in 1964. And women exclusively filled the clerkship positions for the next 18 years. Indeed, even when the Court added a second clerk in 1977, it was a woman who filled the newly created vacancy. Further, once a woman joined the clerk unit within the first decade of its existence, there is never a year wherein there are no female clerks. This stands in marked contrast to the experience of women in the much more robustly studied U.S. Supreme Court clerk unit. There, it took nearly half a century before the first woman clerk was hired in 1944 and then almost another quarter-century before a second woman joined the clerks' ranks in 1966 (Peppers 2006:20). In those intervening 20 odd years, there were no women clerks at all. And whereas the Norwegian Supreme Court simultaneously employed two female clerks at its earliest opportunity (i.e. the moment the clerk unit was expanded to a second clerk), almost a full century would pass before two women clerks simultaneously worked in the chambers of U.S. Supreme Court justices (Szmer, Kaheny, and Christensen 2014:268).

Figure 6.1 Proportion of female clerks

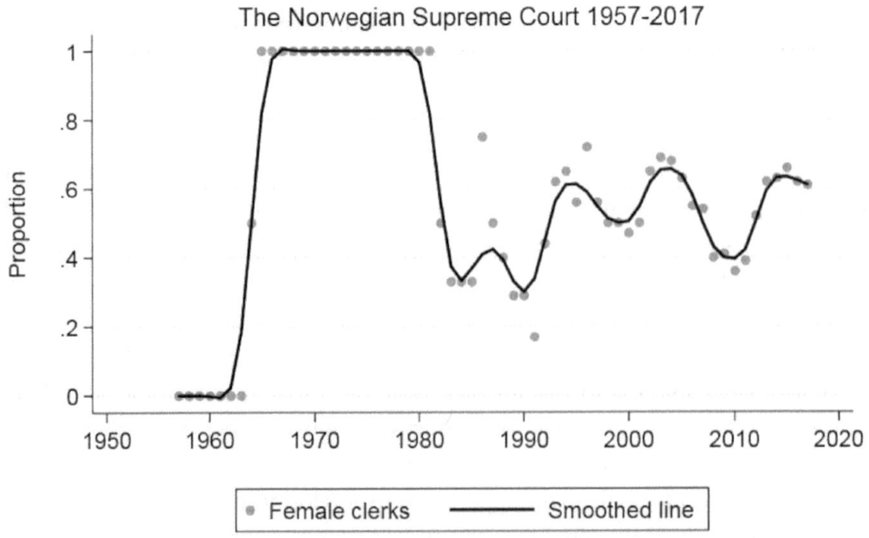

Note: Dots show proportion of female clerks in any given year. Line smoothed by the '4253eh,twice' function. Data source: The Norwegian Supreme Court.

Figure 6.1 nicely displays the well-established presence of women in Norway's clerk unit. It shows the proportion of female clerks for any given year across the time span of our analysis. Early in the time series, the volatility in gender distributions is quite high, owing to the very small number of clerks composing the clerk unit. Beginning in the 1980s, however, the volatility is tamped down as the number of clerks increases and, thus, the male and female proportions become more stable.

Broadly speaking, three subperiods can be identified. First, from 1983 to 1992, the proportion of female clerks hovered around .40. This proportion is significantly low for the series from 1980 to 2017. This, however, should be read with some caution. During this time period, the number of clerks ranged between two and six, averaging just a tick above four. Consequently, the small number of clerks wreaks havoc on the stability of the proportions being reported. Indeed, the addition or subtraction of a single female clerk would have profound effects on the proportion of women in the clerk unit.

Second, the steep rise in the proportion of female clerks in 1992 coincides with the expansive hiring Chief Justice Carsten Smith undertook to implement his vision of transforming the Supreme Court from a court of appeal to a court of precedent. As we have discussed in earlier chapters, this vision placed a premium on the presence of clerks to assist the Appeals Selection Committee (ASC) in the identification of consequential appeals worthy of the Court's review on their full merits. During Smith's tenure as chief justice (1991-2002), the number of clerks increased from six to 16. This expansion of the number of clerks brought more women into the clerk unit, in part as the result of an effort, supported by the Ministry of Justice, to hire more women in the name of diversity. In addition, the increase in the number of women in the unit may be a consequence of the composition of the pool of applicants. As we noted earlier, between 2007 and 2017, women constituted well over 60 per cent of the applicants. It seems likely that the same forces that brought an over-representation of women in to the clerk pool in the period for which we have data were at work in earlier periods as well. The statistical correlation between the lagged proportion of women in the clerk unit and women in the clerk pool is .76.

Finally, during the 2008-2012 period, the proportion of female clerks dipped below .50 only to rebound quickly. This rapid increase in the proportion of female clerks that followed in the subsequent years was in large part a consequence of the successful recruitment of female lawyers by Øistein Aamodt, the newly appointed head of the clerk unit in 2011. Of the first 20 clerks to be hired during his leadership, 18 were women. This 90 per cent rate of hiring significantly outstripped the proportion of women in the clerk pool during this time period.

6.2 AGE

The age at which a clerk is recruited into the clerk unit can serve as a crude proxy for that individual's legal experience. In the United States, for example, after finishing a four-year BA degree the median age of a law school applicant is 24,[4] and a typical legal education requires three years to complete. Thus, a threshold age for a clerk with the U.S. Supreme Court is 27. Twenty-seven, though, establishes what is likely the barest minimum. It is becoming increasingly commonplace for clerks to the High Court to have first acquired some clerkship experience in one of the lower federal courts, especially in a circuit court of appeals (Ward and Weiden 2006:77). And Peppers reports that there is a "new wrinkle to the hiring process – law clerks who work in top law firms or elite government posts between their clerkship with lower federal court judges and Supreme Court justices" (Peppers 2006:32). These actions to gain credible legal experience will necessarily delay the arrival of these freshly minted lawyers on the steps of the marble palace. Indeed, it probably is to state the obvious that for these legal high fliers, the magnitude of legal experience and age are positively related.

With this likely correlation in mind, then, what does the age distribution look like for clerks in the Norwegian Supreme Court? Typically, after graduating from high school at the age of 19, Norwegian law students would go straight to a five-year master's degree at a law school. Prior to the European reform in higher education in 2002/2003, law degrees were a six-year run. According to OECD educational data, the typical age of Norwegian law school graduates ranges from 23 to 29 years.[5] Thus, the threshold age of Norwegian clerks would be somewhere in the mid- to upper twenties.

Overall, in our data the mean age of the clerks at the time they joined the clerk unit is 32.75, indicating that the typical clerk did not join the clerk unit immediately upon his or her graduation from law school (see Figure 6.2). (The average age at which men and women joined the clerk unit is statistically the same.) Like their American counterparts, it appears that prospective clerks in Norway perceive a benefit to acquiring experience in the law prior to applying for a clerkship. Indeed, that clerks possessed some experience with top law firms or in government offices (e.g. the Legislative Department) and that this was an important criterion in the selection process was a recurring theme in our interviews. Moreover, data[6] for the applicant pool indicates that more than a quarter of the applicants

4 https://www.lsac.org/docs/default-source/data-(lsac-resources)-docs/analysis-applicants-by-age-group.pdf (last accessed 14 June 2018).

5 https://www.lsac.org/docs/default-source/data-(lsac-resources)-docs/analysis-applicants-by-age-group.pdf (last accessed 14 June 2018).

6 We have data on the self-reported occupations for 441 applicants for 12 calls between 2008 and 2017. We standardized the self-reported occupations into 14 categories: deputy/interim judge, lawyer (employed in a law firm or equivalent), trainee lawyer (holding an apprenticeship position with a law firm), adviser,

to the clerk unit between 2008 and 2017 fall into one of three occupational categories (deputy/interim judge, lawyer or trainee lawyer) that are of particular relevance to the qualifications for a clerkship.

Figure 6.2 Mean Age of Graduate and Freshman Clerks

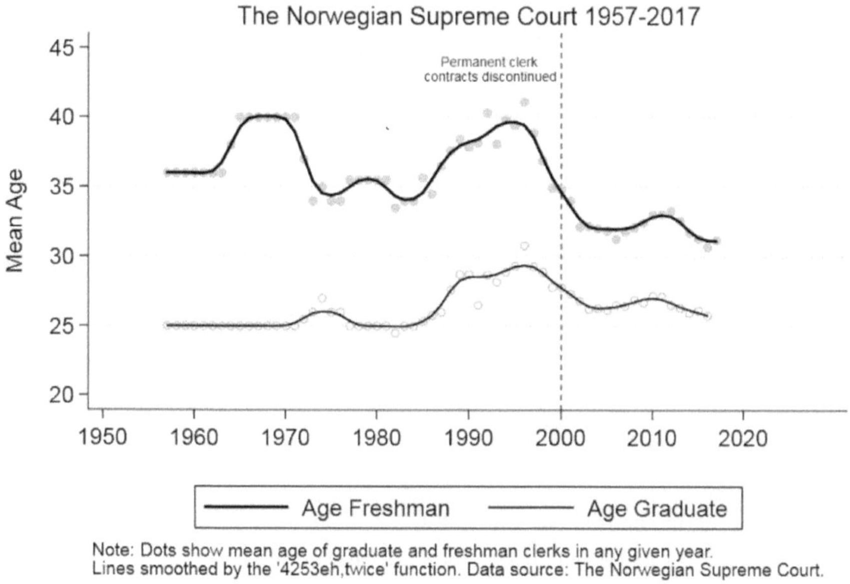

Figure 6.2 displays the mean age of the clerks at the time they joined the clerk unit for any given year. Three features deserve comment. First, the means early in the time series must be interpreted cautiously, inasmuch as they are computed on a very small number of clerks. It is only after 1989 that the clerk unit comprised six clerks.

consultant, jurist, other jurist, senior advisor, clerk, government, other, student, research assistant, unemployed. Unfortunately, we do not have systematic occupation data for the Supreme Court clerks prior to their recruitment. Nor are we able to determine whether having any of these occupations increased the likelihood of an applicant being hired into the clerk unit.

Figure 6.3 Mean Age Clerk Pool v. Clerk Unit

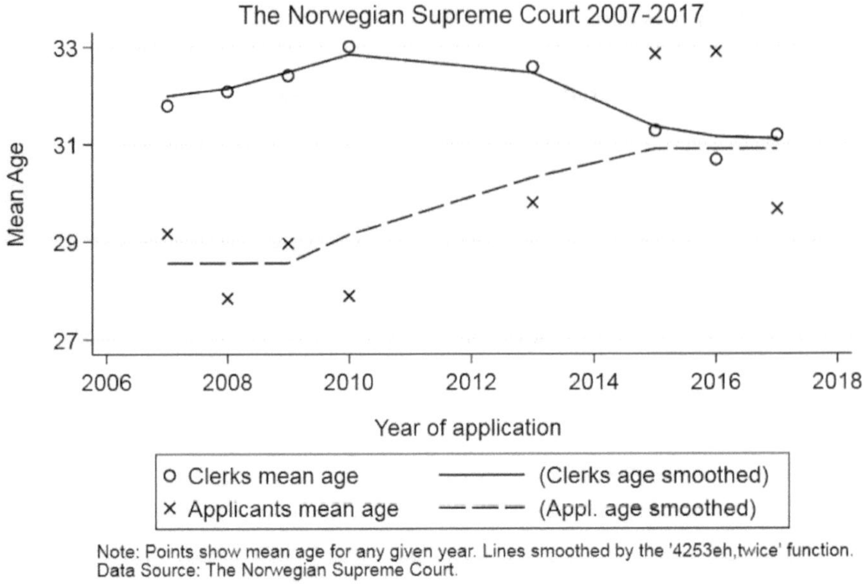

Second, beginning in the mid- to late 1980s, the mean age of the freshman clerks rose steeply, peaking at 41 in 1996. During this same time period, the number of clerks grew by more than 300 per cent. Thus, there were substantial opportunities to fill vacancies with more seasoned lawyers. Unfortunately, we lack the data to determine whether the sharp uptick in the selection of experienced lawyers was the product of design or the result of a more aged pool of applicants.

Finally, regardless of its cause, the increasing mean age of the clerks in the clerk unit began to reverse after 1996. A constraint on the clerk unit's capacity to bring on younger clerks, however, was the permanent contracts under which clerks were hired prior to 2001.[7] Operationally, of course, turnover in the clerks' ranks occurred. The mean tenure of clerks between 1996 and 2001 was about six years; so, clerks were being replaced. Meanwhile, the size of the clerk unit grew by 15 per cent. In 2000 the Court hired the last clerks on permanent contracts. By 2001 clerks were being hired to shorter-term contracts (five years), and in 2002 another clerk position was added. For the next 15 years the number of clerks would increase by almost one-half a clerk per year, growing from 16 clerks in 2002 to 23 clerks in 2017. The opportunity was ripe, therefore, to institute a younger, more dynamic clerk unit. And empirically, that is just what happened. The mean age of freshman clerks

7 In Chapter 3, Section 9, we discuss the implications of offering short-term contracts.

fell from 41 in 1996 to about 32 in 2002, and it has remained around this age since. Moreover, even as the mean age of the clerk pool rose from 2007 to 2017, the mean age of clerks recruited from that pool dropped over the same period (see Figure 6.3). Circumstantially, there is also evidence that bringing about a young, energetic clerk unit was the plan. Our interview sources report that it is an aim of the clerk unit to recruit younger clerks to better complement the higher ages of the justices.

6.3 LAW SCHOOL

Unlike the United States, Norway, consistent with the rest of Scandinavia, has very few law schools. Indeed, for the first 22 years of the clerk unit's existence, only the University of Oslo operated a college of law. In 1969 the University of Bergen opened its law school, and in 1987 the University of Tromsø became the third (and as of this writing, last) Norwegian university to have a law school.

Given the College of Law at the University of Oslo's much longer history, it comes as no surprise that its graduates dominate the ranks of the clerk unit (see Table 6.1). By 2000, the law schools at Bergen and Tromsø had sufficient time to become institutionalized and gain national recognition. (The first clerk to graduate from Bergen's law school joined the clerk unit in 1988; the first clerk with a law degree from the University of Tromsø, 1998.) Yet, even after the turn of the century, graduates from the University of Oslo continue to fill most of the positions in the clerk unit (see Table 6.2).[8]

Table 6.1 Law Schools Attended by Clerks 1957-2017. The Norwegian Supreme Court

	N	Percentage
Oslo	93	76.86
Bergen	21	17.36
Tromsø	7	5.79
	121	100.0

Data source: The Norwegian Supreme Court and the authors.

8 Neither for the complete time series nor for the 2000-2017 period is there a statistical difference in the proportion of male and female clerks graduating from the different law schools.

Table 6.2 Law Schools Attended by Clerks, 2000-2017. The Norwegian Supreme Court

	N	Percentage
Oslo	60	71.43
Bergen	18	21.43
Tromsø	6	7.14
	84	100.0

Data source: The Norwegian Supreme Court and the authors.

Figure 6.4 Law School Graduates in the Clerk Unit

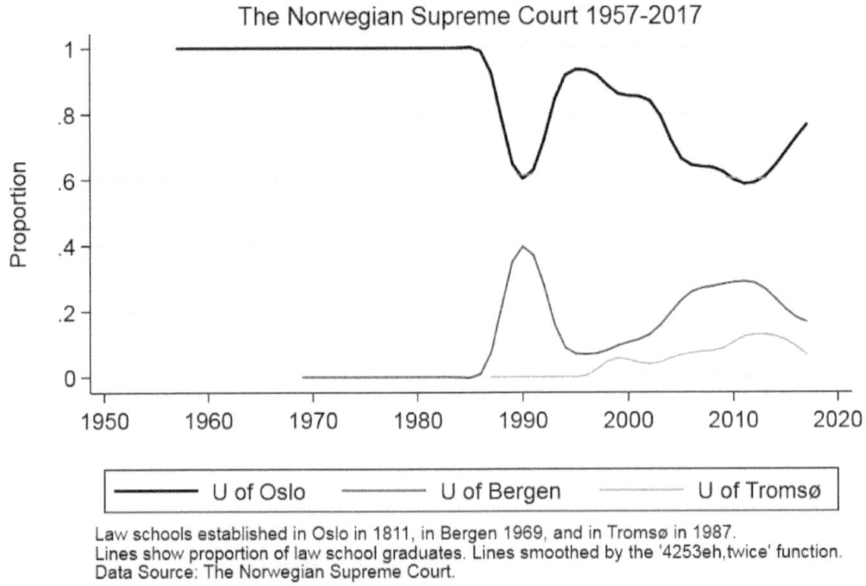

Figure 6.4 displays the relative distributions of graduates from Norway's three law schools across time. Two features are worthy of comment. First, beginning in the late 1980s, there is a notable dip in the proportion of clerks who hail from the University of Oslo with a concomitant increase in the proportion of clerks with law degrees from the University of Bergen. This relative parity among the nation's only two law schools (at the time), however, was short-lived. As the clerk unit more than doubled in size through the 1990s, the relative dominance of the University of Oslo reasserted itself. Although we lack the data to test for this, it seems likely that the University of Oslo benefitted from the Court's demand for more clerks. To state it simply, the University of Oslo's law school had more graduates to supply the clerk pool. Proximity is a factor too. Once established as a law student in Oslo

and graduating from the university, there are lower geographical thresholds and lower transaction costs to apply for a clerkship position. Second, a similar trend is observed at the end of the time series. From 2011 to 2017, the proportion of clerks with law degrees from the University of Oslo increased from 60 per cent to nearly 80 per cent. This 33 per cent increase coincided with the growth in the size of the clerk unit from 17 (2011) to 23 (2017) – a 35 per cent increase.

Through the first two decades of the twenty-first century, Oslo increasingly became the national centre of legal practice, culture and norms. Yet, at the same time, the number of graduates from the Oslo law school began to decline. (By 2017 the number of graduates would be at last 40 per cent lower than the number of graduates in 2011.) This needs an explanation. A function of the clerk unit is to learn from the Court what is important in a case, and to later use that specialized knowledge when the clerks write decisions that might be appealed to the Court or when they are the advocates writing the appeals themselves. Clerks recruited from Oslo likely will return to legal jobs in Oslo at the conclusion of their clerkship. Now, this tendency was a problem in the 1990s because less of the nation's total legal business took place in Oslo. As noted earlier, that has changed. At present, the Oslo city court and appeal court have about 170 of the approximately 500 judges in the country, and the major law firms are all located in Oslo, with only ancillary offices in other cities. Hence, the centralization of legal business that has taken place in the last decades makes it less pressing to recruit from all three law schools and other parts of the country. The institutionalized knowledge the clerks bring out to the rest of the legal system is still effectively transmitted even if it is mostly confined to Oslo.

Along with their domination of the overall recruitment of clerks to the Supreme Court, graduates from the University of Oslo have all but monopolized the clerk unit's leadership positions. Eleven lawyers have held either the leadership or deputy leadership positions since they were made a part of the clerk unit in 1989. For only three years has a law school graduate from the University of Bergen occupied a deputy leadership position.

6.4 Tenure

Figure 6.5 displays the variation in the mean tenure of the clerk unit over time. As we have repeatedly noted, statistics reported at the start of the time series must be viewed and interpreted cautiously because of the very small number of clerks on which the summary statistics are based. Indeed, clerks toiled alone for the first two decades of the clerk unit's institutional history. Each of these clerks served an extended period of time and gave the unit tremendous stability. The highest levels of mean tenure occur prior to 1982 and are the product of this early cohort of clerks. The period during which the clerk unit experienced its most rapid turnover was in the first half of the 1980s, but this era of high replacement in the unit was short-lived. By the 1990s, more mature clerks began to take positions in the clerk unit (see our discussion earlier in this chapter), and stability in employment reasserted itself. At the turn of the century, the Court institutionalized fixed-year contracts, and since then, the mean tenure of the clerk unit has settled at about six years.

Figure 6.5 Mean Tenure of Clerks

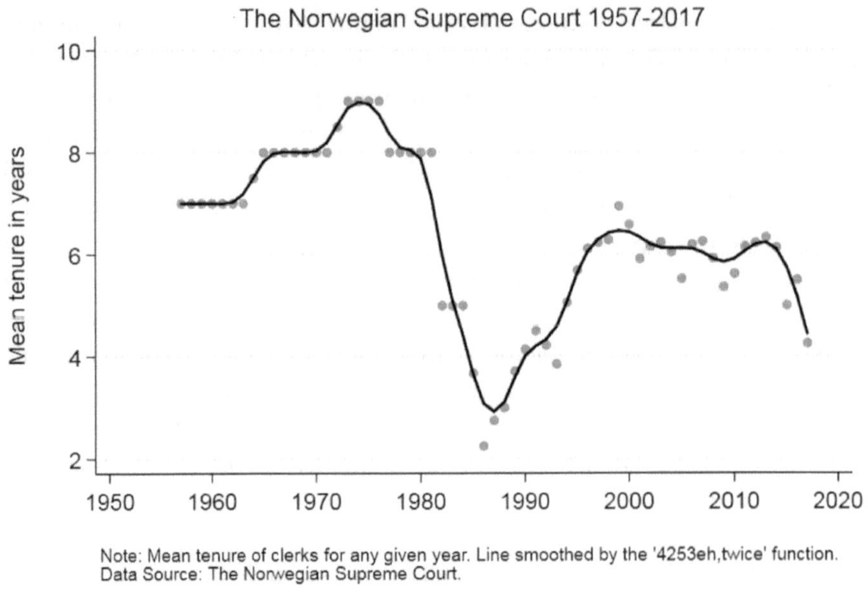

As we noted earlier, the move to hire clerks on fixed-year contracts started in 2001. Clerks hired that year were guaranteed employment (assuming satisfactory job performance) for five years. Contract lengths have been increased twice since then – to six years in 2007 and to seven years in 2011. The average tenure of all the clerks included in the analysis is just under six years, and although clerks hired prior to 2001 were not fixed-year contract employees, there is no statistical difference between their mean tenure and the mean tenure of clerks hired in the twenty-first century.[9]

It bears noting that the Court has tried to balance its interest in preserving some institutional memory within the clerk unit with the capacity to ensure that the clerk unit remains a dynamic institution, that the clerks do not become an entrenched bureaucracy and to guarantee that clerks who are not performing at a satisfactory level may be removed. Indeed, the decision to institutionalize a fixed-year contract system was at least in part an

9 Nor is there a statistical difference in the mean tenure of male and female clerks.

effort to establish a mechanism that would facilitate the removal of a handful of clerks who effectively had overstayed their welcome in the clerk unit. This effort to balance these various concerns is nicely reflected in the history of the length of the fixed-year contracts – moving from five to six years in 2007 and to seven years in 2011. The initial five-year contracts simply were not long enough to bring the necessary stability to the clerk unit.

The highly skilled and excellently trained young lawyers who compose the clerk unit, knowing that their employment with the unit ends on a date certain, will begin to seek out jobs before their contract expires. As a result, the effective mean length of a clerk's tenure on the current Court is about four years, and there is the possibility that contracts will be extended to eight or even nine years in the future.[10]

6.5 Diversity

For some time, there has been a commitment to the principle of diversity when recruiting justices to the Norwegian Supreme Court. As articulated by former law professor and then-chief justice, Carsten Smith,

> it would be to the advantage of the Court if its composition reflected a wide breadth of experience from different areas of the country, professional backgrounds from different areas of legal practice, and, furthermore, if it had a more balanced proportion of men to women (1998:101).

Smith's recommendation effectively has found its way into the Norwegian law. Section 55 of the Court Act explicitly promotes a diverse recruitment of justices. This policy is echoed in the Norwegian Judicial Appointments Board's official statement of recruiting policy: "a pursuit of the principle of a broad recruitment of justices, such that justices who are appointed have prior knowledge from various areas of community and legal life" (Innstillingsrådet for Dommere 2012).

No such formal policies are in effect when it comes to the recruitment of the Court's clerks; yet, given Norway's democratic nature and commitment to egalitarianism, it is likely that, at least informally, attention is paid to composing a clerk unit that is both reflective of the nation's cultural diversity and representative of various legal views. Indeed, when calls for the recruitment of clerks are made, they include clear expressions about

10 The longer mean tenure of the clerks reported in our data is the result of approved leaves of absence not counting against the fixed-year contract clock. We have not had access to detailed data on clerks' leaves of absence. Hence, any absences are not controlled for in our data. Also, initial one-year temporary trial contracts to fill in for a clerk on a leave of absence does not count towards the numbers we use here.

attention to diversity: "It is the goal of the government that the workforce should reflect the composition of the population in general, including general and cultural diversity."[11]

What is more, attention to diversity in the clerk unit is not without consequence. After all, if a diverse bench is to the Court's advantage (in terms of its legitimacy and in performing its role as a court of precedent), then so too would be a diverse clerk unit. As we have discussed in earlier chapters, the clerks serve an important function at the Court's gatekeeping stage. As appeals are processed through the ASC, it is the clerks' duty to identify any principled question(s) in an appeal and make a recommendation as to whether the appeal should be granted or denied. Further, it has become a task of the clerks to identify the proper legal sources to ensure the Court's creation of precedent is sufficiently sound and legitimate. It is here that diversity should matter. Different lived experiences, different professional backgrounds and legal training would presumably bear upon how different questions and legal sources resonate with the clerks, which in turn might affect which cases are identified as principled and worthy of the Court's finite attention on the merits.

Accordingly, we explore the diversity of the clerk unit over time and compare its diversity to the diversity of the Court. To do so, we computed indices of fractionalization or diversity for both institutions from 1957 to 2017. Our measure is derived from a Herfindahl index and is based on the proportion of clerks (justices) in each of the four groupings displayed in Table 6.3. We expect that the combination of attributes associated with a given grouping gives rise to a unique set of lived experiences that would affect the perceptions and thus decisional behaviour of a clerk (justice) and in combination would result in a more heterogeneous institution.

To compute the annual index scores, we calculated the proportion of clerks (justices) who belong to each group and then used these proportions as inputs for the diversity formula.

$$\text{FRACT}_j = 1 - \sum_{i-1}^{N} S_{ij^2}$$

FRACT_j = Fractionalization Index for year i

s_{ij} = Proportion of clerks (justices) in group j for year i

The logic of the formula is simple: as the clerks (justices) are spread across more combinations of groups, greater diversity ensues. (For a more detailed discussion of the measure's computation and its properties, see Shaffer, Grendstad, and Waltenburg 2015).

11 Quotes from various calls for clerk positions at the Court, *e.g.* Jobbnorge-IDs 142598, 117791 and 97550.

Table 6.3 Possible Groupings Contributing to Diversity

Sex	Law School
Female	Oslo
Female	Not Oslo
Male	Oslo
Male	Not Oslo

Figure 6.6 Clerk and Justice Diversity

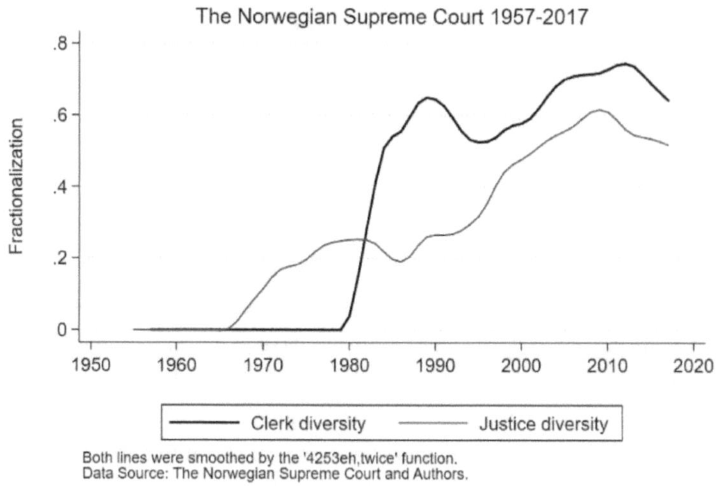

Figure 6.6 reveals that prior to the 1980s there was no diversity in the clerk unit and precious little on the High Bench. This absence of diversity in both institutions stands to reason. In the case of the clerk unit, it comprised only one person until 1977. By definition, then, it was impossible for multiple combinations of groups to be represented. Once more clerks were added, however, the unit's diversity rose sharply. And this was the result of two forces. First, the clerk unit was highly accessible to women. Indeed, as we noted earlier, a woman joined the clerk unit in 1964, less than a decade after the Court employed its first legal secretary and four years prior to the arrival of the first female justice. When the clerk unit expanded to two (in 1977) then three (1984) and then six (1994) clerks, it was natural for men *and* women to be added to the increasing ranks, thereby contributing to the unit's diversity. Second, the period during which the clerk unit experienced its most rapid growth (i.e. 1990-2016) was collinear with the arrival of law school graduates from the two new law schools in Norway – Bergen (1969) and Tromsø (1987). Thus, as these universities'

legal training became institutionalized and nationally recognized, there were more opportunities to place their graduates in the clerk unit.

Although the Court's diversity was not systemically constrained like that of the clerk unit – that is, starting in 1968 with the first female justice being appointed to the Court, there was always a sufficient number of justices for multiple combinations of groups to be represented – its diversity since 1968 was limited first by the relatively small number of female justices and second the lack of opportunity to pursue a legal education other than at the University of Oslo. By the 1990s, however, women and graduates from Bergen began to be appointed to the Court with sufficient frequency to effect a high level of diversity.

By the end of the time period, both the clerk unit and the Court achieved high diversity scores.[12] It appears that both institutions' environments are highly conducive to ensuring that a diverse and representative combination of lived experiences is present and engaged in the decisional environment.

6.6 APPROACHING REPRESENTATIVENESS

The typical clerk is a woman with a law degree from the University of Oslo. Before joining the clerk unit, which she did when she was about 31 years old, she most likely worked as a lawyer (i.e. working in a law firm or its equivalent) or as a 'trainee lawyer' (i.e. an individual holding an apprenticeship position in a law firm). Once she joined the clerk unit, she remained a clerk for almost six years, a tenure long enough to facilitate the transmission of her institutional memory to other clerks, yet short enough to ensure she and her fellow clerks did not become entrenched bureaucrats, although the unit in which she worked clearly had taken on the hallmarks of an institutionalized bureaucracy.

The one attribute we do not discuss is her likely policy preferences or ideology – a phenomenon of some appreciable interest to scholars examining clerks in the U.S. Supreme Court (see, e.g. Baum 2014; Ditslear and Baum 2001; Peppers 2006; Ward and Weiden 2006). And perhaps this makes good sense. After all, the clerks on the Norwegian Supreme Court are neither 'junior justices' nor 'law firm associates' (Peppers 2006; Ward and Weiden 2006). The discontinuation of permanent clerk contracts and introduction of time-limited clerk contracts in 2001 were measures taken exactly to prevent that from happening. The clerks do not play as fundamental a role in the composition of opinions – the articulation of the Court's legal policy – as do their counterparts in the United States. Consequently, it is probably less relevant whether the clerks' ideological or policy preferences are consistent or even negatively collinear with those of the justices for whom they work. Clerks at the Norwegian Supreme Court are almost arbitrarily chosen to prepare an appeal for the three-

12 Given the number of possible group combinations, a maximum diversity score = .750.

justice panel on the ASC. There is never an enduring one-to-one working relationship between a clerk and a justice. There is even less opportunity for the clerks' policy views to find their way into the Court's written opinions. Nevertheless, the degree to which the general views of the clerk unit are broadly representative of Norwegian culture and society is important.

The Norwegian clerks' primary function is to screen cases and to identify and establish the validity and legitimacy of the legal sources undergirding the precedential value of a decision. Now, if the clerk unit is not representative of Norway, important perspectives may be missing from this process. (For a similar argument with respect to the representational consequences of clerks on the U.S. Supreme Court, see Mauro 2014.) In this regard, the clerk unit seems to hit key marks. Our analysis indicates that the unit is broadly representative of the applicant pool from which it is drawn, at least over the time period for which we have data. And in terms of diversity (along the pair of dimensions we consider) the unit is at least as diverse as the Court. To put it simply, when it comes to gender and legal training, the clerk unit achieves nearly as much diversity as possible. Consequently, a range of lived experiences (albeit experiences particularly relevant to legal decision-making) inform the Court's and clerks' selection of cases and identification of legal sources. This does not, however, apply when it comes to law schools, where the development over time has instead been a decrease of diversity. In practice, this means that this important elite social-legal network is less open to lawyers from the periphery than is the position of Supreme Court justice.

7 The Development and Impact of Law Clerks

The Norwegian Supreme Court employed its first legal secretary, or law clerk, in 1957. The number of clerks available to the Court grew slowly throughout most of the twentieth century. Then, as the Court entered the century's final decade, their number began to mushroom. And this rate of growth continued in the new millennium, so that by 2018 the clerk unit comprised 23 clerks, three more clerks than there are justices.

The increase in the number of clerks in the 1990s can be linked to law professor Carsten Smith's proactive court doctrine, which he first articulated in the mid-1970s (Smith 1975, see Chapter 1). When Smith became chief justice in 1991, he was in a better position to effectuate that doctrine by increasing the size of the clerk pool. Yet, it must be noted that Smith was not solely responsible for the addition of clerks. To be sure, their number increased during his chief justiceship, but their presence grew prior to Smith becoming chief, and they continued to be added after Smith's tenure. If the monotonic growth in the institution of the clerk unit cannot be attributed exclusively to Carsten Smith's chief justiceship, the question naturally arises: What does account for it, and this, in turn, prompts the question what has been its effect?

In this chapter, we seek to systematically answer these questions. The answers we offer are significant beyond the specific case of Norway, inasmuch as the transformation of the Norwegian Supreme Court that we are studying here also represents an ongoing transformation of other European courts (Hirschl 2008; Sunde 2017; Tate and Vallinder 1995). While we are looking for the causes of the increase in numbers of clerks and the growth of the clerk unit, as well as any effects resulting from these developments, we are mindful of the fact that organizational change and evolution are not always proximate causes to the object of study.

In Chapter 1 we introduced the concept of institutionalization as a framework for understanding the steady growth of the clerk unit. Generally speaking, the Norwegian Supreme Court exhibits significant levels of "differentiation, durability, and autonomy" (McGuire 2004:130). That is, the Court is identifiable as a distinct organizational entity in the Norwegian political system. It possesses certain aspects (perhaps most notably, budgetary support) that contribute to its persistence and resilience in the face of changes to the political context in which it acts. And it is able to render its "decisions without dictation from outside actors" (McGuire 2004:130-132, quote at p. 132, see also Chapter 1 for a more detailed discussion of these concepts).

7.1 THE GROWTH OF THE CLERK UNIT

Perhaps the most intuitively beguiling explanation for the growth in the size of the clerk unit is that increasing the number of clerks was a simple response to the caseload pressures relentlessly bearing down on the Court. As reported in Chapter 3, between the early 1970s and the mid-1990s, there was a doubling of appeals to be processed by the Appeals Selection Committee (ASC). Not surprisingly, this crush of appeals placed tremendous burdens on the rotating subset of justices serving as the Court's gatekeepers. In the late 1980s and early 1990s, for example, when the average number of appeals stood at nearly 3,200 per year, justices assigned to the ASC anticipated working 18-hour days (plus the weekends) during their five-week stint (Sunde 2015a:148). We have already noted that Carsten Smith, the Court's chief justice from 1991 to 2002, once remarked "that he felt like a general ordering soldiers toward the shower of bullets" as he watched his fellow justices reporting for service on the Committee.

The problem the Court faced, of course, was that as the number of appeals continued to mount, its processing capacity would eventually be overwhelmed. Now, as this looming problem became increasingly concrete, there were three main paths the Court could pursue to address it. First, the Court could ask the legislature to enact laws to provide tools to effectively reduce the inflow of appeals it would adjudicate; by definition, this would lighten the workload of the justices on the ASC and, as appeals were passed on to the merits panels, the full Court as well. Second, the Court could increase its processing capacity by hiring additional clerks. Reducing the inflow of appeals and adding clerks to the Court's support functions would be somewhat more than a subtle display of the institutional standing of the Court. Finally, the Court could also increase the number of justices to augment its processing capacity. Contrary to the two first paths, increasing the number of justices would diminish their standing, as the judicial power of the Court had to be shared among more justices. In other words, there would be a negative marginal utility of increasing the number of justices. Ultimately, the Court pursued all three paths, but it did not remove its foot from the brake pedal when it came to hiring more justices.[1]

In 1995, after the implementation of a criminal procedure reform, the Court gained substantial control of its appellate docket. Prior to 1995, cases involving serious criminal offences were originally tried in the intermediate appellate courts, and any appeals went directly to the Supreme Court. In other words, Norway's highest court was the first-level appeal court, with mandatory appellate jurisdiction, for larger criminal cases. The 1995 reform changed this procedure. It directed that the nation's district courts assume original trial jurisdiction in larger criminal cases too. Appeals of the district court decisions would

1 Minor paths were also available. *E.g.*, the justices could choose to send a case back to the court of appeal for retrial rather than sort out the mess themselves.

then be heard first in the intermediate courts of appeal. Only after this first round of appeals would a criminal case arrive in the Supreme Court, and only the most principled cases were granted leave to appeal by the ASC. The general idea of the criminal reform was that if a criminal case had been heard in two instances, that case had received all the legal attention that could reasonably be expected (Grendstad, Shaffer, and Waltenburg 2015; Sunde 2015a). A third round in the High Court would require that the case attracted special legal or political interest above and beyond itself.

Simply reducing the size and then gaining discretionary control of its criminal appeals docket, however, did not fully resolve the processing challenges the Court faced. First, changing the Court's place in the criminal appeal process did not eliminate criminal appeals. Even after the criminal procedure reform went in to effect, the number of criminal appeals per justice on the ASC averaged over 200 per year (see Figure 4.2). Second, that the Committee could now 'cherry-pick' the criminal appeals it wanted to hear on their merits almost perversely meant that the gatekeeping justices would necessarily be devoting more time and energy to sift through the remaining cases to determine which were worthy of full merits consideration. Third, criminal cases were not the only appeals the ASC processed, even though they were dominating the docket. The Court also started to interpret the civil procedure filtering mechanism in light of the change in criminal procedure, even though the civil procedure was not formally changed until 2005 and implemented in 2008. Hence, through a change in the interpretation of the law and not a change in the substance of the law, the Court achieved much of the same discretionary control over the civil appeals dockets as it did over the criminal appeals. Indeed, after the reform of criminal procedure, the Committee considered nearly equal numbers of civil and criminal cases. Moreover, combined, the total number of criminal and civil appeals was increasing slightly on an annual basis. Consequently, the Court also moved to increase its processing capacity, by adding clerks and, somewhat reluctantly, accepting another justice.

In March 1994 the Minister of Justice called Chief Justice Smith on a Sunday evening, informing him that to deal with their backlog, the Supreme Court would be given one more justice, increasing the number of justices from 18 to 19. The number of justices had remained unchanged since 1939. Smith, knowing full well that his fellow justices had long resisted any increase in their number, attempted a polite refusal. As we noted in Chapter 3, the justices preferred a heavier caseload as a means to burnish the Court's institutional prestige, while their official argument was that increasing the number of justices would rapidly undermine the unity of the law, one of the Court's three loadstars that emerged during the Smith Court. Yet, despite his effort to demur, Smith was informed that he and his Court had no choice. The justices agreed to the offer of a new justice on the basis that it was temporary. The deal was made under the assumption that the next vacancy on the Court would not be replaced. But two years later, when Chief Justice Smith headed the new court commission, the temporary justice was made permanent as the nineteenth justice.

Between the attempts of a polite refusal of a new justice in 1994 and the acceptance of a new permanent justice in 1996 was a realization among the justices that the marginal justice did not challenge the unity of the law that they had feared would happen in the first place (Sunde 2015a:155).

The next new permanent and the twentieth justice on the Court came in 2010. A year earlier, Chief Justice Tore Schei had made several arguments for increasing the Court's size. In his presentation, Schei noted the Court's increasing workload. He pointed out that the new national vacation policy, granting 14 additional days of vacation time for government employees who were at least 63 years old, would disproportionally affect the Court, given the high average age of the justices – a condition unlikely to change if the traditional recruitment patterns of new justices continued to be followed.[2] The Supreme Court will "never become a youth club", Schei said (in Aschehoug 2009). It was improper to expect the relatively younger justices to pick up the slack for senior justices on vacation. Moreover, Schei argued that the addition of a justice was part of a plan to improve the work situation for all the justices, a statement that speaks to the fact that justices do not have policy or even legal goals as their only motivation (Epstein and Knight 2013; Epstein, Landes, and Posner 2013).

Increasing the number of justices on the Court would permit greater flexibility in the Court's decision-making process. Adding a justice would allow an increase in the number of justices assigned to serve on the ASC from four to five, which would provide greater capacity for the Committee's revolving gatekeeping subpanels of three justices. And finally, on occasion the new justice could perform picket service and act as a substitute for a justice who had been assigned to write the majority opinion in a case and needed to be relieved from a panel until the draft of the majority opinion could be circulated (see Chapter 2 for a fuller description of this Court practice).

Although Schei couched at least some of his argument in support of adding a justice in terms of increasing the Court's processing capacity, the most conspicuous measure to augment the processing capacity of the Court has been to hire clerks. (See Figure 1.1, which plots the number of clerks over time, and Chapter 3 for a full description of the growth of the clerk unit.) The Court has continued to pursue this tack in the twenty-first century. Indeed, the official policy and goal of the Supreme Court is to continue to increase the number of clerks to 30 by 2021, while the number of justices is expected to remain at 20 (Høyesteretts Kontor 2017).[3]

2 In 2009, the justices' mean age was nearly 60; almost half of the justices qualified for the additional two weeks of vacation.

3 In the face of a tighter budget situation, there is also an emergent awareness that the Court would be better off hiring clerks: In terms of salary, two clerks are equal to one justice.

In a 2014 article, Supreme Court Justice Arnfinn Bårdsen, speaking for the Court, stated that the clerk unit should increase from 20 (the number of clerks at the time he wrote) to 40 clerks in relatively short order. He argued that the increase in the number of clerks would promote the quality of the Court's decision-making processes and provide the specialization that the Court needed in order to handle the demanding internationalization of the legal field. He also argued that the clerks should assist the ASC in selecting the 'correct' appeals for the merit panels and complement the analyses and documents that currently are left for the parties of the case to provide (Bårdsen 2014).[4]

These last two points - correct selection of cases and complementing analysis - are especially relevant to the transformation of the Norwegian Supreme Court from a court whose role was to resolve individual cases to a court of precedent with the goal of clarifying and developing the law. As we have discussed, pivotal to this transformation was the Court's discretionary power to pluck out specific criminal cases for their broad precedential value with the implementation of the reform in criminal procedure in 1995. But the *instant* 1995 control over its criminal docket did not complete the Court's power to select cases for their broader legal salience. Discretionary jurisdiction expanded *slowly* to civil cases as well, with the justices taking advantage of the inconspicuous fourth clause that was inserted in Section 373 of the old *Dispute Act* in 1960. At the Court's urging, the clause was significantly sharpened when the Act was revised in 1981. And finally, what had been accomplished became established law when the Court's discretionary power in civil cases was fully extended with the implementation of the 2005 *Dispute Act* in 2008 (NOU 2001:A,125-126).[5] At this point, two-thirds of the Court's denial of civil law appeals was based on the once inconspicuous fourth clause. Thus, by 2008, not only did the Supreme Court have the efficient instruments to deny an appeal in civil and criminal cases if the appeal did not promise to shape and/or clarify the law, its workload had also flipped. The Supreme Court no longer had the burden of proof for denying appeals. The burden of proof was shifted to the litigants who now had to convince the Court to grant appeal. If the Court agreed, the appeal was forwarded to the merits panels.

This expanded discretionary authority and the Court's new role, however, came with a price. Namely, if the ASC was to pick only those cases that would allow the High Court to shape the law, the justices on the Committee would necessarily expend greater time and effort on assessing the precedential potential of each appeal. This type of analysis would place a premium on the marshalling of legal arguments and case law that would go beyond

4 The goal of doubling the number of clerks was also advanced by Chief Justice Tore Schei during a speech celebrating the Court's 200-year anniversary in 2015 (Schei 2015c). Since 2015, no one has repeated the lofty goal of 40 clerks. "The clerks are to be organized in different way now", a source informed the authors in 2017.

5 With the 2008 implementation of the *Dispute Act*, passed in 2005, civil law cases too needed the explicit consent of the ASC to be heard by the Court.

those the litigants provided. Moreover, this type of analysis for each appeal could take longer and might strain the finite resources of the justices on the ASC, once again contributing to growing bottlenecks at the gatekeeping stage. It was already well known on the Court that straining finite resources was exactly what happened when the Swedish Supreme Court was reformed in the 1970s (Sunde 2017:67). Adding clerks would enlarge the legal research capacity of the Court's gatekeepers. Indeed, in interviews with current and former clerks as well as several justices, a recurrent theme is the substantial role the clerks play in identifying cases with the greatest potential policy consequence in order to cull the caseload for the Court.

7.2 EXPLAINING THE GROWTH OF THE CLERK UNIT

In the end, then, it appears that the increase in the number of clerks on the Supreme Court took place by design but was justified by the Court's need to meet its gatekeeping responsibility (in the form of the ASC). Whether before or after the implementation of the criminal procedure reform, the justices serving as the Court's gatekeepers had a heavy caseload. From 1970 to 1995, the number of appeals per ASC-justice averaged nearly 730 cases (standard deviation is 123.4). After 1995, the average number of appeals per ASC-justice drops to a still sizeable 431 cases (standard deviation is 44.8). All of these cases had to be examined for their potential utility in clarifying and developing the law.[6] Thus, the need for effective gatekeeping continued to cast its shadow over the Court even after the inflow of appeals to the Court was dramatically reduced in the mid-1990s. Therefore, the Court pursued a policy of hiring more clerks to relieve the workload of the Court's gatekeepers.

It seems likely, then, that the Court's mounting workload and concomitant backlogs stimulated the move to hire more clerks in the first place. Before the turn of the century clerks were hired on permanent contracts, but those who left for other jobs were still replaced by new clerks. Once clerks were added, however, there was no move to reduce their number, even as backlogs dropped. Simply stated, even though the enlarged clerk unit facilitated a more effective management of the increased workload, the Court continued to seek and receive additional clerks.

We suggest that as backlogs were brought under control, expansion of the clerk unit took on a life of its own through a process of *institutionalization*, which we contend underpins the pattern illustrated in Figure 7.1 tracking the number of clerks by year.[7] On

6 Of course, after the 1995 reform in criminal procedure, the share of appeals made to the Court composed of criminal appeals dropped dramatically.

7 In this chapter we analyse clerks and the clerk unit starting approximately in 1970 as this is the time when the unit expands and for which subsequent period we have appropriate variables for expanded analyses.

the basis of the trend depicted, two outcomes are readily apparent. First, a dramatic rise in the number of clerks occurs after 1990, with approximately a fourfold expansion. Second, every time the size of the clerk unit is enlarged, it remains at that level until the next addition of clerks. Note that there is not one year in which the number of clerks is reduced, notwithstanding the reining in of massive workloads. Once underway, growth of the clerk unit gained momentum, expanding in a very steady incremental fashion.

Figure 7.1 Number of Clerks in the Clerk Unit

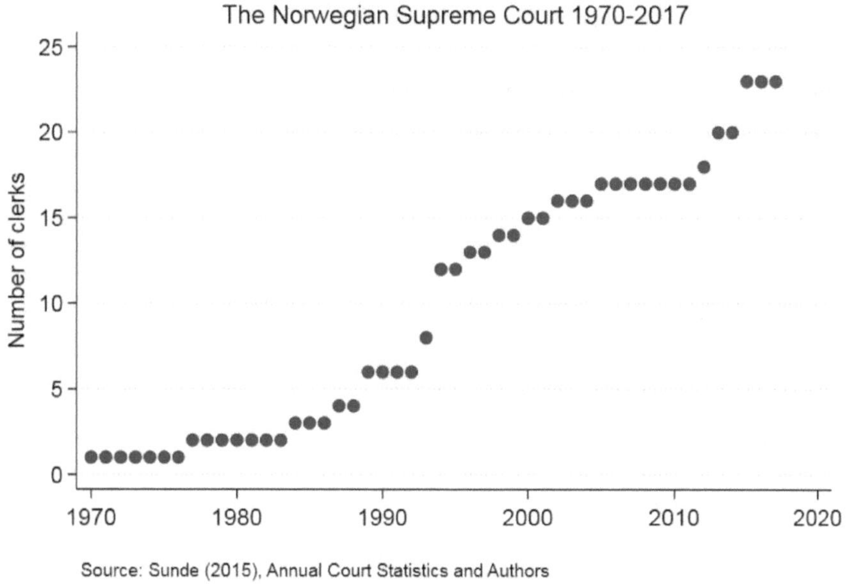

To bring some more analytical leverage to bear on this explanation, we estimated a regression equation of the number of clerks in the clerk unit for any given year that includes the number of clerks lagged one year. Specifically, our regression model is the following:

$$\text{Clerks}_t = \text{Clerks}_{t-1} + \varepsilon(1)$$

The results are displayed in Table 7.1. They provide strong support for the institutionalization explanation. The lagged value of clerks is almost perfectly correlated with the number of clerks at time t ($R^2 = 0.99$), indicating that the previous level of clerks in the clerk unit predicts the number of clerks currently working for the Court with uncanny accuracy. The simple beauty of this relationship is captured by Figure 7.2.

Table 7.1 Regression of Number of Clerks at Time (t) on Clerks at t-1

Ind. Var.	Coeff.	SE
Clerks (t-1)	1.014	0.017*
_cons	0.329	0.207
R^2	0.987	
N	48	

DV = Number of law clerks at time t; DW = 2.060.

*$p < .001$.

Data source: The Norwegian Supreme Court and the authors.

Figure 7.2 Clerks t Regressed on Clerks at t-1

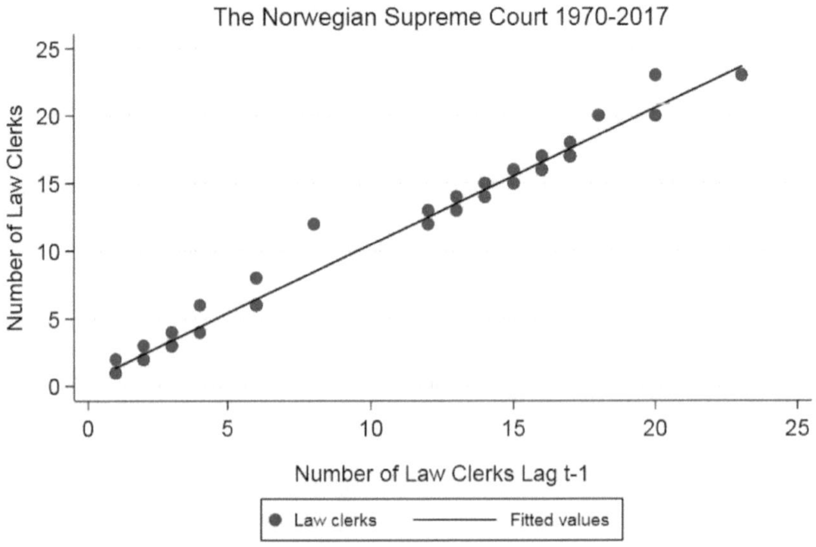

Source: Data compiled by authors.

For the estimated relationship to inform us of subsequent additions to the clerk unit, we must assume that the underlying dynamic reflected in the equation will remain in effect for some time to come. This may be an appropriate assumption in the near term, but tenuous as one moves too far into the future. To think that the trend will continue indefinitely is more than a bit fanciful. Interestingly enough, though, if the relationship remains in effect, Justice Bårdsen's assertion that 40 clerks are required to meet the expanded role assigned the clerks will not be realized anytime soon (Bårdsen 2014:549). Even assuming that the number of clerks remains a function of the lag of the number of clerks at t–1, the level of staffing of the clerk unit that Justice Bårdsen recommends will not be achieved until 2035.

In Chapter 1 we proposed that the extraordinary development of the clerk unit is best understood in the context of the institutionalization of the Supreme Court as it evolved from a reactive court of appeal to a proactive court of precedent. Clearly, the master plan crafted by former Chief Justice Carsten Smith was not designed merely to bring case backlogs under control, but to position the Court as a major policymaking player in the process of developing the law. As pointed out in Chapter 3, backlogs were greatly diminished, thereby no longer accounting for the continued growth of the clerk unit, which instead reflected the continued institutionalization of the Court. For present purposes, we have adopted the general framework of institutionalization proposed by McGuire (2004:130), who identifies three indicators of institutionalization: "differentiation, durability, and autonomy" (see Chapter 1 for a fuller discussion of these concepts).

McGuire's theoretical framework has been adopted to examine the institutionalization of a number of East European and Asian constitutional courts (Bumin, Randazzo, and Walker 2009). In this study, 11 indicators of differentiation, durability and autonomy are factor analysed to produce a factor score tapping the overall viability of the constitutional courts. The authors note that the need for institutionalizing high courts is not confined to Western democracies. Indeed, for the 28 nations in their dataset, they conclude that

> ... in order for judiciaries to play a significant role in democratizing states, they must develop certain levels of organizational sophistication and autonomy that enable the institutions to withstand exogenous influences and/or pressures (Bumin, Randazzo, and Walker 2009:148).

In our view, without a well-developed institutional structure, "... capacity constraints generally force the Court to adopt a posture of deference toward the political process" (Coan 2012:426). For the specific case of the Norwegian Supreme Court, the greatly expanded law clerk unit was a necessary, if not sufficient, condition for transforming the Supreme Court from a reactive one to a court of precedent, one not requiring 'deference towards the political process'.

McGuire's theoretical concept of institutionalization incorporating 'differentiation, durability and autonomy' dimensions includes factors associated with an interconnected concept of 'professionalism', another perspective on explicating the process by which a High Court experiences institutional growth. The most well-developed body of political science research on professionalism has focused on legislative bodies. In general, legislative professionalization is tapped by length of session, salaries and staffing (King 2000; Squire 2007). Professionalized legislatures have lengthy sessions, ample compensation and a substantial support staff.

Measures of this concept of professionalization have been developed for court systems, as well, with some modifications (Squire 2008). For example, session length is replaced by whether or not a High Court has jurisdictional discretion. Staffing is of paramount importance, since a "... court's ability to produce and evaluate information should increase with the number of law clerks working for justices" (Squire 2008:226). Clearly, the institutionalization of the Norwegian Supreme Court has been greatly enhanced by the professionalization brought about by the jurisdictional discretion that is essential to a court of precedent and the development of a highly qualified pool of law clerks. Squire's operational measure of staffing best reflects the indicator we have chosen, the number of clerks. Although both McGuire's and Bumin et al.'s analyses recognize the importance of support staff, the Bumin et al. indicator reflects "equipment and staff" (Bumin, Randazzo, and Walker 2009:135), while McGuire considers the clerks' "initial appearance and subsequent incorporation into the Court's formal structure" (McGuire 2004:132). Judicial professionalization, in particular the substantial growth of the number of clerks, has contributed greatly to the institutionalization of the Norwegian Supreme Court.

Further support of this interpretation is that as clerks were added, at no time were they hired as 'temporary' employees. Recall that initially, the addition of the nineteenth justice was supposed to be temporary. The added justice eventually would be subtracted from the Court through attrition. Not so with the clerks. As they were added to the clerk unit, their formal contracts stated that their new positions would become permanent. On the other hand, it was tacitly assumed and broadly understood that clerks would only stay on for a couple of years before moving on to other jobs within the legal system. When on one occasion a baby bird failed to leave the nest, so to speak, the Court introduced a system of time-limited contracts for clerks. To drive home its intentions and befitting a legal institution, the Court made sure limited contracts for clerks was codified.[8]

This is not to say that processing demands have no bearing on the size of the clerk unit, just that backlogs, *per se*, is not the driving force over the long haul. As we have noted, backlogs likely were a concern to the Court that it wanted to correct, thereby prompting many justices to favour adding clerks. Backlog was the issue that united justices with divergent views on the development of the Court, whether those views supported a reduced workload to improve the Court's performance as a court of appeal, held by the old guard, or to facilitate the Court's transformation to a court of precedent, as promoted by Carsten Smith. Backlogs have not steadily increased. In fact, as we have already noted, they have been contained, if not for all practical purposes eliminated, as stated by the leader of the clerk unit in 2017 (Aamodt 2017). The increase in the number of the clerks, however, was relentless. To put it simply, never in the period under study did the clerk unit experience a decline of so much as one staff member despite the growth in backlogs flattening out.

8 The *Court Act*, Section 61.

The turn of the century, at the same time that backlogs began to come under control, was also a time when a wave of international law crashed into the Norwegian legal system. European Human Rights and European Union laws challenged the untrained justices and inexperienced law clerks and required more time to process. As these laws now are a staple of legal sources and are included in the curriculum of law schools, generational replacement of justices and turnover among clerks reduced the amount of resources needed to process these types of cases.

Clearly, the development of the clerk unit was a prerequisite for the series of changes that Chief Justice Smith desired and foresaw already in the 1970s: an increase in the number of clerks was an instrument to enable more filtering of cases, which would give the justices more time to concentrate on the principled issues of law, which in the end would enable the Court to have the development of law as its main task. However, the chain of changes has not stopped here. Since around 2010, the increased presence of clerks changed the character not only of the Court but of the ASC too.

7.3 Clerks and the Transformation of the ASC[9]

First established for criminal cases by legislation in 1887 and expanded to include civil cases by legislation in 1915, the ASC was originally a court in its own right. However, since it had a gatekeeping role for the Supreme Court, was staffed by Supreme Court justices and run by the Court Administration, being a court in its own right was in name only. Then with the civil procedure reform implemented in 2008, the ASC lost its titular status as a separate court and became a fully integrated unit within the Supreme Court. Simultaneously, the increased number of clerks and their contribution to the filtering of cases on the Committee increased the importance of the Committee and the quality of its decisions.

Paradoxically, from around 2010, the ASC has turned towards being more of a court than just a gatekeeping unit within the Supreme Court. First, at a meeting in 2010, the justices decided that appealed cases concerning a miscarriage of justice should be quashed by the Committee and returned to the intermediate court of appeal for retrial rather than being granted leave of appeal. The preliminary work by a clerk was sufficient to clarify the appeal, and no oral arguments or deliberations by the justices were needed. A draft of the change in the civil and criminal procedure was sent from the Court to the Parliament, and the proposal for change was approved in 2012.

Second, at about the same time arguments as to why some of the appeals were denied by the ASC became more elaborate and exceeded what had been standard practice and what was required by law. Again, this procedural change was discussed among the justices

9 *See* Chapter 2 for a more complete description of the ASC.

during internal meetings. The new procedure, it was argued, was a way of compensating for the decrease in the number of merits cases the Court decided. Even though the cases decided on their merits concerned principled questions of law, the number of these decisions was still low compared to the many fields of law in need of clarification and development. Hence, the justices decided to create 'mini-precedents' (Bårdsen 2014). That is, the Court would use some of the appeals denied by the Committee as vehicles to still develop the law, thereby increasing the overall number of consequential decisions, or precedents, decided by the Court.

In contrast to the decisional procedure in five-justice merits panels involving oral arguments in public and then deliberation in conference, the three-justice ASC decides cases based on written documents and communications only. The difference in quality of the procedures in these two different types of decision-making has been equalized by the assistance and support of clerks to the ASC. Basically, the clerks bring to the ASC justices the entire domain of relevant legal records, thereby ensuring their decisions are fully informed.

The question is why the rhetoric of backlogs has prevailed while the number of clerks has not tracked more closely with the magnitude of the backlogs.[10] We suggest that the institutionalization of the clerk unit facilitates a different type of processing. Namely, the clerks support the justices' identification of those cases most likely to clarify and develop the law. Clarifying and developing law as a task increased the demand for quality in the processing of cases from gate to judgement passed. And this process would again increase the workload for clerks beyond their more traditional role of support staff at the gatekeeping stage to becoming case managers from beginning to end. In short, the institutionalization of the clerk unit has been an important contribution to the Norwegian Supreme Court's emergence as a court of precedent (see extensive discussions in Sunde 2015a).

7.4 The Effects of the Institutionalized Clerk Unit

In this section we systematically examine the effects of the institutionalized clerk unit on the Norwegian Supreme Court's case processing. Our exploration focuses on three expectations:

- a declining rate of appeals being accepted for merits review,
- the trend in the number of legal sources cited in written opinions and
- the increasing rates of non-unanimous decisions.

10 Moreover, since 2001 there has been a discrepancy between the number of backlogs published in the Court's annual reports and the actual and lower number of backlogs that the Court reported internally (email correspondence between one of the authors and the Supreme Court in March 2018).

Our initial impulse is to treat criminal appeals reform and the number of clerks as distinct independent variables. They are not. That the two indicators in our dataset are correlated at .91 makes plain the fact that empirically we seem to be examining separate measures of the same phenomenon. A further complication arises if one includes both indicators as independent variables in a regression equation – outsized multicollinearity. When the two measures are subjected to a factor analysis, they reduce to one dimension and each one loads on the single factor at greater than .93. On the basis of this factor analysis solution, we computed a single factor score, which we label 'Institutionalism'. Our preferred theoretical interpretation rests on the assumption that appeals reform and the addition of law clerks are not distinct measures that can form the basis of such an interaction term.[11] Instead, they clearly are measures of a single phenomenon – institutionalism. Given that former Chief Justice Smith and his successors view the clerk unit as a crucial feature of an increasingly professional Supreme Court, we argue that the growth of the clerk unit prior to the appeals reform, rising to about half its current size, was contributing to institutionalization *before* the appeals reform. Institutionalism, comprised of the monotonically increasing number of clerks and the criminal appeals reform, is shown in Figure 7.3. The figure demonstrates that the professional contribution of the clerk unit was not entirely dependent upon rolling back criminal appeals. Let us now examine the effects of this institutionalization.

7.4.1 Institutionalism and Merits Review

First, the impact of institutionalism should result in a declining rate of appeals being accepted for merits review. As a court of precedent, the Court's gatekeepers would aim to select appeals strategically in order to develop the law, and the clerks would provide support in this endeavour. Thus, we expect that as the number of clerks increases and criminal appeals declines, the percent of appeals granted review will drop.

This hypothesized negative relationship cannot be confirmed by the regression results reported in Table 7.2.[12] After correcting for serial correlation, the continued institutionalization of the Supreme Court does not have a statistically significant relationship with the

---

11 Typically, factor analysis is employed as a data reduction technique. Here, we are using factor analysis simply for index construction. Interacting the criminal appeals reform and the number of law clerks is another way to express the dual influence of the number of clerks and criminal appeals reform. Appendix A illustrates the trend of such an interaction term, a trend that does not exhibit verisimilitude with the actual process of institutionalizing the Supreme Court.

12 The requirement that appeals be first heard by the lower appellate courts effectively bleeds off the less salient and consequential cases to begin with. That is, those appellants most resource rich and pursing a litigation strategy (or those with basically no other choice) will continue to pursue appeals beyond the lower appellate courts. Thus, the pool of appeals that the clerks plumb for merits grants might be relatively rich.

percent of merits appeals granted. Figure 7.4 offers a graphic display of the regression equation, suggesting that even if the impact of the institutionalism factor score had been significant, the change in appeals granted would be modest at best. For example, when the institutionalism factor score is set at its lowest level, one would predict that the appeals granted is 26.3 per cent, and when institutionalism is set at its maxim value, 23.4 per cent of the appeals is predicted to be granted.

Figure 7.3 Institutionalism

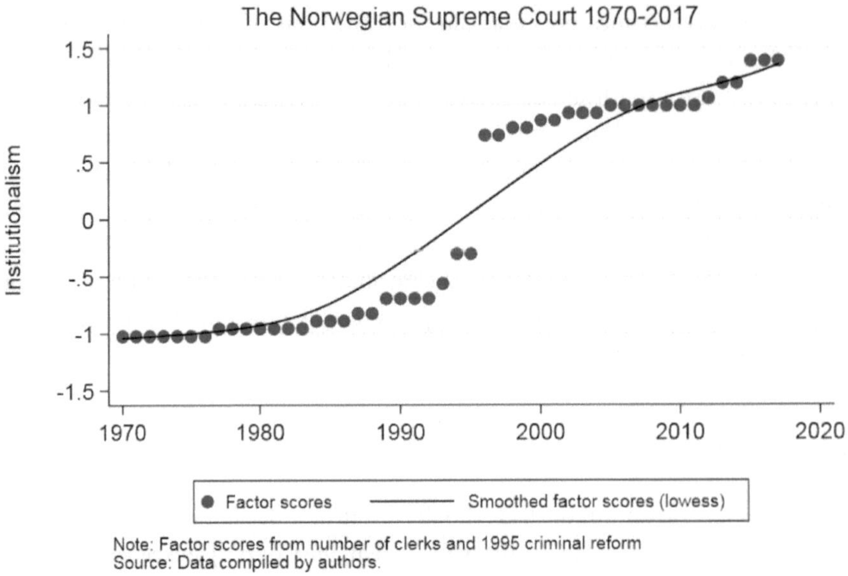

Table 7.2 Regression of Number of Merits Appeals Granted on Institutionalism

Appeals[a]	Coeff.	se
Institutionalism	-1.057	1.661*
_cons	20.768	1.772
R^2	0.009	
N	47	

DV = Merit appeals accepted; DW = 2.239.

*p = .527 (ns).

[a] Corrected for serial correlation.

Data source: The Norwegian Supreme Court and the authors.

Figure 7.4 Merits appeals granted by institutionalism

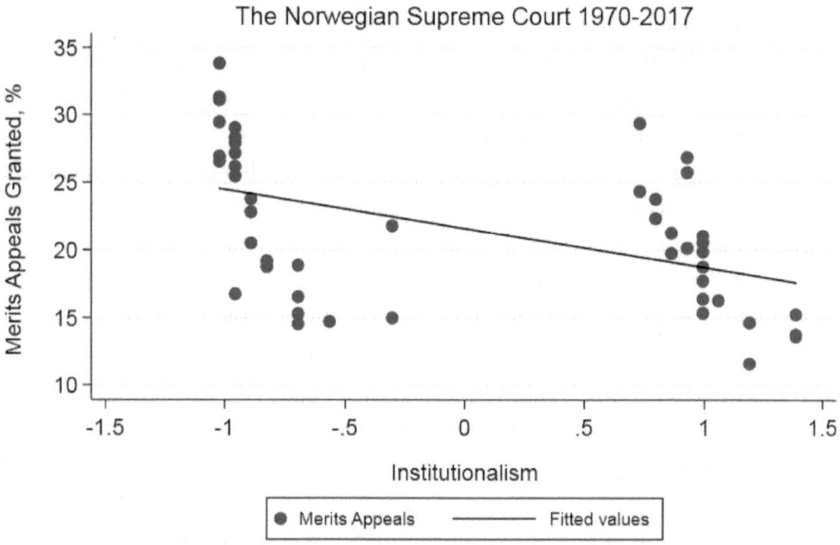

Source: Norwegian Supreme Court Annual Reports and the authors.

7.4.2 *Institutionalism and Legal Grounding of Opinions*

While the Court's institutionalism does not significantly affect the incidence of merit appeals acceptances, the growth of the clerk unit, combined with criminal appeals reform, bolsters the legal grounding of opinions handed down by the High Court. We have taken advantage of extensive mining of data in Supreme Court decisions that Nadim (2017) did in order to establish the number of legal sources incorporated in the written opinions submitted by the justices.[13] Nadim documented legal sources for a number of areas of law. Our main focus of attention is on the mean number of legal sources offered in expropriation and labour law cases. Nadim chose to study expropriation cases and labour cases because both types of cases are politically controversial and usually pit a weaker party against a stronger party (2017:329, 390-391).

Turning first to expropriation disputes, Section 105 of the Norwegian Constitution unambiguously guarantees that expropriation of private property must be fully compensated. This is an area of conflict addressed in a number of extremely important Supreme Court cases, perhaps most prominently in the oft-discussed *Ship Owners Taxation* case,

13 We are grateful to Morten Nadim (2017) who shared his data in these areas of law with us. Nadim covers the years 1971-2014 in the expropriation time series. He reports no data for 2010 and 2013.

in which a 6-5 majority, falling roughly along ideological lines, decided against the government and in favour of the shipping companies (see also Grendstad, Shaffer, and Waltenburg 2015 for a fuller discussion).

We contend that the institutionalization of the Supreme Court has not only facilitated the processing of a high volume of cases, but arguably has *deepened* the quality of the decisions. The ever-increasing number of clerks, a mark of judicial professionalization, is hypothesized to generate a corresponding surge in the number of legal sources presented in the Court's merits opinions. Initially, an equation in which the number of legal sources cited in expropriation cases was regressed on the institutionalism factor score.

As indicated in Table 7.3, we needed to correct for heteroscedasticity. The final equation reveals a highly significant relationship ($p = .008$) with an explained variance (R^2) of .161 between institutionalism and the number of legal sources cited in expropriation cases. This bivariate relationship is graphically displayed in Figure 7.5. The slope of the regression line appears shallow, owing primarily to the fact that the dependent variable is expressed as a natural logarithm.

Table 7.3 Regression of Log of Expropriation Sources on Institutionalism

[a]	**Coeff.**	**SE**
Institutionalism	0.251	0.089*
_cons	3.043	0.080
R^2	0.161	
N	43	

DV = Expropriation legal sources; DW = 1.939.

*$p = .008$.

[a] Corrected for heteroscedasticity.

Data source: The Norwegian Supreme Court, Nadim (2017) and the authors.

Figure 7.5 Expropriation legal sources (log) on institutionalism

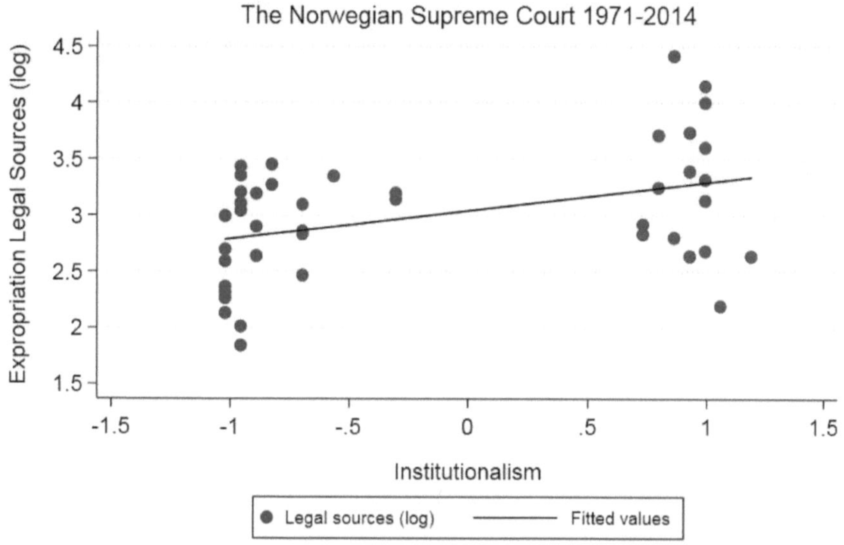

Source: Nadim 2017 and the authors.

To gain a sense of the impact of the increasing number of clerks, we calculated the regression equation prediction of the number of expropriation legal sources cited in a case at the lowest and highest institutionalism factor score. To do so, the log values of the legal sources variable were calculated and converted to anti-logs. These computations reveal that the number of legal sources cited at the low end of the institutionalism scale is nearly 16, and at the high end of institutionalism that number doubles to over 32 legal sources mentioned in written opinions.

We repeat this process for cases involving labour law, a legal domain of central importance to government policymaking. Nadim underscores that labour law is private law but is also heavily regulated by the Parliament (2017:330,390).[14] We measure the average number of legal sources in labour law decisions per year. The regression results, reported in Table 7.4, exhibit a substantially stronger impact of institutionalism on the number of labour law legal sources cited, as reflected in the highly significant (p = .000) R^2 of .383. The relationship is displayed in Figure 7.6. Repeating the previous exercise of calculating regression values reveals that when the institutionalism factor score is set at its lowest value the number of labour law sources offered is greater than 16, but balloons nearly threefold to over 44 at the maximum level of institutionalism.

14 Nadim (2017) covers the years 1971-2016 in the labour law time series.

Table 7.4 Regression of Labour Law Sources on Institutionalism

	Coeff.	SE
Institutionalism	9.752	1.907*
_cons	26.989	1.772
R^2	0.383	
N	44	

DV = Labour law sources; DW = 1.789.

*$p < .001$.

Data source: The Norwegian Supreme Court, Nadim (2017) and the authors.

Figure 7.6 Labour law legal sources on institutionalism

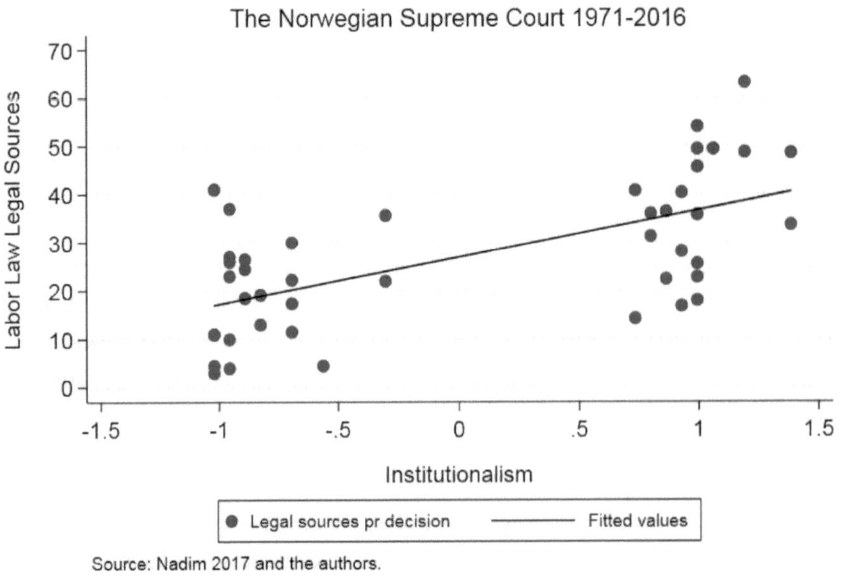

As we have noted, increasingly Supreme Court deliberation has been attentive to international law, moving beyond a singular focus upon Norwegian constitutional and statutory legal principles. Accommodating this jurisprudential globalization certainly has been facilitated by the persistent increases in the level of Court institutionalism. We hypothesize that the higher the level of institutionalism, the greater the incidence of legal citations for each area of law. For these regression equations, the dependent variable is the proportion of cases in each year for which there was a citation of human rights (European Convention of Human Rights, ECHR) law and European Economic Area-European Union (EEA-EU) law.[15]

Performing a regression analysis for human rights law, the results are clear – institutionalism matters a great deal. Again, once correcting for serial correlation and heteroscedasticity, the coefficient of determination of .813 indicates that 81.3 per cent of the variance in human rights citations is accounted for by the variance in institutionalism (see Table 7.5).[16] A plot of this relationship illustrates the strength of the relationship (see Figure 7.7). Predicting the log values of human rights citations for the lowest and highest values of institutionalism and converting them to the original unit of measure, we find that the predicted range of human rights citations vary between 0.5 and 26.5 per cent.

Table 7.5 Regression of Human Rights Legal Sources on Institutionalism

Human Rights[a]	**Coeff.**	**SE**
Institutionalism	1.625	0.145*
_cons	-3.609	0.135
R^2	0.813	
N	31	

DV = Log of number of sources; DW = 1.999.

*$p < .001$.

[a] Corrected for heteroscedasticity and serial correlation.

Data source: The Norwegian Supreme Court and the authors.

15 Jon Kåre Skiple, Henrik L. Bentsen and Petter Kristiansen Arnesen coded law citations in Supreme Court case decisions. The case citations on EEA-EU law relies also in part on Fredriksen (2011). The annual proportions used here are generated from the data on the individual decisions in the *Doranoh* database (Grendstad, Shaffer, and Waltenburg 2019).

16 There are eight years with no reported human rights law cases primarily in the beginning of the 1974-2016 time series we use here.

Figure 7.7 Human rights law legal sources (log) on institutionalism

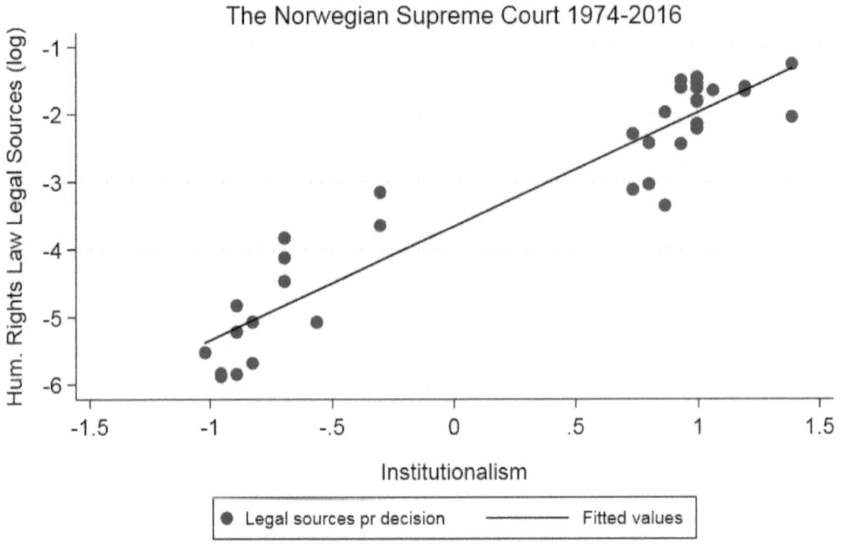

Source: Doranoh and Data compiled by authors.

Finally, on a number of occasions, a case attracted a citation of EEA-EU legal references. Executing a regression analysis for these cases required corrections for serial correlation and heteroscedasticity. The resulting R^2 of .658 signifies that 65.8 per cent of the variance in EEA-EU legal references is explained by the variance in institutionalism (see Table 7.6).[17] The plot depicted in Figure 7.8 illustrates the substantial link between institutionalism and EEA-EU legal citations. Predicting the log values of EEA-EU citations for the lowest and highest values of institutionalism and converting them to the original unit of measure generates a predicted range of EEA-EU citations to vary between 0.4 and 7.0 per cent.

17 There are ten years with no reported EEA-EU law cases primarily in the beginning of the 1971-2016 time series we use here.

Table 7.6 Regression of EEA-EU Legal Sources on Institutionalism

EEA-EU[a]	Coeff.	SE
Institutionalism	1.233	0.174*
_cons	-4.360	0.167
R^2	0.658	
N	28	

DV = Log of number of sources; DW = 1.899.

*$p < .001$.

[a] Corrected for heteroscedasticity and serial correlation.

Data source: The Norwegian Supreme Court and the authors.

Figure 7.8 EEA-EU law legal sources (log) on institutionalism

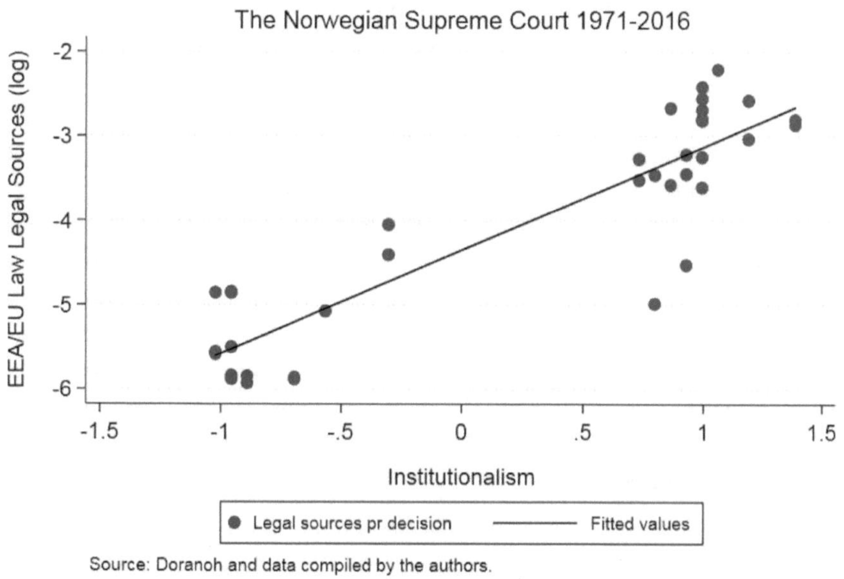

We suggest that at least part of the rise in the number of legal sources cited is a direct function of Supreme Court institutionalism in the form of a well-developed clerk system and relief from a burdensome level of criminal appeals. Identifying legal sources for arriving at a decision does not speak to the volume of cases processed or an all-out assault on backlogs. Instead, in this instance the impact of an increased clerk staff is of a *qualitative* nature. In order to fulfil its evolving role as a court of precedent, the Supreme Court benefits greatly from a highly professional staff able to contribute to the *quality* of decisional outputs. The contribution of the clerk unit in the context of criminal appeals reform is made manifest in the surge in tying a greater number of legal sources to the justices' decisions. Undeniably, the Court's legal research has been enhanced greatly.

7.4.3 *Institutionalism and Non-unanimous Decisions*

A robust clerk unit can exhibit yet another impact related to the fall in the number of merits cases for review. Inasmuch as the cases that are granted full review are those that have greater policy and/or legal consequence, they likely are more complex and thus given to more division among the justices.[18] Researchers have been specifically attracted to the abrupt increase in non-unanimous decisions in the 1990s. Bentsen writes that

> [t]he annual proportion of nonunanimous decisions was well below 10% in the late 1980s. Then, in the 1990s, the level of nonunanimous decisions increased to a record high of 29% in 1999 before plateauing at 20% in the early 21st century (Bentsen 2018a:196).[19]

Several factors have been tested to explain the occurrence of non-unanimous decisions on the Norwegian Supreme Court. None of them have included the role of clerks. Bentsen discusses and tests three sets of proximate forces that may account for variation in the rate of non-unanimous opinions: court leadership, composition of justices and docket control. Using 5,886 five-justice-panel cases decided between 1987 and 2014, Bentsen finds that only the presence of legal academics on the panel, whether the case addresses an issue related to ECHR, and the 1995 docket reform affecting criminal cases had effects across both types of non-unanimous opinions (i.e. concurrences and dissents), while the leadership of Smith only increased the likelihood of dissent.[20] Bentsen finds the strongest effect linked to the 1995 discretionary reform:

---

18 *See* Baum (1997) for the effect of complex cases on decisional behaviour.

19 To be sure, the rate of dissent is lower at the Norwegian Supreme Court than in, for example, the U.S. Supreme Court. Two institutional factors contribute to account for this difference: size and rotation. In the U.S. Supreme Court nine justices resolve all cases while in the Norwegian Supreme Court two parallel five-justice panels rotate on a five-week basis within a larger rotation of the 20 justices (*see* Chapter 2). Absent rotation of justices, which undermines development of stable factions (at the institutional level there are 15,504 combinations of five justices being drawn from a pool of 20 justices), size itself is an important factor since "the likelihood of disagreement grows with the size of the panel" (Epstein, Landes, and Posner 2013:267).

20 The third category of non-unanimous decisions – disagreements on sentencing in criminal cases and compensation in civil cases – was not treated separately in Bentsen's study.

> [t]he findings strongly suggest that the unleashing of time and discretion to focus on the more complex and contentious criminal issues following the reform in turn influenced the justices' propensity to author dissents and concurrences (Bentsen 2018a:209).

As we have argued in this chapter, this 1995 discretionary reform is part and parcel of the broader dimension of Supreme Court institutionalism. Moreover, an integral component of the Court's level of institutionalism, which includes criminal appeals reform, is the inception and steady growth and development of the law clerk unit. In keeping with findings to date regarding dissent rates, we hypothesize that as institutionalism increases, the percentage of non-unanimous votes rises correspondingly.

To test this hypothesis, we estimated a regression equation linking dissent rates to the level of institutionalism (see Table 7.7). After correcting for serial correlation, we find that the institutionalism factor score explains 31.7 per cent of the variance in dissent ($R^2 = .317$; $p = .000$). Figure 7.9 indicates that as institutionalism increases, a greater proportion of the Court's merits decisions are decided non-unanimously. Based on this regression equation we would predict that with institutionalism at its lowest level, the dissent rate would be expected to be approximately 7.2 per cent, and when institutionalism is at its maximum, the dissent rate jumps to 17.8 per cent.

Table 7.7 Regression of Merits Dissent Percentage on Institutionalism

Dissent[a]	Coeff.	SE
Institutionalism	3.737	0.818*
_cons	15.663	0.783
R^2	0.317	
N	47	

DV = Merits dissent percentage; DW = 2.324.

*$p < .001$.

[a] Corrected for serial correlation.

Data source: The Norwegian Supreme Court, Bentsen (2018) and the authors.

Figure 7.9 Non-unanimous decisions on institutionalism

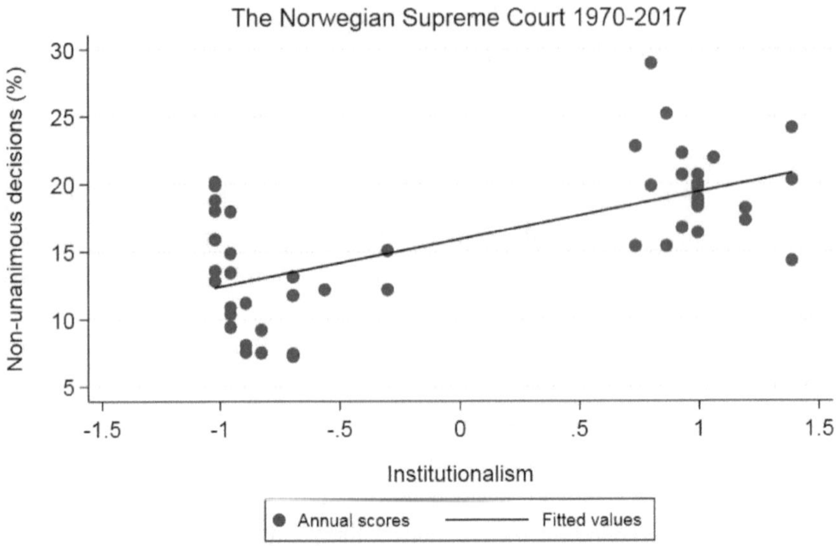

Source: Bentsen (2018), Doranoh and data compiled by the authors.

The growth of the law clerk unit, which, along with the criminal appeals reform, taps a broader institutionalism dimension, exhibits a major impact on much of the Supreme Court's decision-making. While the 'institutionalism' factor score bears no statistically significant relationship to the percentage of merits appeals granted, it is a powerful determinant of an increased emphasis on legal reasoning across a number of policy areas, including expropriation, labour issues, human rights and EEA-EU policy, as well as higher levels of dissent. Thus, not only has the clerk unit contributed to the Court's management of cases with which it deals, it also has enhanced the quality of the Supreme Court's deliberative process.

7.5 The Growth of the Law Clerk Unit Matters

Absent the secular discretionary reform in civil procedure law between 1981 and 2008 and the critical discretionary reform in criminal procedure law that was abruptly implemented in 1995 – both of which replaced the citizens' right to appeal with the Court's power to deny, thereby giving the Supreme Court complete discretionary power to choose the appeals it found most interesting and consequential – the growth of the clerk unit has been the most important institutional development at the Norwegian Supreme Court over the last six decades.

While the original impulse to greatly expand the clerk unit arose from the burdensome caseloads and the corresponding backlog of cases awaiting review, the sustained increase in the number of clerks is best understood as the long-term institutionalization of the Supreme Court. After all, when backlog pressure diminished in any given year, the number of clerks did not drop. Alternatively, we find that the number of clerks at time t is a function of the number of clerks at time t–1, as reflected in a nearly perfect correlation coefficient. Once committed to bolstering the legal professionalism of the Court, clerks became an indispensable form of staff support.

In any event, the observed growth of the clerk unit clearly was a goal that all justices could agree on even if they did not see eye to eye on the rationale for that goal. Some justices supported the addition of clerks to reduce the Court's backlog and its workload. Other justices sought out clerks in order to assist in the selection of the most consequential cases for review. Regardless of the point of view rationalizing the moves, the outcomes would be the same: Clerks were added; backlogs have been reduced; the justices have an overall lighter workload. In the end, the clerks are not only assisting the ASC in selecting cases for review, they are also assisting the justices in the complete decision-making process. The Court today has completed Chief Justice Carsten Smith's vision of transforming itself from a passive court of appeal to a proactive court of precedent.

Although our primary purpose here is to focus upon the development and impact of the clerk unit, we hasten to add that the number of clerks is not a stand-alone, independent force affecting the Supreme Court's performance. Instead, the size of the clerk unit is but one indicator of a larger phenomenon, namely institutionalization. As discussed earlier, institutionalism is a multifaceted concept and, in this instance, cannot be disentangled from the 1995 criminal appeals reform. In order to tap the larger dimension of institutionalism, we produced a simple factor score comprising the number of law clerks and the criminal appeals reform measure (0 if pre-reform and 1 if post-reform). Given that these two indicators are correlated at slightly greater than .9, it is nearly self-evident that each variable taps into just the sort of broad reform that Carsten Smith envisioned would yield a more professionalized court of precedent.

Documenting the rise and growth of the law clerk unit provides an interesting tale of institutional development, but does it matter? Our initial analysis suggests that it matters a good deal, certainly for the legal reasoning informing decisions, as well as the incidence of non-unanimous decisions. Yet, our hypothesis that increased institutionalism also would reduce the incidence of appeals granted is rejected, although the non-significant relationship runs in the direction expected.

Perhaps one of the most consequential ways in which institutionalism enhances the professional quality of Supreme Court deliberation is to be found in the increase in the citation of legal sources relevant to the cases adjudicated. We find that with the ever-increasing institutionalization of the Court, the number of legal sources accompanying expropriation and labour law cases climbs steadily over the period under study. Furthermore, institutionalism exhibits an extremely powerful impact upon the proportion of cases referencing human rights and EEA-EU provisions. Slashing the number of criminal cases heard on appeal and bulking up the clerk unit combine to materially improve the quality of the Court's policymaking. Moreover, an increasingly institutionalized Court hearing progressively more complex cases, accompanied by a greater number of legal principles, resulted in a pronounced increase in the percentage of non-unanimous decisions. Overall, the law clerk unit has had a profound impact upon the quality of the deliberative process by enhancing the Supreme Court's level of institutionalization.

7.6 APPENDIX A

We briefly entertained the possibility that the two indicators of institutionalism, criminal appeals reform and the growth of the clerk unit, might best be modelled as an interaction term. Figure 7A shows a plot of the interaction term computed by multiplying the number of clerks by a criminal appeals reform dichotomous variable (0 = pre-form; 1 = post-reform). Modelled this way, the expanding clerk unit does not contribute to Supreme Court institutionalization unless and until the criminal appeals reform dramatically slashes the number of cases brought to the Court in the post-reform era.

Figure 7.A Criminal Appeals Reform and Clerks Interaction Term

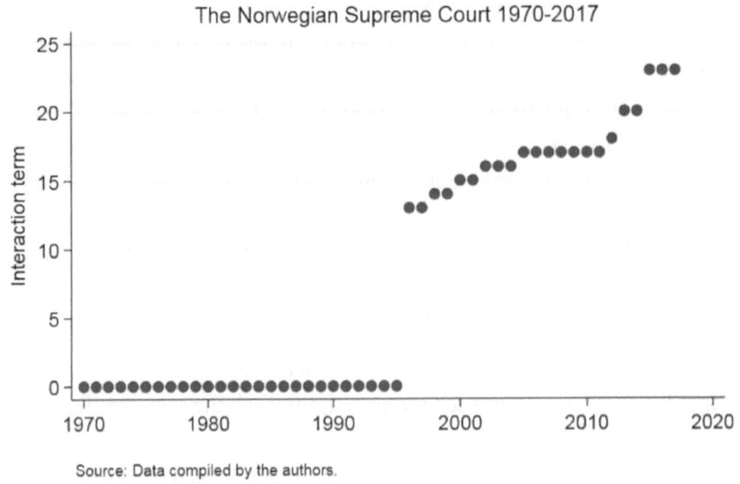

8 A Nordic Comparative Perspective

As we have seen, the Norwegian Supreme Court became a more consequential player in Norwegian politics with its transformation from a court of appeal to a court of precedent and control over its docket. We have claimed that this was possible due to the growth of the clerk unit. What, then, about the role of the clerks in the other Nordic Supreme Courts? The Swedish and Finnish Supreme Courts became courts of precedent by the 1970s and 1980s. The Danish Supreme Court took the same turn in the 1990s, together with the Norwegian Supreme Court. Iceland, however, followed suit only recently. Its transformation into a court of precedent became possible only after a three-tier court hierarchy was introduced in 2016, which became effective in 2018.

A comparison between the role of the clerks in the Nordic Supreme Courts has a twofold purpose.[1] First, our study of the Norwegian Supreme Court tells us that institutionalization is an important condition for the rise of a court of precedent. We can pursue the hypothesis that there is a link between the clerk unit and a court of precedent on a larger body of data. Second, we can explore the extent to which there is common trajectory across courts in the degree of institutionalization of the clerk unit over time. We hasten to add that neither attempt can be definitive. Lack of data prevents us from studying the development of the clerk unit in the other Nordic countries at the same level as we did in Norway. Nonetheless, our comparative analysis will serve as a partial, tentative application of our institutionalization hypothesis. At the very least, it will indicate whether our understanding tracks with more generalizable data or if our hypothesis needs to be reconsidered and retooled. Furthermore, we hope that this effort to expand the analytical scope beyond a single country will encourage other comparisons between the role of clerks in European Supreme Courts.

'Culture' is also a framework for the use of the interviews that are at the base of this chapter. In legal comparison, as with all comparisons, it is important that the information being analysed is similar across the comparative context. The first part of this chapter deals with the framework for clerking in the Nordic Supreme Courts. Here, we compare the number of clerks, their qualifications and specialization, and the organizational model for the clerk unit. This comparison is partly based on numbers and other factors that are easily comparable. Our goal is to ensure that we are comparing apples with apples, to employ an old phrase much used in the comparative context. Once we establish that the clerk unit's basic form, organizational structure, duties and specializations align, we turn to an

1 There is no uniform term used for the Supreme Court clerks in the Nordic countries. They are called *aðstoðarmaður dómara* in Iceland, *utredere* in Norway, *dommerfuldmægtig* in Denmark, *justitiesekreterare* in Sweden, and *oikeussihteereitä* and *esittelijäneuvoksia/ justitiesekreterar* and *referendarieråd* in Finland.

examination of how the clerks actually work. Accordingly, a central component of our interview schedule was to query the clerks about their work tasks and how they performed them. During the interviews, we allowed the interviewees to discuss the details of their work according to their own conversational preferences. That is, the clerks related the details of their work responsibilities in whatever order and using whatever categories they thought best rather than us guiding the interview through a predetermined index of tasks and responsibilities. Following this approach allows us not only to obtain important information on the functions and performance of the different clerk units but also to get a glimpse of the operating culture in a given Court.

For instance, when Guðlaug Jónasdóttir noted that the clerks in the Icelandic Supreme Court rarely alter or elaborate the party's arguments in their memoranda to the reviewing justices, we did not ask her for any specific figures on the addition of legal sources. Rather than dry numeric data, the important point we gleaned was that the clerks (and presumably the Court) perceived that the advocates before the Icelandic Supreme Court provide the justices with documents of sufficient quality that it is unnecessary for the clerks to augment them. This is very different from the other Nordic Supreme Courts and probably can be explained by the fact that the Icelandic Supreme Court is in the very first phase of being a court of precedent.

The other Nordic Supreme Courts, in contrast, have been courts of precedent for at least two decades. They and their clerks recognize that, as a court of precedent, it cannot be left to the parties' lawyers to do the crucial work of identifying and collecting the relevant legal arguments essential to make new law through precedent. Of particular import here is that since we did not ask clerks in the other Nordic Courts about the incidence of legal arguments they added to a case, had we done so in the Icelandic interview, we might have begun a comparison of apples with oranges. Nevertheless, our more conversational and unstructured interview strategy provided us with fruits we might otherwise have missed (Holvast 2016:11). This is the cultural bit of this analysis.

8.1 The Nordic Legal Family

The Nordic countries are – from west to east – Iceland, Norway, Denmark, Sweden and Finland. Although collectively referred to as 'Nordic' (Knutsen 2017), there are many differences between them in terms of crucial factors such as geography, population size, politics, economic system and history. It might be claimed that Iceland – with a population of nearly 350,000, an economy based on fishing, and a close political association with the United States – has little in common with Finland, with a population nearly 16 times larger, an economy dominated by forestry and a long border with the West's Cold War adversary, the Soviet Union (Russia).

In a legal context there are two important differences between the Nordic countries. First, Sweden and Finland have administrative courts, which is typical throughout Europe; Iceland, Norway and Denmark, however, do not follow this structure. This difference is due largely to the fact that the Danish-Norwegian kingdom, of which Iceland was a part, never developed administrative courts, while Sweden did, and Finland was a part of the Swedish state. Second, the influence of American legal science in general was larger in the western portion of the Nordic countries, while in the eastern portion, German legal science predominated, especially after the Second World War.

These internal differences, however, pale in comparison to the unifying factors. This is why the legal system in the Nordic countries often is regarded as a separate family of law next to the common and civil law families in Europe (Backer 2014:106; Husa, Nuotio, and Pihlajamäki 2007; Nylund 2010). Important common features of the Nordic countries include rather constant national borders; predominantly Lutheran and rural societies with a low degree of professionalization; a long tradition of governance through legislation; early development of a centralized, bureaucratic state; and high levels of public trust. Typically, the Nordic countries are perceived as homogenous. Although this can be disputed, it is important that within the Nordic countries themselves society is both seen and experienced as homogenous. Citizens have taken pride in it and perceive themselves as different due to it. Most importantly, the Nordic countries remain aligned as a distinct bloc in Europe (Kershaw 2019). The Nordic council, with members from the different Nordic parliaments, was formed in 1952. Two years later, the Nordic passport union and free labour mobility went into effect. And it bears noting that with respect to the legal landscape, connections across the Nordic states had been ongoing since the late nineteenth century. Beginning in 1872, Nordic lawyers were meeting at three-year intervals, and this enabled extensive legal cooperation and common Nordic legislation throughout the twentieth century (Nylund and Sunde 2018:212; Sunde 2017:54-58).

8.2 Courts of Precedent

Just around the First World War, procedural reforms of the legal system were undertaken in all the Nordic countries. Only Sweden, however, decided to solve the problem of backlogged cases by making its Supreme Court a court of precedent; this change was made in 1915. The transformation was relatively short-lived. By 1942 the operating nature of the Swedish Supreme Court was returned to that of a court of appeal, bringing it back into line with the other Nordic Supreme Courts. In 1969 the Swedes were preparing to change their Supreme Court yet again, reinstituting the 1915 reform of the Court to a court of precedent. Sweden's 1969 reforms did not go unnoticed. Finland discussed making a similar change to its High Court. In Denmark there was also a move towards empowering its Court to reject appeals if they did not have importance beyond the case in question.

At the 1969 Nordic Meeting for Lawyers in Oslo, a topic of discussion among the several hundred Nordic lawyers present had been law-making outside the legislative process. To put it simply, then, throughout the last third of the twentieth century, the concept of Supreme Courts as courts of precedent was being considered, although it was not always at the core of legal discussion. One reason was the procedural reform in Sweden, where preparations for the transformation of the Swedish Supreme Court from a court of appeal to a court of precedent were being made. Indeed, in Sweden the transformation of its Supreme Court had been an ongoing discussion and theme for procedural reforms throughout the entire century. Carsten Smith, participating at the Nordic Meeting for Lawyers in Oslo in 1969, observed all of this and used these developments as arguments for a similar reform in Norway in his speech in Tromsø in 1974 (Sunde 2015a:258, and Chapter 1 in this book).

By 1987, a 1971 procedural reform in Sweden had turned its Supreme Court, for the third and last time, into a court of precedent. (An important adjustment with a new reform to the Court took place in 1981.) In Finland the change of its Court to a court of precedent was initiated with a procedural reform in 1979 and in force from 1980. In Norway Carsten Smith, whose vision for the Supreme Court as a court of precedent had been so harshly rejected in 1974 (see Chapter 1), had sat on the Supreme Court as an interim justice, and Smith was present at the Helsinki meeting in 1987. There, he could observe how Hans Michelsen, senior justice on the Norwegian Supreme Court and lecturer in civil procedure at the Faculty of Law in Oslo, elegantly ridiculed the role of the Swedish and Finnish Supreme Courts. Michelsen probably bent forward, stretching his neck and lifting both his hands up in the air, gesticulating and looking much like a lion ready to attack its prey – a countenance he often adopted when arguing with force and enthusiasm. This time, however, the prey was out of reach. The Swedish and Finnish High Courts as courts of precedent would not easily be dismembered. Their transformation would serve as a useful model for the Norwegian experience. Michelsen should have known as much (Sunde 2015a:259-261).

The Norwegian Supreme Court on which Michelsen sat was experiencing a backlog crisis (see Chapter 3) and rejected more and more cases on the grounds that they bore no importance beyond the case itself. Moreover, the clerk unit was slowly growing, thereby making the transformation that had taken place in Sweden and Finland possible in Norway as well. (A similar transformation was taking place at about the same time in Denmark.) Only in Iceland did the Supreme Court's legal and political role remain frozen; it continued to operate as a court of appeal in a two-tier system for three decades following the 1987 Helsinki Meeting of Nordic Lawyers.

With this as context, then, what are the similarities and differences between the clerk units across the Nordic Supreme Courts? Table 8.1 juxtaposes the information on the Norwegian clerks with those of their Nordic counterparts and summarizes our comparative discussion of the clerk units, the clerk's gatekeeping tasks and their judgment tasks in the five Nordic countries.

Table 8.1 Nordic Clerks Compared

	Iceland	Norway	Denmark	Sweden	Finland
Clerk Unit					
Size	5	23	12	30	27
Organization	Common Pool	Common Pool	Common Pool	Common Pool	1 Pool Civil (12); 1 Pool Criminal (15)
Qualifications	Law degree; prior work experience expected	Law degree; prior work experience expected	Law degree; prior work experience expected	Law degree[a]	Law degree; prior work experience expected
Specialization	No	Informal	No	Yes[b]	Yes[c]
Tenure	Life	Single 7-year contract	Life, but common to transfer across courts	4-year contracts with two 2-year extensions possible	Life or fixed term contracts; more experienced judges hired on 5-year contracts
Gatekeeping Tasks					
Appeals Processed	All	All	Only extraordinary appeals are treated by the Court and its clerks	All	All
Written Memo	Yes	Yes	Yes, and oral presentation	Yes	Yes
Add Legal Arguments	Yes	Yes	Yes	Yes	Yes
Contact with Parties	Contact respondent for comments	Yes	Yes, one round of comments for extraordinary appeal. Two rounds of comments on cases granted leave of appeal	Yes (but only clarifying formalities)	No

	Iceland	Norway	Denmark	Sweden	Finland
Contact with Justices	Yes	Yes	Yes	Yes	Yes
Judgment Tasks					
Present at Deliberations	No	Yes	Yes	Yes	Yes
Voice/Vote	No	No	No	No	Yes
Draft part of Judgment	Yes	Increasingly yes	Yes	Yes	Yes
Proof Text/Sources	Yes	Yes	Yes	Yes	Yes

Data compiled by the authors.

[a] Law degree, 2 years as a law clerk in a district court, 1 year as a legal clerk in an appeal court, 2 years as a junior judge in a district court, 1 year as acting associate judge in an appeal court. (Drafting law clerk: 2 years as a law clerk in a district court.)

[b] Yes: (3) land and environmental law; (2) intellectual property; (3) to complex and/or consequential cases.

[c] Yes: one group civil and one group criminal.

8.3 The Clerking Framework

8.3.1 The Number of Clerks

With only 20 justices, the Norwegian Supreme Court is rather small in a European context, although it is the largest of the Nordic High Courts (Sunde 2017:67-68). As we discussed in Chapter 3, the justices are very reluctant to add to their numbers for fear of the deleterious effect such an addition would have on the Court's capacity to fulfil its role as a unifier of law. Rather than adding justices, then, the Court has expanded its clerk unit. Reluctance to increase the number of justices and/or expanding the clerk unit has been a common theme across the Nordic Supreme Courts. When transforming the Swedish and Finnish Supreme Courts into courts of precedent in the 1970s and 1980s, the aim was not to reduce backlogs alone but also to reduce the number of justices on the Supreme Court. In Sweden the number of ordinary justices was reduced from 25 to 16; in Finland, from 25 to 19. In Denmark there are 18 justices, and in Iceland, there are only 9 justices and the number will be reduced to 7.[2]

In general, clerks outnumber the justices in the Nordic Supreme Courts. In Norway there are 23 clerks and 20 justices – or 1.1 clerks per justice. At the time of the interviews

2 Legislation has already been passed reducing the number of justices from nine to seven, but it will take effect as the justices retire from the court.

for this book there were five clerks and eight justices on the Icelandic Court – 0.6 clerk per justice. With its transformation to a court of precedent, the Court has decided to operate with four clerks only during the time it takes to reduce the number of justices. This means that the relationship between clerks and justices will remain unchanged. In Denmark there are 12 clerks and 18 justices, which results in the same relationship between the number of justices and clerks as in Iceland. In Sweden there are 30 clerks and 16 justices on the Court, which results in 1.9 clerks per justice. In Finland there are 1.4 clerks per justice (27 clerks and 19 justices). These relative distributions indicate that those Courts that have striven hardest to keep the number of justices down have the largest number of clerks per justice. We also can conclude that the Courts that first were transformed from courts of appeal to courts of precedent have the largest number of clerks.

The future development of the Icelandic clerk unit will be interesting to observe. In the interview the clerk reported that when she left the Court in the fall of 2018, she would not be replaced because the Supreme Court anticipated that the Court's workload would lessen significantly once an Icelandic Court of Appeal went into operation in 2018, thereby giving Iceland a three-tier court hierarchy for the first time since 1920 (Sunde 2017:58-59).

The number of cases heard and decided on their merits has dropped significantly in all the Nordic Supreme Courts with their transformations from a court of appeal to a court of precedent. At the same time, the number of clerks has risen (a pattern we described in detail for Norway). Accordingly, before its reform, the Icelandic Supreme Court decided 264 civil cases and 92 criminal cases. Five clerks served the Court, which gives a relation of 71 cases per clerk annually. In 2016 (the same year as the Icelandic reform) the Norwegian Court decided 108 cases with the assistance of 20 clerks, which gives a relation of 5.4 cases per clerk. In 2016 in Denmark, 12 clerks served the Court, and 123 cases were decided (10 cases per clerk). The figures for Sweden and Finland are 104 cases decided and 30 clerks and 135 precedent cases decided and 27 clerks, respectively – resulting in 3.5 and 5 cases per clerk for each Court.[3]

The work tasks of the clerks in the Nordic Supreme Courts vary substantially – a point we will take up in more detail later in this chapter – hence the comparison is partly between apples and oranges. Not at least since a substantial part of a court of precedent's workload is appeal selection. However, the figures show that a decrease in the number of cases decided does not lead to a decrease in the clerk unit unless that is a deliberate policy. The continuous call for more clerks in the Norwegian Supreme Court, with a continuous fall in the number of cases decided and no large increase in appeals to the court, underlines this conclusion.

---

3 The number of cases is taken from Nylund and Sunde (2018:209, 211).

8.3.2 A Pool of Clerks and Specialization

As we have seen, Smith envisioned a system of personal clerks in the Norwegian Supreme Court when he became chief justice in 1991. At that time there were too few clerks for such a system, and the growth of the number of clerks was too slow for a system of personal clerks to develop; it was not until 2013 that the number of clerks matched the number of justices. Instead, the clerk unit remained a pool of clerks. This is typical across the Nordic states. In Sweden, a clerk pool is effectively an institutional necessity. Only 20 of the clerks actually work in Stockholm, the capital city where the High Court sits. The other ten clerks have their workplaces in Gothenburg and Malmö, only travelling to Stockholm and the Court to attend meetings.

This general system of a pool of clerks operates with some slightly different features in Finland and Denmark. In Finland, there is a pool of 12 clerks for the civil division and 15 clerks for the criminal division[4]; thus, there are two clerk pools in the Finnish Supreme Court. In Denmark the Court's procedure is that the two most junior justices in both chambers (i.e. four justices in total) are responsible for summarizing one-half of the cases being reviewed in terms of their facts and relevant law. Each of these justices is assigned a clerk who has at least one year of experience to assist them in this laborious task (Dahl 2014:46). The most junior justices have this duty for up to four years, but the individual clerks who are assigned to them serve for only six months and then are replaced. The other half of the cases that each chamber decides are assigned to more experienced justices, who in turn are assigned a clerk to assist them on each case. The Appeals Selection Committee (ASC) has a presiding justice or chair who is responsible for making case assignments. These justices have a clerk who serves as a secretary for the Committee to assist him or her during the two-year period they possess this office. Hence, in Denmark there is a touch of personal clerks, but it is limited in time and the clerks are taken from and returned to the general pool of clerks.

Although there is a pool of clerks, this does not preclude a system of some specialization among the clerks. As we have seen, in Norway the Supreme Court is a generalized court that deals with civil, criminal, administrative and constitutional cases in rotating decisional panels. This is the general rule in the Nordic countries, even though the sequences for the rotation of chambers vary. The major difference across the five nations is that Sweden and Finland have administrative courts; consequently, the Swedish and Finnish Supreme Courts do not handle administrative cases. On the one hand, there might be an advantage to the presence of specialized clerks working with generalist justices. On the other hand, this could cause a knowledge imbalance in the Court in favour of the clerks. It is the justices,

4 As in other European countries, the Finnish Supreme Court experienced a decline in appeals in civil cases, and the number of clerks in the civil division will probably be reduced.

and not the clerks, who enjoy the protection that the principle of independence of the judiciary renders and who are subject to the scrutiny springing from the principle of accountability.[5]

In Norway, Iceland and Denmark there are no formal specializations among the clerks, and they must – as is true for the justices – be able to deal with all kinds of cases. In Finland, some sort of specialization derives from the fact that there are separate pools of clerks for the civil and criminal chambers.[6] The clerks in each division are headed by a chief referendary. It is only in the Swedish Supreme Court that we find actual specialization among clerks. Here, three clerks are assigned to the cases concerning environmental law, two clerks to cases dealing with intellectual property law and yet another three clerks are assigned to what are considered complex and comprehensive cases. When such a specialized job is vacant, the experienced clerks in the Court can apply to fill the vacancy. Clerks with such a specialization enjoy an increased salary.

Again, we can conclude that the specialization among the clerks has been most pronounced in the Nordic Supreme Courts that transformed earliest from courts of appeal to courts of precedent. Moreover, these Courts have the largest clerking unit and a rather small number of justices. We cannot conclude, but we can speculate, whether this is a development that will take place if there is no deliberate policy creating a barrier.

8.3.3 *Qualification Criteria*

As we have seen, there are no other formal qualification criteria for clerks in the Norwegian Supreme Court other than a law degree. Nonetheless, it has become a norm that clerks have previous legal work experience (see Chapter 6). The situation is quite similar in Iceland; the formal qualification criterion for a law clerk in the Supreme Court is simply possession of a law degree, while legal work experience is an informal criterion. Only recently has the position been advertised. Earlier, the practice was that justices asked clerks and other referents for potential candidates, who were then selected for the clerk position. Often the justices asked clerks and other acquaintances for potential candidates, who were then selected for the clerk position. Only recently has it become more normal that a clerk position is advertised.

Like Norway and Iceland, the only formal qualification criterion for clerks in the Danish Supreme Court is a law degree. As of the writing of this book, there are no clerks who came to the Court directly from law school. Indeed, currently, every clerk has at least

5 It is important to keep in mind that the clerks in the Danish and Finnish Supreme Courts have life tenure, which renders the clerks a large degree of independence.

6 In the Finnish Supreme Court there is also voluntary specialization among the clerks within the chambers as to types of cases in order to promote in-depth competence among the clerks in specific areas of law.

four years of work experience with the Ministry of Justice, as clerks in a lower court, or with similar prestigious workplaces. The clerks have life tenure. However, they are employed by the Danish Court Administration, which can move clerks from the Supreme Court to other courts. This transfer across courts is common; it is usual to clerk in the Supreme Court for two to three years (Dahl 2014:42).

As we have seen, there are about 30 clerks in the Swedish Supreme Court. However, that is not the whole story. These are only the judge-referees (*justitiesekreterare*), the original clerks in the Court.[7] Recently another group of clerks, six to seven law clerks (*beredningsjurist*), has been added to the lot and can be viewed as a kind of clerk assistants.[8] The formal qualification criterion for both kinds of clerks is a law degree. The actual criteria are different for the two groups of clerks. A law clerk must have completed the two-year service as a clerk in a district court (*notarie*), while the judge-referees must complete one year as a clerk in a court of appeal, two years of training as a judge in a district court and finally one year of training as a judge in a court of appeal. For the time being, about two-thirds of the judge-referees in the Swedish Supreme Court have gained more experience before taking on clerk position in the Court. Judge-referees are hired on four-year contracts and are eligible for a pair of two-year extensions.[9]

In Finland, the clerks must have a law degree. There is no formal requirement as to the length of work experience, but many of the clerks have previously worked as a clerk in an appeal court or as a district court judge and may have five to 15 years of relevant work experience. More than half of the clerks have permanent tenure. Some of the upper-level clerks are appointed to their position for a period of five years. This practice is one way to recruit the more experienced lawyers – appeal court or district court judges, university lecturers or professors – to the court. It should be noted that several clerks have also been promoted to justices although more often the clerk will hold some other position elsewhere before being nominated to justiceship. Even though a couple of clerks in the Finnish Supreme Court are now in their fifties and may retire from their current office, the average period for staying at the court is four to eight years.

In Sweden, and to some extent in Finland, there is an informal criterion that the clerks have training in court. The law clerks need only have service as a law clerk in a district court, while a judge-referee must have training at the level of the appeal court. Again, the clerking framework in Sweden and Finland is different from that in Iceland, Norway and Denmark, which have shorter histories of Supreme Courts as courts of precedent.

7 That is why we in this chapter mean a judge-referee when speaking of a "clerk" in the Swedish Supreme Court.

8 The law clerks were introduced in 2016.

9 It is not normal to have contract extensions.

8.4 The Task of the Clerks

As we have seen, the clerk unit in the Norwegian Supreme Court expanded as a result of a backlog crisis, which largely was solved by limiting access to the Court. Indeed, it was assisting in the crucial gatekeeping task that was understood to be *the* role of the Norwegian clerk unit, at least until recently. Clerks play a role in gatekeeping in all the Nordic Supreme Courts. But gatekeeping is not the only task they perform. Indeed, when it comes to the duties of the clerks, there is quite a bit of variation.

8.4.1 Iceland

In Iceland the clerks spend much of their time preparing cases for the justices in chamber. It is common for two clerks to work on procedural cases and two clerks to work on the cases concerning substantive law. When a clerk is assigned to a case, he or she is responsible for sending it to the respondent for comments. If deemed necessary, the clerk can on rare occasions send the case to both the petitioner and respondent for a further round of comments. After comments are received, the clerk would write a memo that summarizes the facts and elaborates on the law. The clerks also compose a conclusion that suggests how the question of appeal should be answered. After the Court was made a court of precedent, a new system was tested where the clerk instead of writing a memo would discuss the case with the justices and draft a conclusion on the appeal question.

If the case is granted leave for appeal, the clerk will look at it again two to three weeks before the oral hearing. Occasionally, the parties add new information, or the justice in charge of the case might also ask the clerk to examine special legal questions. If either of these occur, it is necessary for the clerk to review the case again and write an updated summary. This practice continued after the Court became a court of precedent, but the practice will be reviewed as the Court gains more experience. Historically, three less experienced justices decided legally simple cases, while one to five more experienced justices decided more complicated cases. As a court of precedent, the Icelandic Court will only have one chamber consisting of five justices deciding cases.

After the case is decided in chamber, the justice writing the decision might ask a clerk for a draft of the decision. Not all justices do so, and some justices only ask for a draft of the facts. The practice varies among the justices in the Icelandic Supreme Court. The clerks might also be asked to assist a justice writing a dissenting opinion. However, dissenting opinions are rare; consequently, this is a rather unusual task for the clerks. Clerks also assist in proofreading the final decision and collect the references to legal sources.

Lunch is not overly organized in the Icelandic Supreme Court, but at times the clerks eat lunch with the justices. This fits in well with the general informality characterizing clerking in the Court. All in all, the clerks in the Icelandic Supreme Court appear as much as assistants as members of a pool of clerks. The clerks do not have formal meetings, unlike their Norwegian counterparts. Nor do they have their own organizational hierarchy, and there are no formal memoranda written. Instead, the clerks often have one-on-one conversations with fellow clerks and the justices. This less institutionalized and somewhat informal character of the clerkship might be due to the fact that the Court is only on the verge of transformation from a court of appeal to a court of precedent. Clerking is still about getting the work done and deciding each case efficiently, rather than making law through precedential decisions. However, a Court with eight justices and five clerks, aiming to soon become a Court of seven justices and four clerks (perhaps even less), may not become overly formal under any circumstance. This can serve as a reminder that there are factors other than the character of the Court that determine the nature of the clerkship at the Court.

8.4.2 Denmark

In Denmark a separate body – the Appeals Permission Board (*Procesbevillingsnævnet*) – has decided the question of whether an appeal merits review for both the appeal court and the Supreme Court since 1996 (Skiple, McKenzie, and Bentsen 2017). A Supreme Court justice heads this body, with an appeal court judge, a city court judge, a professor and an advocate constituting the remaining members. The Appeals Permission Board has its own clerk unit, larger than the one at the Supreme Court.[10] At the Supreme Court, the clerks serve as gatekeepers primarily by preparing appeals in extraordinary cases, typically appeals not submitted in due time. The clerk unit in the Danish Supreme Court, therefore, is primarily engaged in the actual decision-making process.

When the Appeals Permission Board grants appeal to a case, the clerk who serves as the secretary for the Appeals Committee logs the case into the computer system. If the case concerns procedural law, the procedure is normally all written. The clerk sends the case to the parties' lawyers for two rounds of comments. The clerk then writes a memo to the justices in chamber. A memo of five half pages would be short; a memo of 50 half pages would be long. The typical memo ranges from 12 to 15 half pages. These memoranda deal with facts and the law, include legal reasoning and a suggested conclusion. There is no fixed time for when a memo must be delivered to the justices, but the clerks strive to

10 https://www.domstol.dk/PROCESBEVILLINGSNAEVNET/OMPROCESBEVILLINGSNAEVNET/MEDARBEJDEREISEKRETARIATET/Pages/default.aspx (last accessed 12 August 2019). Those entitled 'fuldmægtig' are counted as clerks.

complete a memo within three months; the typical amount of time required is one month.[11] The clerk also will draft a decision. Cases are decided by one, three, five or even seven justices in very complicated cases.[12]

If it is a case on substantive law, the chair and the clerk begin the process with a telephone meeting with the parties' lawyers to discuss procedural questions, including whether a chamber of five or seven justices would be most appropriate when deciding the case. The chair's clerk will then write a short recommendation on these procedural questions. This task is assigned to a separate clerk if the matter is complicated and time consuming. A clerk will also take statements from witnesses before the oral hearing. This material is then given to the justice assigned to the case and his or her clerk, and they will have a meeting on the case where the clerk might be asked to examine specific legal questions. The clerk might be asked to write a draft decision that comprises the introduction and a summary of the facts. Most justices, however, will write the legal reasoning themselves (Dahl 2014:48). The clerk does not write a memo but will give an oral presentation of the case to the justice. During the deliberations after the oral hearing, the clerk assisting the justice assigned to the case takes notes.[13]

Of the 12 clerks in the Danish Supreme Court, four clerks also clerk for the Complaint Court (*Den Særlige Klageret*), which deals with complaints concerning judges in Danish Courts, including courts on the Faroes Islands and Greenland.

The clerks and justices eat lunch at the same time, but in different rooms. This fits well with the general image of the clerk as an assistant to the justices, with a very different role from the justices in the Court – much like in Norway. (The Norwegian clerks visited Denmark in 2017.) The tasks of the clerks in the Danish Supreme Court vary with the procedural form. Hence, at first glance, clerking in this Court looks very different from clerking in the Norwegian and Icelandic Supreme Courts. However, the clerks are involved in preparing the cases for decision and in drafting decisions as they are in Iceland and – when it comes to drafting decisions – to an increased degree in Norway. The memoranda written in procedural cases are longer than what in general is written in Iceland but not in Norway. No memo is written in cases on substantive law; only an oral presentation is given.

11 If a memo is not complete within three months, the chair's clerk will contact he clerk in question to see how the matter can be solved.

12 Cases concerning procedural law subject to oral procedure are decided by the five justices and a clerk serves as a referent during the oral hearing. Cases arriving in the Court on extraordinary appeal – an overdue appeal or a request for reopening a case – have only one round of comments from the lawyers; the memo is normally shorter, and the case is decided by the chair of the ASC alone.

13 For about ten years the deliberations have also been recorded.

8.4.3 *Sweden*

The law clerks in the Swedish Supreme Court have fewer qualifications than the judge-referees and thus are assigned less demanding tasks – mainly in the gatekeeping process. Appeals are filed at the Supreme Court at the Registrar's office. Then the appeals are allocated to one of the two drafting units where it is decided whether a law clerk or a judge-referee will handle the case.[14] The vast majority of the several thousand appeals to the Supreme Court are denied leave to appeal. In many cases it is obvious that the appeal will not be successful, and these cases are dealt with by the law clerks. Judge-referees take those cases that initially appear to have a good chance of being granted appeal. Comments from the parties' lawyers are not received before the question of appeal is decided – as in Iceland and Denmark.[15] The clerk writes a first memo after having read all the documents, often adding legal arguments. The aim of the examination of the case is to see if it has the potential to become precedent, or if there has been a miscarriage of justice.

Along with suggesting a conclusion in the memo, the clerk also decides if the question of appeal should be heard by one, three or five justices. The reason the clerk performs this role is that if the clerk finds that the appeal should not be granted, it is a one-justice case. Should the justice later conclude otherwise, two more justices will have to be brought in to decide the case. (A single justice can only deny a leave to appeal.) A three-justice panel can decide in favour of the petitioning party with a simple majority.[16] Five-justice panels are only used in the most complicated cases.

For the one-justice cases the clerk writes a rather short memo on three to ten pages. No formal layout is used, and the memo is given to the justice on paper with copies of the relevant legal sources. If the case is to be decided by a three- or five-justice panel, the memo will be on ten pages or more; a formal layout is used, and it is distributed to the justices electronically with attachments. The clerk also writes a draft of the decision before the three or five justices meet. At the meeting, the clerk is present. The clerk does not participate in the deliberations but might be asked to clarify the memo. Clerks stationed in Gothenburg or Malmö will participate via a video link.

If leave of appeal is granted, the respondent is asked to comment on the case, and afterwards there is a round of comments from both parties' lawyers.[17] The memo is often written by the same clerk who prepared the case for appeal selection. This time the memo

14 For an outline of the case handling process in the Swedish Supreme Court, *see* Høgsta Domstolen (2019:19-29).

15 We are then talking of the extraordinary appeals sent directly to the Danish Supreme Court.

16 Dissents are rare and not recorded.

17 This is not the case with the Other Cases (*øvrige mål*), which are cases on bankruptcy, debt restructuring, procedural questions in ongoing cases and in the Extraordinary Cases (*extraodinära mål*), which are cases of evidence error, trial error or overdue appeal.

will often be between 30 and 40 pages with several attachments. Normally, the memo takes three weeks to write. The memo is sent to the justices two weeks before they meet to decide the case. Here they will also have a draft of a suggested decision. Clerks stationed in Gothenburg or Malmö will be personally present in the deliberations in a five-justice case.[18]

The clerks and justices do not eat lunch together. Indeed, we might have expected clerks and justices to have lunch together because their work intersects so consistently. The clerks are even present during the deliberations and might speak. Overall, the number of clerks, their assistants, their specialization and the actual qualification criteria suggest that clerks in the Swedish Supreme Court are not there just to help the justices to get the work done but to increase the quality of the precedent-making process. This impression is confirmed by the actual work tasks of the clerks. Cases with and without the potential of becoming precedent are immediately steered into two different tracks in the Court. The allocation of resources continues to favour the precedent cases. The clerks write long memoranda. The same clerk follows the case from beginning to end, and clerks are even present in the deliberations and might speak.

8.4.4 *Finland*

In the Finnish Supreme Court, the chief referendary in each of the two divisions browses through new cases to assign the workload evenly among the clerks of the chamber and to determine at the outset which cases may have the potential to be a precedent-setting case. These cases are then taken to a secretary, who writes the introduction for a memo with the basic information. The case and the draft of the memo are then given to a clerk, who makes an independent evaluation of the case with an eye towards the potential for precedent. The greater the potential, the more urgent the case is, and it is given priority accordingly. The clerk then completes what often is six- to ten-page memo for the leave to appeal decision. In this memo the clerk always adds legal arguments and writes a suggested conclusion.

The cases found clearly to have no precedent potential will be decided by one justice together with the clerk, while the other cases will predominantly be decided by two justices and the clerk. In all cases justices vote; the clerk also votes. The clerk's vote, however, cannot be decisive when there is a draw. If the two justices cannot agree on the leave to appeal, a third justice will join the panel.[19] Clerks rarely dissent in leave to appeal cases, but it does happen at least once a year.

---

18 There are relatively few cases with oral proceeding in the Swedish Supreme Court. When these occur, a clerk is present and handles the technical equipment.

19 This happens only a couple of times every year.

If leave of appeal is granted, the respondent is informed and is given one month to comment on the case. Usually, there are no further rounds of comments, which is different from the procedure in the other Nordic Supreme Courts.[20] The same clerk who prepared the case for the appeal selection will prepare the case for the final decision. The memo will be expanded considerably, as in Sweden. In a small case composing the memo will take a week. In a large case three to four weeks is the norm, but up to five weeks might be taken by the clerk to finish the memo. Each clerk can write between two to ten such memoranda a year, and five is typical.

When the case is decided on the merits, the clerk has a vote and may give a dissenting opinion, just as he or she did on the question concerning the leave of appeal. The clerk's vote cannot be decisive in minimum winning decisions. The clerk speaks during the deliberations but only after the chair, who presents the case to the panel of justices. The same procedure for deliberations is applied in the vast majority of cases with written procedure and the few cases with oral procedure. If there is consensus, the suggested draft for a conclusion is used. If there is dissent, the dissenting justice or justices write the dissenting opinion, while the clerk writes the majority opinion as long at the clerk votes with the majority. All opinions in the precedent are published, including the one by the clerk.

The Finnish Supreme Court handles extraordinary appeals like the Danish and Swedish Supreme Courts. Such cases are decided by one justice and one clerk, or three justices and one clerk when dismissing the appeal. Five justices and one clerk decide the case when ruling in favour of the appellant.

All Supreme Court employees have lunch together. This fits well with the image of the Finnish Supreme Court as a precedent factory more than a court with a strict hierarchy. In the Finnish Supreme Court the clerks not only help the justices process the workload, they also assist the justices when making precedents and hence increasing the quality of the law-making process. The clerks even participate in this process with a vote at the final stage. That the clerks vote in the merits decision process can be seen as a consequence of the work the clerks have put into the case – clerks get a thorough understanding of the case when writing the lengthy memo. However, this is again a consequence of the Court's transformation from a court of appeal to a court of precedent that began in the early 1980s. This transformation was much inspired by the procedural reforms in Sweden from 1971 on.

20 The is also only one round of comments in extraordinary appeals handled by the Danish Supreme Court, but then both parties get a chance to give their comments.

8.5 Conclusion

When performing a legal comparison between the Nordic countries, often the west Nordic countries – Iceland, Norway and Denmark – group together on one hand, and the east Nordic countries – Sweden and Finland – on the other. This is due to the legal commonalities these countries developed during the many centuries they were either part of the Danish-Norwegian or the Swedish realm. The fact that you find administrative courts in Sweden and Finland, and not in Iceland, Norway and Denmark, largely is the result of historical forces. However, the long-term history does not offer much explanatory leverage in this study, while the short-term history does.

At the same time, even if there are good reasons to conclude that there is a strong relationship between the transformation from a court of appeal to a court of precedent, we should be aware that each of these Courts has a history and operates within a legal culture with its own traits and context. History and culture must also have played a role in shaping the organizational structures of the Courts we have examined, including the institutional variations of the clerk units and the clerks' gatekeeping tasks that we detailed in Table 8.1 and discussed in the chapter. However, the purpose of this study was not to explore the organizational structures in full, but to find indications that our hypothesis of a relationship between the transformation from a court of appeal to a court of precedent and the clerking unit has some traction. This we have done.

9 Conclusion: Clerks Count, Justices Decide

The central focus of this book is the development of the Norwegian Supreme Court's law clerk unit, which should be understood in the context of the concerted effort to thrust the Court into a more active role in shaping public policy. The sustained increase in the number of clerks (and their expanding responsibilities) can be best understood as an integral part of the systematic institutionalization of the Supreme Court. 'Institutionalization', McGuire (2004:129-131) informs us, "refers to the development of a regularized system of policy making". Institutionalization can be measured by *differentiation*, the degree to which an organization is a well-defined entity in the political system; *durability*, an organization's capacity to persist and pursue its institutional goals even in the face of appreciable environmental change; and *autonomy*, the ability to make decisions "without dictation from outside actors" (Keohane 1969:862).

9.1 Building a More Powerful Court

The general process of institutionalizing the Norwegian Supreme Court discussed throughout the book is depicted in Figure 9.1. Two paths are available through which greater institutionalization and also political power can be achieved. The figure can be read like a simplified flow diagram in which one can proceed from the bottom left corner with a determination as to whether the Court seeks added political clout. Given Carsten Smith's active interest in empowering the Supreme Court, first as law professor and later as chief justice, the answer to that question is a resounding 'yes'. Otherwise, the status quo, characterized by a passive court of appeal rather than a proactive court of precedent, would prevail.

Figure 9.1 A More Powerful Court

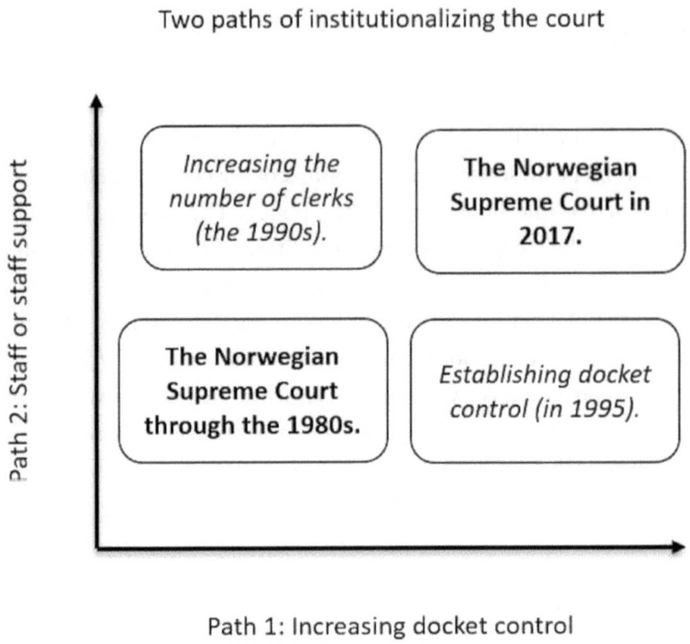

One path, or decision point, requires the reform movement to consider the potential need to increase the Court's control of its docket, which broadly speaking might be achieved by adding an intermediate layer to the Court structure and/or allowing the Court to exercise discretion in accepting cases for review. Smith and allies aggressively sought to reduce dramatically the number of cases given leave to appeal. Indeed, an enormous chunk of the criminal appeals were directed towards intermediate courts of appeals. Moreover, the ability to restrict the volume of civil cases also served to skew the Court's merits caseload toward more politically important cases. Whether or not a reduction in the number of cases was considered a necessary course of action, added staff support may be another crucial step along the path in the institutionalization of the Supreme Court's power. Naturally, the government would have to approve the required funding to underwrite the increase in personnel.

Of course, while appeals reform helped to address the pressure of a massive caseload, was it enough to enhance the Court's position in the political system? Would increasing staff support by adding more justices be sufficient? Or would a robust law clerk unit be required to achieve the desired outcome? If not, then no additional staff would be sought, as specified in the flow diagram. In the case of the Norwegian experience, Chief Justices

Smith, Schei and Øie enthusiastically endorsed the broad expansion of the law clerk unit. In the final analysis the increased institutional power of the Court was justified, in large part, first by managing backlogs. However, the increase in the number of clerks took on an unchecked momentum, well after backlogs were no longer a real issue. Indeed, backlogs have not been a serious problem for about a quarter of a century, a time during which the number of clerks nearly tripled.

The genesis of the institutional reform was Carsten Smith's 1974 (1975) address to the annual meeting of the Norwegian Association of Judges, in which he issued a clarion call for the Supreme Court to take the lead in 'developing the law'. To do so required a number of significant changes, if the Court was to perform a meaningful political function. Perhaps the most important of these was a dramatic reduction in the number of appeals the Court accepted. Reducing appeals would allow the justices to focus upon crucial, policy-relevant cases, thereby clearing the way for the Supreme Court to engage in what Smith referred to as 'judicial legislation'. Eventually, such docket control was swiftly facilitated by the criminal appeals reform of the mid-1990s and more slowly established by the changing interpretation of the Dispute Act across an almost twenty-year period finalized by the implementation of the revised Dispute Act in 2008.

However, accepting appeals of more complex statutory and constitutional disputes would require a research arm to assist the Court in the processing and review of those cases. Enter the clerks. The growth of the clerk unit was meagre during the first couple of decades of its existence, but its expansion began in earnest in the mid-1990s and continued apace during the time frame examined in this study. A convenient hook for securing additional law clerks was a period of case backlogs, which challenged the Court's capacity to adequately process appeals. While backlogs provided the rationale for an expanded clerk unit, the number of clerks continued to grow even after backlogs were brought under control. Indeed, during Carsten Smith's tenure as chief justice, the clerk unit increased at a steady rate. The result was a more autonomous Norwegian Supreme Court "... assimilated into the system of (...) policy making" (McGuire 2004:130).

The contribution of the law clerk unit to the Supreme Court's institutionalization developed gradually over time. Undoubtedly, the clerks' most consequential role has been their capacity to shape the Court's agenda through their participation on the Appeals Selection Committee (ASC). A clerk is assigned to undertake background research on legal material to determine whether or not there is a need for 'developing the law'. If an appeal is deemed important, the ASC grants a leave of appeal. All of this sounds rather mundane, until one considers that 85 to 90 per cent of appeals to the Court are rejected, and by all indications, the ASC accepts the recommendations of the law clerks approximately 90 per cent of the time. Clearly, the law clerks have a significant hand in shaping the constellation of cases, the issues and legal questions that the Court hears and decides.

Over time, the responsibilities assigned to the law clerks have been expanded to include greater involvement in the decision-making process. One is a clerk's occasional participation in the ASC when justices convene to grant or deny appeals. Another is a clerk's presence at the justices' table in the courtroom during oral arguments, since the clerk later in the decision-making process may be called upon to answer questions posed by the justices. In addition, law clerks often assist the justices in the composition of the boilerplate sections of the opinion. And although the prevailing norm is that clerks are expected to be legal 'generalists', with the increased relevance of international law, some specialization may be required.

After introducing Smith's master plan in Chapter 1 and describing the structure of the Court's decisional process in Chapter 2, in Chapter 3 we track the development of the law clerk unit. We begin with a mapping of the Supreme Court caseload, which was quite heavy until the 1995 Criminal Procedure Reform eliminated the automatic right to appeal criminal case decisions to the Supreme Court. Subsequently, the number of appeals began to rise, even with the added docket control. Nevertheless, the actual number of decisions rendered declined, thanks in large part to the gatekeeping function of the ASC. The case backlogs were substantial, but after the turn of the century, they remained low as the number of clerks doubled from 1995 onwards; appeals increased at about half that rate.

During Carsten Smith's tenure as chief justice, the Norwegian Supreme Court witnessed a dramatic institutionalization with respect to its *differentiation*, *durability* and *autonomy*. The criminal procedure reform we noted earlier took place midway through his leadership. It had a profound effect on the number of appeals the Court processed. In addition to achieving greater docket control during that period, Smith oversaw a surge in the number of clerks from six to 16, an increase of 167 per cent. His successor, Tore Schei, doggedly pursued the goal of reducing backlogs, which nevertheless were at a relatively low point at the outset of his tenure as chief justice. More telling in our view is the desire Schei expressed to guarantee the 'quality' and 'efficiency' of the Court's decision-making, both of which were required to 'develop the law', thereby making the Høyesterett a more consequential political actor.

A thorough explanation of the gatekeeping function of the ASC and the major role performed by the law clerks is provided in Chapter 4. We cannot stress enough the predominant impact of the clerk who is assigned to any given case. At the outset he or she formally summarizes the case facts, identifies the relevant legal issues and notes whether the appeal offers the opportunity to clarify the law or establish a precedent. The clerk also is responsible for assessing if any of the justices have a conflict of interest, which could lead to one or more of them being recused from participating in that particular case. Central to the ASC deliberations is the clerk's memo laying out the most important and relevant information for the Committee to process the appeal. Arguably, given that the justices serving on the Committee follow the clerk's recommendation to grant or deny 90 per cent of the time, one could reasonably assert that the law clerks were the principal gatekeepers of the Norwegian Supreme Court.

The active role of clerks in preparing material for deciding which cases the Court hears on their merits has resulted in justices handling fewer appeals, further increasing the clout of the clerks in controlling the number of cases adjudicated. However, as the role of the clerk unit has continued to evolve, the influence of the clerks may extend well beyond the gatekeeping function. Currently, once a case is assigned to a clerk, he or she may occasionally follow the case through oral argument and the justices' opinion writing. And the influence of the law clerks may be further magnified if they were chosen to manage a case because they possessed a special legal competence such as in international law.

In Chapter 5 we recount a defining moment in the expanding role of law clerks in the Supreme Court's decisional process. In a 2010 landmark 6-5 decision, generally referred to as the *Ship Owner's Taxation* case (Rt-2010-143), the Court ruled that the government's tax on the shipping companies violated the Norwegian Constitution's prohibition of *ex post facto* laws. Constitutional review cases like this are policymaking at its finest. Owing to the case's substantive complexity, a clerk with substantial tax law experience was assigned to it. Not only did the clerk prepare the customary memo, but he also was in the courtroom during oral argument, sat in on the justices' deliberations and was available while the justices crafted the opinion for the Court. As suggested in the *Ship Owner's* case, the Supreme Court was evolving into a more powerful force in the nation's politics, and, simultaneously, the clerk unit was becoming more influential in the Court's policymaking.

Carsten Smith pioneered the effort to transform a court of appeal into a court of precedent, and his successor as chief justice, Tore Schei, was clearly on board with Smith's reform project. During his tenure as chief justice, Schei sought to recruit more clerks to be engaged in a full range of activities, including drafting of opinions and adding legal material over and above that offered by the attorneys representing the parties to a case. In our view, in his effort to 'develop the law', Schei was pursuing the goal of realizing a Supreme Court that would have a policymaking role as important as that of the other branches of government. And Schei succeeded in this effort (see, generally, Grendstad, Shaffer, and Waltenburg 2015; Sunde 2015a; 2017).

Chapter 6 is devoted to providing a demographic profile of the clerks over time, with an eye towards assessing the level of diversity of the unit. Given the unit's gatekeeping role, the sociopolitical backgrounds and experiences of the clerks are a salient concern, particularly in light of Norway's egalitarian culture. Of special importance in this regard is the presence of women. Recognizing that in the early years there were so few clerks, often just one, little can be said about diversity until the 1980s. With a couple of exceptions, the data suggest that there have been substantial proportions of men and women in the clerk unit. Indeed, over time slightly more than half of all clerks have been female. Women have found the clerk unit to be family-friendly because it permits prioritizing a work-life balance.

We should add that a number of male clerks share this same view of employment in the clerk unit. The presence of women clerks is not likely to be a short-term phenomenon. If anything, we expect the percentage of women to increase, since they constitute a major share of Norway's law school graduates and currently most applicants to the clerk unit are female.

Prior to the turn of the century, the average age of a beginning law clerk could have been as high as the upper thirties to the low forties. Since then the mean age of a beginning clerk has been about 33 years, while the average age of the current set of Supreme Court justices hovers around 60. The relative youth of clerks can be viewed as a means to bring fresh ideas and perspectives to adjudication before the Court.[1] Not to belabour the obvious, but the clerks are younger than their justice counterparts. Consequently, the clerks will have graduated from law school more recently and therefore are more certain to have a legal education that includes the most current legal models and philosophies. This currency, in turn, may be especially important in an era of increased complexity of the law, fuelled in part by Norway's embrace of international law. It goes without saying that although the more recently minted lawyers may be eligible for a clerk position, they would never be credible applicants for a seat on the High Court's bench at such a tender age.

Norway has three law schools – one in the nation's capital (Oslo), one on the west coast (Bergen) and one far north of the Arctic Circle (Tromsø). While the University of Oslo has been the alma mater of most law clerks, there were a couple of times that the University of Bergen supplied a percentage of clerks larger than its proportion of law school graduates. In recent years the significant growth of the clerk unit re-established the University of Oslo as the principal source of law clerks. Given its location in the capital and the fact it produces the most lawyers makes the University of Oslo a major training ground for new clerks.

Chief Justice Carsten Smith and his successors have been committed to the principle of diversity of the justices on the High Court Bench, and developing a heterogeneous clerk unit also brings a level of diversification of the lived experiences of those vital staff members. Naturally, in the years prior to the 1980s there simply was no diversity; diversity cannot be achieved with only one clerk. After the mid-1980s, the diversity score for the clerk unit (see Shaffer, Grendstad, and Waltenburg 2015, and Chapter 6 for the score's computation) basically tracks the diversity score for the High Bench and generally exceeded the value computed for the justices. Having a broad representation of Norwegian social and economic characteristics present in the clerk unit should produce a greater quality of gatekeeping than a homogeneous clerk unit.

1 A similar result was achieved when clerks began to be hired on fixed-year contracts. Effectively terming clerks out would ensure sufficient turnover in the clerk unit so that there would always be a stream of clerks knowledgeable of current legal reasoning.

Chapter 7 is devoted to the impact of the institutionalization of the Supreme Court, a process central to its conversion from a court of appeal to a court of precedent. We began by creating a factor score for 'institutionalism' composed of criminal appeals reform and the size of the clerk unit. While higher levels of institutionalism resulted in fewer merits appeals being accepted, the relationship is statistically non-significant. Otherwise, institutionalism exhibits a significant and theoretically meaningful effect on a variety of judicial actions.

A well-developed law clerk unit combined with strong docket control could facilitate an intense review of more complex cases, thereby unearthing a greater number of legal sources. Indeed, that is precisely what occurs for both expropriation and labour law cases. Moreover, the higher the institutionalism score, the greater the number of citations of human rights law and EEA-EU law. Finally, institutionalism was positively correlated with dissent rates. Given the increased complexity of cases granted review by the Supreme Court, a more bureaucratized institution, especially the maintenance of a robust clerk unit, is necessary to assure the quality of the judicial decision-making process.

In Chapter 8 we saw that the Supreme Courts in Sweden and Finland were the first to undergo the transformation from a court of appeal to a court of precedent in the 1970s and 1980s. And in those Courts, we find the largest clerking units, the largest (although still small) degree of specialization and the most demanding qualification criteria for the clerks. We also find the most conscious allocation of resources to the handling of cases with a precedent potential and the longest and most thorough memoranda written. Here we also find that the clerks follow the case; they participate in the deliberations. In Finland the clerks even have a vote. All in all, there is a very strong indication that the longer the tradition for a precedent producing Supreme Court – and hence a court that is a more consequential political player – the more developed and institutionalized the clerk unit is. The most prominent example of this development is the clerk unit in the Swedish Supreme Court.

The long-term development in the Swedish and Finnish Supreme Courts does not tell us how the clerk unit in the Norwegian Supreme Court – or the Icelandic or Danish – will continue to develop. But given the five countries' braided history and the still common culture and interaction of the five countries, the Swedish and Finnish Supreme Courts provide sufficient examples and inspiration for the other Courts to emulate. The Swedish and Finnish examples also inform us in what direction the driving forces will take them even without deliberate choices being made.

9.2 The Supreme Court as a Political Actor

As we have noted, perhaps the most compelling case for the development and steady expansion of the law clerk unit was the growing pressure on the Supreme Court to manage a rapidly increasing caseload. Arguably, the sheer size of the workload and cumulative growth of backlogs placed an undue burden on the institution. By 1988 the number of appeals reached crisis proportions. However, adding a justice or two to the High Court was not an adequate solution; more personnel in the form of law clerks was deemed critical to the effective functioning of the Supreme Court.

We have documented the rise and expansion of the law clerk unit, an effective remedy to the increasing expectations that the Court must address important social and political issues. We noted, however, that the growth of the clerk unit, an antidote to caseload pressures, continued apace well *after* backlogs were brought under control. Those readers who have managed to get this far in the book will know that we suggest that the unrelenting increase in the number of law clerks was part and parcel of the Norwegian Supreme Court's institutionalization and concomitant transformation into a major political actor (on institutionalization and its effects, see Mahoney and Thelen 2010; McGuire 2004).

In terms of governmental design, Norway's parliamentary system has three separate branches, each of which possesses a degree of political autonomy. In characterizing the Supreme Court's role in politics, we adopt two qualities identified by Rehder (2010). First, while in the U.S. presidential system one might conclude that the Court is an "[e]xtension of [the] political system", in Europe the Court might best be considered as occupying an "[a]utonomous sphere". Second, in American jurisprudence "[p]olitics invades the legal sphere", while in Europe "[j]udicial action invades or displaces politics" (Rehder 2010:115). The U.S. Supreme Court can be considered an "[e]xtension of [the] political system" (Rehder 2010:115) if for no other reason than the fact that justices tend to share the ideological propensities of the president nominating them (Epstein, Landes, and Posner 2013; Epstein and Posner 2018), while simply basing their votes on their personal ideology (Segal and Spaeth 2002). Of course, strategic considerations might temper ideological enthusiasm in order to achieve an outcome most closely reflecting a justice's value preferences (Epstein, Landes, and Posner 2013).

While some evidence demonstrating a link to the politics of the party system has been unearthed for the Norwegian Supreme Court, the relationship is anaemic relative to that manifested in the American system (Grendstad, Shaffer, and Waltenburg 2015; Skiple et al. 2016). The Norwegian Supreme Court does indeed appear to be relatively 'autonomous', perhaps largely because the appointment process is not a mere reflection of the colour of the government in place at the time a new justice is selected. The ruling coalition does not compile a list of preferred candidates and then forward the name of the top contender. Instead, lawyers can apply for a seat on the Supreme Court, and a commission based in

Trondheim, a city allegedly far removed from the legal-political powers that be in the nation's capital of Oslo, forwards a list of three ranked candidates, from which the government makes a final decision. Typically, the applicant ranked first by the commission has been approved by the sitting government. Although this appointment process is not driven by crass party influences, nevertheless we contend that

> ... political and legal ideologies are inseparable in many ways. Political predispositions, consciously or unconsciously, form the foundations for the legal theories that judges ultimately embrace. Such is the nature of human reasoning, analysis, and decision making (Joondeph 2009:358).

Returning to American shores, accepting the notion that the U.S. High Court is an "[e]xtension of [the] political system", it would follow that "[p]olitics invades [the] legal system" (Rehder 2010:115). President Obama nominates liberals; President Trump nominates conservatives. And the tracking of the Court's ideological centre of gravity with the tilt of the nation's law-making majority has been going on for a very long time (Dahl 2001 [1957]).

By way of contrast, the Norwegian system appears to be one in which "judicial action invades or displaces politics" (Rehder 2010:115). There is scant to no evidence that either the government or the Storting directly manipulates the Supreme Court's ideological composition to achieve policy goals. The relationship between appointing government and a justice's treatment of cases, while statistically significant, is modest. Nevertheless, we hasten to add that the Norwegian Supreme Court is an important player in Norwegian politics. That the Supreme Court is a political organ (Seip 1965) is no longer in dispute, and the pioneering efforts of Carsten Smith spurred the development of an even more consequential judicial policymaker.

Smith created a blueprint for the expansion of the Supreme Court's political power or, more euphemistically stated, for enabling the Høyesterett to take the lead in 'developing the law'. In order to do so, the Court would exercise rigorous judicial review, acknowledging the political function of the courts. (Parenthetically, we note that given the changing role of the Supreme Court, Smith (1975:316) suggested that political experience might be a relevant consideration in the appointment of justices.) In an effort to transform the Supreme Court from a court of appeal to a court of precedent, Smith proposed that the number of appeals accepted should be dramatically reduced. Such a reform would permit the Høyesterett to produce 'judicial legislation', further intensifying the Court's political power (Feteris 2017). The criminal appeals reform implemented in 1995 enhanced the Supreme Court's docket control by eliminating its responsibility to act as a first-level appellate court in criminal cases. It had its intended effect. As documented earlier, there was an extraordinary decline in the number of such cases.

We have treated the criminal appeals reform as one indicator of 'institutionalism', but Smith also called for hiring many more law clerks. Their increasing number is another integral part of the institutionalization of the Norwegian Supreme Court (see Figure 9.1). A robust clerk unit would undertake a remarkable share of the processing of cases, including preparing legal documents, identifying the full set of legal questions and provisions, participating when justices convened to resolve difficult appeals on the ASC, occasionally sitting in on oral arguments in civil cases and helping the justices in drafting opinions. As already noted, even after bringing backlogs under control, additional clerks were recruited. When stepping down as chief justice in 2016, Tore Schei (2015c) had already called for doubling the number of clerks, and his successor, current Chief Justice Toril Marie Øie, seeks approximately a 30 per cent increase in the number of law clerks (Øie 2019).

Why the heartfelt interest in beefing up the Supreme Court's bureaucratic apparatus? Are case backlogs a credible reason? Clearly not, owing to the fact that there are no appreciable backlogs. Alternatively, given the complexity of the cases granted leave, perhaps a large and growing clerk unit is necessary to ensure the 'quality' of the Court's overall performance (Schei 2015b). The need for assuring 'quality' was made necessary by virtue of its more politicized role enabled by Smith's reforms, which have been embraced by his successors Schei and Øie. 'Quality' may be a kinder, gentler term for enhanced political effectiveness. In this regard, was the 'quality' of the Supreme Court's performance lacklustre prior to the clarion call for many more law clerks? We suspect not. Instead, we posit that the concern about quality was occasioned by the intense focus on policy consequential cases, the sort of which enhances the policy-making role of the judiciary. Therefore, in order for the Court to achieve its goal of increased political power, the institutionalization of the Supreme Court was essential. The Supreme Court is now a serious player in Norwegian politics.

Since the Supreme Court, now a court of precedent, focuses on cases involving crucial legal and constitutional issues, one might posit that far greater staff support is required. In other words, the Supreme Court has created a demand for more law clerks in its quest for a vital political role contributing to the 'judicialization of politics' (Tate and Vallinder 1995). Unfortunately, the notion that judges are 'political' is occasionally a sensitive topic, one over which there has been a good deal of intellectual controversy. The finding that ideology, as crudely measured by the nature of the appointing government, has a significant yet modest effect on decisions rendered by the Norwegian Supreme Court (Grendstad, Shaffer, and Waltenburg 2010; 2015) has prompted significant pushback from former Associate Justice Jens Edvin Skoghøy (2010) and former Chief Justice Tore Schei (2011). They aver that justices do not take a 'party line' on public policy. Justices apply legal principles and the legal method rather than hew to an ideological line. For that matter experimental work by Kahan and colleagues (2016) demonstrates that the legal training that equips a future justice with solid 'professional judgment' dampens or eliminates the influence of 'cultural world views', as measured by 'hierarchy-egalitarianism' and 'individualism-communitarianism'.

Although professional standards may override personal cultural orientation, one astute observer notes that, in addition to the role that the partisanship of the appointing government might play in judicial decision-making, judges are part of government. They make public policy, their "background ideological views" shape their decisional behaviour and their decisions "shape the outcome of major political issues of the day" (Tamanaha 2012:773). For our purposes, we differentiate "'political influence' from 'partisanship'" (Tamanaha 2012:767). In the final analysis, a nuanced understanding of the decisional behaviour of justices recognizes that their behaviour is guided by professional legal standards and preferences about major policy questions (Bailey and Maltzman 2011; Epstein, Landes, and Posner 2013). With or without political party influence, the idea that judges 'legislate' is widely accepted (Tamanaha 2009).

In order to transform the Norwegian Supreme Court to a more prominent political actor, the development and expansion of the law clerk unit was critical. Not only did a robust clerk unit enable judicial policymaking, it became a participant in the Supreme Court's rulings, largely by virtue of its role as gatekeeper for the ASC. However, are clerks apolitical? That very notion stretches credulity. Like the justices, the clerks have the requisite legal training to inculcate professional standards. But also like the justices, the clerks' background experiences will shape their perceptions of policy questions, legal principles and standards. With the emergence of a robust clerk unit, the Norwegian Supreme Court enjoyed a level of 'institutionalism', which enhanced its policymaking role in Norwegian politics.

During the decades we have analysed in this book, the number of clerks on the Supreme Court has increased, the type and significance of their tasks have expanded and the lines of division of labour between clerks and justices have become less distinct. Nevertheless, during our research on the Court we were repeatedly told that the influence of clerks was checked and the ultimate division of labour between the clerks and justices was still clear. These disclaimers reminded us of the axiom by the political sociologist Stein Rokkan who in his analyses of the numerical and corporatist channels of influence on government decision-making stated that "[v]otes count in the choice of governing personnel but other resources decide the actual policies pursued by the authorities" (Rokkan 1966:106).

Analogously, clerks have counted, and justices decided. But given the transformation of the Supreme Court, that analogy too might be morphing into a new political reality. Law clerks may be enjoying increased political influence, by virtue of their gatekeeping function, the increased complexity of the law, their presence in the courtroom and their growing participation in assisting with the justices' opinions. This outcome is a product of the institutionalization of the Supreme Court.

Compared to the other four Nordic countries, as we saw in Chapter 8, the role of the clerk unit in the Norwegian Supreme Court occupies a middle position. On the one hand, in the Icelandic and Danish Supreme Courts, whose role as courts of precedent are more subdued, the clerks have little influence on court operations. On the other hand, the Swedish and Finnish Supreme Courts have been courts of precedent for about 40 years. Here the clerks play a much more prominent role. In Finland the clerks vote on the outcome of the case; they enjoy the same independence as do the justices, and they are often recruited as justices at a later point in their career. The Nordic examples do not give us a detailed line of development of the role of law clerks as a Supreme Court moves from a court of appeal to a court of precedent. However, the examples provide rough templates of the role of the clerks and their political influence. The templates also offer insights as to which types of institutionalization to emulate and which types of institutionalization to avoid.

The Nordic comparison also reminds us that the clerk-driven institutionalization of a Supreme Court is a question about policy. In the Nordic countries the Supreme Courts themselves are at liberty to decide how they want to organize, including the division of labour between the justices and the clerks. However, it is the individual government that passes the final budget within which a Supreme Court must operate. In Norway, the state budget is decided by Parliament after a government proposal. Hence, at the end of the day, the level of institutionalization of the Norwegian Supreme Court is determined not by the Court alone but through a decision-making procedure that involves all branches of government.

In closing we revisit the institutional paths to court power depicted in Figure 9.1. While docket control and the level of staff support can enhance the policymaking role of an apex court, the pattern of institutionalization can vary across political systems. In this context one can view the Norwegian Supreme Court in the aggregate and assess its activity in relation to Parliament and the government. Successfully moving from a court of appeal to a court of precedent, the Høyesterett became a more consequential player in Norwegian politics. Shedding the burdensome criminal appeals cases enabled the Court to direct its energies to produce 'judicial legislation'.

The Court's resulting institutional clout would not have been achieved had it not been for the unrelenting expansion of the law clerk unit. After all, the Supreme Court no longer busied itself with criminal appeals, but with consequential matters of public policy, thereby necessitating added legal staff to deal with the increasing complexity of cases under adjudication. Additional staffing was achieved, not by appointing more justices, but by recruiting an ever-increasing number of law clerks. While a robust clerk unit has enabled the Court as a unitary actor to be a more powerful agent vis-à-vis Parliament and the government, within the Supreme Court, some of its power has shifted from the justices to the law clerks.

10 References

Aamodt, Øistein. 2017. Juridisk utredningsenhet før og nå. Tale ved 60-årsjubileum for Juridisk utredningsenhet, Norges Høyesterett, Oslo, 15 Mars 2017.

Arnesen, Finn, and Are Stenvik. 2009. *Internasjonalisering og Juridisk Metode*. Oslo: Universitetsforlaget.

Arnesen, Petter Kristiansen, Henrik L. Bentsen, and Gunnar Grendstad. 2018. Internasjonalisering, sakskompleksitet og arbeidsmengde i Norges Høyesterett. *Lov og Rett* 57 (7):391-411.

Arnstad, Iwar. 2017. Rekordhøy tiltro til domstolene – igjen. *Rett på Sak* (4):4-5.

Aschehoug, Marit. 2009. Ny dommerstilling i Høyesterett. *Advokatbladet*, December, 14-15.

Askeland, Bjarte. 2018. Nyere utviklingslinjer i norsk rettskildelære 1999-2018. *Lov og Rett* 57 (9):519-536.

Backer, Inge Lorange. 2014. Goals of Civil Justice in Norway: Readiness for a Pragmatic Reform. In *Goals of Civil Justice and Civil Procedure in Contemporary Judicial Systems*, edited by A. Uzelac. New York: Springer.

Bailey, Michael A., and Forrest Maltzman. 2011. *The Constrained Court. Law, Politics, and the Decisions Justices Make*. Princeton, NJ: Princeton University Press.

Bårdsen, Arnfinn. 2014. Anketillatelse til Norges Høyesterett. *Lov og Rett* 53 (9):529-549.

Bårdsen, Arnfinn. 2015. Norges Høyesterett som konstitusjonsdomstol. In *Lov, sannhet, rett. Høyesterett 200 år*, edited by T. Schei, J. E. A. Skoghøy and T. M. Øie. Oslo: Universitetsforlaget.

Baum, Lawrence. 1997. *The Puzzle of Judicial Behavior*. Ann Arbor, MI: The University of Michigan Press.

Baum, Lawrence. 2014. Hiring Supreme Court Law Clerks: Probing the Ideological Linkage Between Judges and Justices. *Marquette Law Review* 98 (1):333-360.

Baum, Lawrence, and Corey Ditslear. 2010. Supreme Court Clerkships and "Feeder" Judges. *Justice System Journal* 31 (1):36-48.

Bentsen, Henrik Litleré. 2018a. Court Leadership, Agenda Transformation, and Judicial Dissent: A European Case of a 'Mysterious Demise of Consensual Norms'. *Journal of Law and Courts* 6 (1):189-213.

Bentsen, Henrik Litleré. 2018b. Determinants and Public Policy Consequences of Dissent in the Supreme Court of Norway, PhD dissertation. Department of Comparative Politics. University of Bergen, Bergen.

Best, Bradley J. 2002. *Law Clerks, Support Personnel, and the Decline of Consensual Norms On the United States Supreme Court, 1935-1995*. New York: LFB Scholarly Publishing.

Bieri, Peter. 2016. Law Clerks In Switzerland – A Solution To Cope With The Caseload? *International Journal for Court Administration* 7 (2):29-38.

Black, Ryan C., Timothy R. Johnson, and Ryan James Owens. 2018. Chief Justice Burger and the Bench: How Physically Changing the Shape of the Court's Bench Reduced Interruptions during Oral Argument. *Journal of Supreme Court History* 43 (1):83-98.

Black, Ryan C., and Ryan J. Owens. 2012. *The Solicitor General and the United States Supreme Court: Executive Branch Influence and Judicial Decisions*. Cambridge: Cambridge University Press.

Black, Ryan C., and Ryan J. Owens. 2013. A Built-In Advantage: The office of the Solicitor General and the U.S. Supreme Court. *Political Research Quarterly* 66 (2):454-466.

Bruzelius, Karin M. 2016. Gjeldende rettsregler – hvor er de nå? *Lov og Rett* 56 (10):589-590.

Bumin, Kirill M., Kirk A. Randazzo, and Lee D. Walker. 2009. Institutional Viability and High Courts: A Comparative Analysis of Post-Communist States. *Australian Journal of Political Science* 44 (1):127-153.

Coan, Andrew B. 2012. Judicial Capacity and the Substance of Constitutional Law. *The Yale Law Journal* 122 (2):422-458.

Coonan, Genevieve. 2006. The Role of Judicial Research Assistants in Supporting the Decisionsmaking Role of the Irish Judiciary. *Judicial Studies Institute Journal* 6 (1):171-196.

Cushman, Clare, and Todd C Peppers. 2015. *Of Courtiers and Kings: More Stories of Supreme Court Law Clerks and Their Justices.* Charlottesville: University of Virginia Press.

Dahl, Børge. 2014. Højesteret og dommerfuldmægtigene. In *Jubilæumsskrift for Dommerfuldmægtigforeningen*, edited by R. P. Skovby, N. P. Bonde and D. P. Asanovski. Copenhagen: DJØF Forlag.

Dahl, Robert A. 2001 [1957]. Decision Making in a Democracy: The Supreme Court as a National Policy Maker. *Emory Law Journal* 50 (2):563-582.

Ditslear, Corey, and Lawrence Baum. 2001. Selection of Law Clerks and Polarization in the U.S. Supreme Court. *The Journal of Politics* 63 (3):869-885.

Drucker, Peter F. 1954. *The Practice of Management.* New York: Harper.

Dyevre, Arthur. 2010. Unifying the Field of Comparative Judicial Politics. Towards a General Theory of Judicial Behaviour. *European Political Science Review* 2 (2):297-227.

Epstein, Lee, and Jack Knight. 2013. Reconsidering Judicial Preferences. *Annual Review of Political Science* 16:11-31.

Epstein, Lee, and Eric Posner. 2018. If the Supreme Court is Nakedly Political, Can it be Just? *The New York Times*, July 9.

Epstein, Lee, William M. Landes, and Richard A. Posner. 2013. *The Behavior of Federal Judges. A Theoretical and Empirical Study of Rational Choice.* Cambridge, MA: Harvard University Press.

Feteris, Maarten. 2017. Development of the Law by Supreme Courts in Europe. *Utrecht Law Review* 13 (1):155-160.

Fredriksen, Halvard Haukeland. 2011. *EU/EØS-rett i norske domstoler.* Oslo: Europautredningen.

Galanter, Marc. 1974. Why the "Haves" Come Out Ahead: Speculations on the Limits of Legal Change. *Law & Society Review* 9 (1):95-160.

Gilmore, Grant. 1977. *The Ages of American Law.* New Haven, CT: Yale University Press.

Grendstad, Gunnar, William R. Shaffer, and Eric N. Waltenburg. 2010. Revealed Preferences of Norwegian Supreme Court Justices. *Tidsskrift for Rettsvitenskap* 123 (1):73-101.

Grendstad, Gunnar, William R. Shaffer, and Eric N. Waltenburg. 2015. *Policy Making in an Independent Judiciary. The Norwegian Supreme Court.* Colchester: ECPR Press.

Grendstad, Gunnar, William R. Shaffer, and Eric N. Waltenburg. 2017. Norway - Managed Openness and Transparency. In *Justices and Journalists: The Global Perspective*, edited by R. Davis and D. Taras. New York: Cambridge University Press.

Grendstad, Gunnar, William R. Shaffer, and Eric N. Waltenburg. 2019. *Judicial Behavior on The Supreme Court of Norway. The Doranoh Database.* University of Bergen and Purdue University.

Heidar, Knut. 2000. *Norway. Elites on Trial.* Boulder, CO: Westview Press.

Hirschl, Ran. 2008. The Judicialization of Politics. In *The Oxford Handbook of Law and Politics*, edited by G. A. Caldeira, D. R. Kelemen and K. E. Whittington. New York: Oxford University Press.

Hjellbrekke, Johs., and Olav Korsnes. 2010. Nedturar. Deklassering i det seinmoderne Noreg. *Nytt Norsk Tidsskrift* 27 (1-2):44-57.

Hjellbrekke, Johs., and Olav Korsnes. 2014. Intergenerasjonell mobilitet og sirkulasjon i norske elitar og profesjonar. In *Elite og klasse i et egalitært samfunn*, edited by O. Korsnes, M. N. Hansen and J. Hjellbrekke. Oslo: Universitetsforlaget.

Hoekstra, Valerie, Miki Caul Kittilson, and Elizabeth Andrews Bond. 2014. Gender, High Courts, and Ideas about Representation in Western Europe. In *Representation: The Case of Women*, edited by M. Escobar-Lemmon and M. M. Taylor-Robinson. New York: Oxford University Press.

Holvast, Nina L. 2016. The Power of the Judicial Assistant/Law Clerk: Looking Behind the Scenes at Courts in the United States, England and Wales, and the Netherlands. *International Journal for Court Administration* 7 (2):10-28.

Holvast, Nina L. 2017. *In the Shadow of the Judge: The Involvement of Judicial Assistants in Dutch District Courts.* The Hague: Eleven International Publishing.

Husa, Jaakko, Kimmo Nuotio, and Heikki Pihlajamäki. 2007. Nordic Law – Between Traditionalism and Dynamism. In *Nordic Law – Between Traditionalism and Dynamism,* edited by J. Husa, K. Nuotio and H. Pihlajamäki, 1-39. Antwerpen/Oxford: Intersentia.

Høgsta Domstolen. 2019. HD 2018 – Activity Report of the Supreme Court. http://www.hogstadomstolen.se/Domstolar/hogstadomstolen/dokument/2018%20Activity%20report.pdf (last accessed 29 August 2019).

Høyesteretts Kontor. 2017. Høring – Forslag til økonomiplan for domstolene 2019-2022 – revidert versjon. Letter to the National Court Administration, September 5.

Innstillingsrådet for Dommere. 2012. Innstillingsrådets Praksis-/Policynotat. http://www.domstol.no/Enkelt-domstol/Innstillingsradet/Publikasjoner/PraksisPolicynotat/ (last accessed 21 February 2013).

Jimeno-Bulnes, Mar, and Valerie P. Hans. 2016. Legal Interpreter for the Jury: The Role of the Clerk of the Court in Spain. *Oñati Socio-Legal Series* 6 (2):197-215.

Joondeph, Bradley W. 2009. The Many Meanings of "Politics" in Judicial Decision Making. *University of Missouri-Kansas City Law Review* 77 (2):347-379.

Justis- og politidepartementet. 1962-63. *Om landsvikoppgjøret.* Oslo: Stortingsmelding 17.

Kahan, Dan M., David Hoffman, Daniel Evans, Neal Devins, Eugene Lucci, and Katherine Cheng. 2016. "Ideology" or "Situation Sense"? An Experimental Investigation of Motivated Reasoning and Professional Judgment. *University of Pennsylvania Law Review* 164 (2):349-439.

Kenney, Sally J. 2000. Beyond Principals and Agents. Seeing Courts as Organizations by Comparing Référendaires at the European Court of Justice and Law Clerks at the U.S. Supreme Court. *Comparative Political Studies* 33 (5):593-625.

Keohane, Robert O. 1969. Institutionalization in the United Nations General Assembly. *International Organization* 23 (4):859-896.

Kershaw, Ian. 2019. *The Global Age. Europe, 1950-2017.* New York: Viking.

King, James D. 2000. Changes in Professionalism in U.S. State Legislatures. *Legislative Studies Quarterly* 25 (2):327-343.

Knutsen, Oddbjørn, ed. 2017. *Nordic Models in Political Science. Challenged, But Still Viable?* Bergen: Fagbokforlaget.

Kristjánsson, Mímir. 2010. Er gift med staten. *Klassekampen*, February 22.

Kromphardt, Christopher D. 2014. Fielding an Excellent Team: Law Clerk Selection and Chambers Structure at the US Supreme Court. *Marquette Law Review* 98 (1):289-312.

Mahoney, James, and Katleen Thelen, eds. 2010. *Explaining Institutional Change: Ambiguity, Agency, and Power.* Cambridge: Cambridge University Press.

Massing, Otwin. 2016. The Legal Assistants at the German Federal Constitutional Court: A "Black Box" of Research? In *Constitutional Courts in Comparison: The US Supreme Court and the German Federal Constitutional Court*, edited by R. Rogowski and T. Gawron. New York: Berghahn Books.

Matheson, Wilhelm. 2016. Høyesteretts Sivile Saker. Noen strukturelle utviklingstrekk. In *Rettsavklaring og rettsutvikling. Festskrift til Tore Schei*, edited by G. Bergby, M. Matningsdal, J.E.A. Skoghøy and T.M. Øie. Oslo: Universitetsforlaget.

Matningsdal, Magnus. 1996. *To-instansreformen.* Oslo: Universitetsforlaget.

Mauro, Tony. 2014. Diversity and Supreme Court Law Clerks. *Marquette Law Review* 98 (1):361-366.

McGuire, Kevin T. 2004. The Institutionalization of the U.S. Supreme Court. *Political Analysis* 12 (2):128-142.

Menkel-Meadow, Carrie. 1996. The Feminization of the Legal Profession: The Comparative Sociology of Women Lawyers. In *Lawyers in Society: An Overview*, edited by R. Label and P.S.C. Lewis. Berkeley, CA: University of California Press.

Nadim, Morten. 2017. *Precedents in the 21st Century. The Evolution of Case Law in the Norwegian Supreme Court 1970-2016*, PhD Dissertation, Faculty of Law, University of Bergen, Bergen.

Nesterchuk, Tetyana. 2013. The View from Behind the Bench: The Role of Judicial Assistants in the UK Supreme Court. In *Judge and Jurist: Essays in Memory of Lord Rodger of Earlsferry*, edited by A. Burrows, D. Johnston and R. Zimmermann. Oxford: Oxford University Press.

Norges Høyesterett. 2013. Høyesteretts årsmelding 2012. Oslo: Norges Høyesterett.

Norges Høyesterett. 2015. Høyesteretts årsmelding 2014. Oslo: Norges Høyesterett.

Norges Høyesterett. 2017. Årsmelding 2016. Oslo: Norges Høyesterett.

Norges Høyesterett. 2018a. Anke, saksforberedelse og prosedyre for Høyesterett. Oslo: Norges Høyesterett.

Norges Høyesterett. 2018b. Årsmelding 2017. Oslo: Norges Høyesterett. https://indd.adobe.com/view/1bc9c6b9-75c2-4d3d-8af2-c950e08fff40 (last accessed 07 October 2019).

NOU. 1992. To-instansbehandling, anke og juryordning i straffesaker. Oslo: Department of Justice.

NOU. 1999. Domstolene i samfunnet. Administrativ styring av domstolene. Utnevnelser, sidegjøremål, disiplinærtiltak. Midlertidige dommere. Oslo: Justisdepartementet. http://www.regjeringen.no/nb/dep/jd/dok/NOUer/1999/NOU-1999-19.html?id=141812 (last accessed 10 June 2015).

NOU. 2001. Rett på sak. Lov om tvisteløsning (tvisteloven). NOU 2001: 32.

NOU. 2015. *Advokaten i samfunnet. Lov om advokater og andre som yter rettslig bistand.* Oslo: Justisdepartementet.

NTB. 1996. Endelig har Høyestrett fått sitt eget hus. *NTB*, September 2.

NTB. 2008. Storberget vil ha flere kvinner til Høyesterett, October 31.

NTB. 2010. Rederiene kjemper mot milliardsmell. *NTB*, January 1.

NTB. 2014. Søkere til Høyesterett får endelig være anonyme. *NTB*, March 9.

Nylund, Anna. 2010. Mixing Past and Future. The Making of a Nordic Legal Culture 1850-2050. In *Rendezvous of European Legal Cultures*, edited by J.Ø. Sunde and K.E. Skodvin. Bergen: Fagbokforlaget.

Nylund, Anna, and Jørn Øyrehagen Sunde. 2018. Courts and Court Proceedings. In *Nordic Law in European Context*, edited by P. Letto-Vanamo, D. Tamm and B.O.G. Mortensen. Cham: Springer.

Ot.prp. nr. 41. 1980-1981. Om lov om endringer i rettergangslovgivningen. Oslo: Ministry of Justice.

Ot.prp. nr. 44. 2000-2001. Om lov om endringer i domstolloven m.m. (den sentrale domstoladministrasjon og dommernes arbeidsrettslige stilling). Oslo: Department of Justice. http://www.regjeringen.no/nb/dep/jd/dok/regpubl/otprp/20002001/otprp-nr-44-2000-2001-.html?id=164074 (last accessed 07 October 2019).

Ot.prp. nr. 51. 2004-2005. Om lov om mekling og rettergang i sivile tvister (tvisteloven). Oslo: Ministry of Justice.

Ot.prp. nr. 78. 1992-1993. Om lov om endringer i straffeprosessloven m.v (toinstansbehandling, anke og juryordning). Oslo: Ministry of Justice.

Paterson, Alan. 2013. *Final Judgment: The Last Law Lords and the Supreme Court*. Oxford: Hart Publishing.

Peppers, Todd C. 2006. *Courtiers of the Marble Palace: The Rise and Influence of the Supreme Court Law Clerk*. Stanford, CA: Stanford University Press.

Perry, Hersel W. 2009. *Deciding to Decide: Agenda Setting in the United States Supreme Court*. Cambridge, MA: Harvard University Press.

Qvigstad, Jan Fredrik, and Tore Schei. 2018. Criteria for "good" justifications. Working papers fra Norges Bank #6. https://static.norges-bank.no/contentassets/6c4730e4787045bfa5c2778ae6c25c2b/working_paper_6_18_eng.pdf?v=04/30/2018094939&ft=.pdf (last accessed 4 June 2018).

Regjeringen. (Various years). Stortingsproposisjon nr. 1.

Rehder, Britta. 2010. What Is Political about Jurisprudence? Courts, Politics and Political Science in Europe and the United States. *Contemporary Readings in Law and Social Justice* 2 (1):100-129.

Rhinehart, Lynn K. 1994. Is There Gender Bias in the Judicial Law Clerk Selection Process?". *Georgetown Law Review* 83:575-578.

Rokkan, Stein. 1966. Norway: Numerical Democracy and Corporate Pluralism. In *Political Oppositions in Western Democracies*, edited by R.A. Dahl. New Haven: Yale University Press.

Ryssdal, Andres. 2015. Prøvelsesretten. *Lov og Rett* 54 (10):579-580.

Sandmo, Erling. 2005. *Siste ord. Høyesterett i norsk historie. 1905-1965.* Oslo: Cappelen.

Schei, Tore. 2010. Arbeidet med domsskriving i Høyesterett. In *Domsnøkkel. Privatrettslige emner*, edited by W.K. Bergli, L. Fauske, M. Garborg, J.G. Fliflet and I.H. Rørvik. Oslo: Gyldendal Akademisk.

Schei, Tore. 2011. Har Høyesterett en politisk funksjon? *Lov og Rett* 50 (6):319-335.

Schei, Tore. 2015a. Norges Høyesterett – 200 år 30. juni 1815 – 30. juni 2015. Rt-2015-769: Lovdata.

Schei, Tore. 2015b. Norges Høyesterett ved 200-årsjubileet. In *Lov, sannhet, rett. Høyesterett 200 år*, edited by T. Schei, J.E.A. Skoghøy and T. M. Øie. Oslo: Universitetsforlaget.

Schei, Tore. 2015c. The Supreme Court of Norway and international collaboration with courts and justices. Address at International Conference 'Supreme Courts in Context', University of Bergen, Bergen, September 21-22, 2015.

Schmidt, Nina. 2017. Vil ha flere straffesaker i Høyesterett. *Advokatbladet*, 4-5.

Segal, Jeffrey A., and Harold J. Spaeth. 2002. *The Supreme Court and the Attitudinal Model Revisited.* New York: Cambridge University Press.

Seip, Jens Arup. 1965. Den norske høyesterett som politisk organ. *Lov og Rett*: 1-21.

Sejersted, Fredrik. 2016. Hilsen fra Regjeringsadvokatembetet. Speech to Chief Schei on the occasion of Schei stepping down from the Court on February 29, 2016 https://www.domstol.no/globalassets/upload/hret/artikler-og-foredrag/fredrik-sejersted-tale-ved-tore-schei-fratredelse-29.2.2016.pdf (last accessed 21 October 2016).

Shaffer, William R., Gunnar Grendstad, and Eric N. Waltenburg. 2015. Is Diversity Just for Show? Diversity and Appointment to the Norwegian Supreme Court 1945-2011. *Retfærd* 38 (1):18-42.

Skiple, Jon Kåre, Gunnar Grendstad, William R. Shaffer, and Eric N. Waltenburg. 2016. Supreme Court Justices' Economic Behavior. A Multi-Level Model Analysis. *Scandinavian Political Studies* 39 (1):73-94.

Skiple, Jon Kåre, Mark Jonathan McKenzie, and Henrik Litleré Bentsen. 2017. Judicial Protectors of the Scandinavian Welfare State? A Comparative Analysis of Tax Decisions in the Norwegian and Danish Supreme Courts. Paper presented at the 75nd Annual Meeting of the Midwest Political Science Association, Chicago, IL, April 6-9, 2017.

Skoghøy, Jens Edvin A. 2008. Anketillatelse til Norges Høyesterett. In *Festskrift til Lars Heuman*, edited by J. Kleineman, P. Westberg and S. Carlsson. Stockholm: Jure.

Skoghøy, Jens Edvin A. 2010. Dommeratferd og dommerbakgrunn. Særlig om yrkesbakgrunnens betydning for utfallet av tvister mellom private og det offentlige. In *Festskrift till Torgny Håstad*, edited by G. Lambertz, S. Lindskog and M. Möller. Uppsala: Iustus.

Skoghøy, Jens Edvin A. 2016. Høyesteretts rolle og arbeidsmåte. *Lov og Rett* 56 (5):302-328.

Smith, Carsten. 1975. Domstolene og rettsutviklingen. *Lov og Rett* 11:292-319.

Smith, Carsten. 1998. Høyesterett i dagens samfunn. In *Norges Høyesterett*, edited by S. Tschudi-Madsen. Oslo: Aschehoug.

Smith, Eivind. 2016. Norges Høyesterett – en «konstitusjonsdomstol»? In *Festskrift til Jens Peter Christensen*, edited by M. H. Jensen, S. H. Mørup and B. Dahl. Copenhagen: Jurist- og Økonomforbundets Forlag.

Squire, Peverill. 2007. Measuring State Legislative Professionalism: The Squire Index Revisited. *State Politics & Policy Quarterly* 7 (2):211-227.

Squire, Peverill. 2008. Measuring the Professionalization of U.S. State Courts of Last Resort. *State Politics & Policy Quarterly* 8 (3):223-238.

Statistisk Sentralbyrå. 2018. Konsumprisindeks, historisk serie fra 1924 (2015=100). https://www.ssb.no/kpi?fane=tabell (last accessed 22 February 2019).

Steenstrup, Bjørn. 1973. *Hvem er Hvem?* Oslo: Aschehoug. http://runeberg.org/hvemer-hvem/1973/ (last accessed 07 October 2019).

Stone, Alec. 1992. *The Birth of Judicial Politics in France*. Oxford: Oxford University Press.

Stortingsproposisjon nr. 1, 1983-1984. [Government budget proposal].

Stub, Marius. 2016. Noen Kommentater til Rt. 2015 s. 1388. *Jussens venner* 51 (2):92-118.

Sunde, Jørn Øyrehagen. 2015a. *Høgsteretts historie 1965-2015 – At dømme i sidste Instans*. Bergen: Fagbokforlaget.

Sunde, Jørn Øyrehagen. 2017. From Courts of Appeal to Courts of Precedent – Access to the Highest Courts in the Nordic Countries. In *Supreme Courts in Transition in China and the West: Adjudication at the Service of Public Goals*, edited by C. H. van Rhee and Y. Fu. Cham: Springer.

Sunde, Jørn Øyrehagen, and Frode Ulvund. 2014. Vaktbikkja fyller 200, October 26, 16-17.

Szmer, John J., Erin B. Kaheny, and Robert K. Christensen. 2014. Taking a Dip in the Supreme Court Clerk Pool: Gender-Based Discrepancies in Clerk Selection. *Marquette Law Review* 98 (1):261-288.

Tamanaha, Brian Z. 2009. *Beyond the Formalist-Realist Divide: The Role of Politics in Judging*. Princeton, NJ: Princeton University Press.

Tamanaha, Brian Z. 2012. The Several Meanings of "Politics" in Judicial Politics Studies: Why "Ideological Influence" is not "Partisanship". *Emory Law Journal* 61 (4):759-778.

Tate, Neal, and Torbjörn Vallinder, eds. 1995. *The Global Expansion of Judicial Power*. New York: New York University Press.

Valdini, Melody E., and Christopher Shortell. 2016. Women's Representation in the Highest Court: A Comparative Analysis of the Appointment of Female Justices. *Political Research Quarterly* 69 (4):865-876.

Ward, Artemus. 2017. Law Clerks. In *The Oxford Handbook of U.S. Judicial Behavior*, edited by L. Epstein and S. A. Lindquist. Oxford: Oxford University Press.

Ward, Artemus, and David L Weiden. 2006. *Sorcerers'Apprentices: 100 Years of Law Clerks at the United States Supreme Court*. New York: NYU Press.

Wieland, Joachim. 2002. The Role of the Legal Assistants at the German Federal Constitutional Court. In *Constitutional Courts in Comparison: The U.S. Supreme Court and the German Federal Constitutional Court*, edited by R. Rogowski and T. Gawron. New York: Berghahn Books.

Øie, Toril Marie. 2016. Tale til justitiarius Tore Schei ved hans fratreden, 29 februar 2016. Speech to Chief Schei on the occation of Schei stepping down from the Court on February 29, 2016. http://www.domstol.no/globalassets/upload/hret/artikler-og-foredrag/toril-m.-oie-tale-ved-tore-schei-fratredelse-29.2.2016.pdf (last accessed 21 October 2016).

Øie, Toril Marie. 2017. Høyesterett i 2016. Supreme Court Annual Report 2016.

Øie, Toril Marie. 2019. Norges Høyesterett i 2018. Norges Høyesterett 2018. Årsmelding, Oslo.

Index

D

Printed by Libri Plureos GmbH in Hamburg,
Germany

9 789462 369788